Praise for Phillip Done

"Phillip Done gets it—he gets how kids think, he gets how kids learn, and he gets how to inspire them to do both. His comical, warm, and insightful memoir brings you right into the classroom, following his incredibly colorful class of characters through an entire school year, capturing the magic and wonder of being a kid."
> —Erin Gruwell, author of *The Freedom Writer's Diary* and *Teach with Your Heart*

"Phillip Done reminds us of the excitement and joy of learning."
> —Hal Urban, author of *Life's Greatest Lessons* and *Positive Words, Powerful Results*

"Phil Done is my hero."
> —Roy Blount, Jr., author of *Robert E. Lee* and *I Am the Cat, Don't Forget That*

Close Encounters
of the
Third-Grade Kind

Thoughts on Teacherhood

PHILLIP DONE

CENTER
STREET

NEW YORK   BOSTON   NASHVILLE

Center Street
Hachette Book Group
237 Park Avenue
New York, NY 10017

Visit our Web site at www.centerstreet.com.

Center Street is a division of Hachette Book Group, Inc.
The Center Street name and logo are trademarks of
Hachette Book Group, Inc.

Book design by Fearn Cutler de Vicq
Printed in the United States of America

FIRST EDITION: September 2009

10 9 8 7 6 5 4 3 2 1

Library of Congress Cataloging-in-Publication Data

Done, Phillip.
  Close encounters of the third-grade kind : thoughts on teacherhood / Phillip Done.—1st ed.
      p. cm.
  Summary: "With the wit, warmth, and wisdom unique to a third-grade teacher, Phil Done offers priceless lessons in life and learning from a true lover of education"—Provided by the publisher
  ISBN 978-1-59995-148-5
  1. Done, Phillip. 2. Elementary school teachers—United States—Biography. 3. Elementary school teaching—United States. 4. Teaching—Philosophy. 5. Education—Philosophy. 6. Conduct of life. I. Title.

LA2317.D615A3 2009
  372.11—dc22   2009001162

Dedicated to:

Mrs. Ranada who taught me how to read,
Mrs. Murayama who taught me how to think,
And Mr. Stretch—who taught me how to teach.

Contents

Contents

CONTENTS

August

Now all I have to teach you is one word—everything.

—*The Miracle Worker*

TEACHERHOOD

On my desk at school there is a treasure chest. It is filled with construction paper cards decorated with glitter glue, school photos framed with Popsicle sticks, and pictures drawn with tropical marker and colored pencil and love. If I'm in the drawings, I am usually as tall as the schoolhouse in the background. My head is bigger than the sun.

Next to parents, teachers are the most influential people in children's lives. We love, care, guide, and nurture. We collect baby teeth, check foreheads for fevers, and can punch the little silver dots on top of juice boxes with one swift poke of the straw. We are used to being called Mom and Dad. I wonder: Why don't we have a word that captures the essence of being a teacher—a word that encompasses the spirit of teaching? *Motherhood* and *fatherhood* are words. *Parenthood* is a word. I think *teacherhood* should be a word, too.

Teacherhood is knowing that softer voices are more effective than louder ones, that students read better under their desks, that you always hand out birthday treats at the end of the day, that kids will not hear the difference between *than* and *then,* that children will always choose chocolate chip cookies before oatmeal and raisin, and that if the office supply store is having a Back to School sale on folders but will only let you purchase twenty folders at a time—buy twenty, leave the store, return, grab another twenty, and go to a new register.

Teacherhood is understanding that you should never try to

teach anything on Halloween, that when kids start learning cursive they forget how to spell, that students who are usually quiet will become chatty the week before Christmas break, that desks swallow papers, that at any given moment a child could announce something random like he's been to Denver and saw a banana slug, that the best lessons on paper can tank in real life, that children who are about to throw up get clingy, that reading nothing but comics is like eating only pasta your whole life, and that for Show and Tell you do not ask Sarah to bring in her cat and Trevor to share his dog on the *same* day.

Teacherhood is knowing that when kids hold up their multi-plication flash cards to the light they can see the answers on the back, that children will leave the *t* out of *watch* and the second *m* out of *remember,* that you always explain the instructions *before* handing out the blocks (or beans or marshmallows), that cupcake paper is edible, that the pile of red construction paper in the supply room will be lowest in February, that when the air-conditioner man comes into the classroom and starts remov-ing the ceiling tiles — stop teaching, and that when children see their teacher burst out laughing or fight back tears while read-ing a book — they witness two of reading's greatest rewards.

Teacherhood is prying staples out of the stapler with a pair of scissors, following mud tracks to a student's desk, asking ques-tions about things when you already know the answers, laugh-ing at knock-knock jokes you've heard three hundred times, being able to make thirty-seven different things out of a paper plate, locating the exact book that a child is searching for when all she knows is that it has a yellow cover, knowing that a storm is coming without looking outside, pushing desks that have crept up throughout the day back to their original places, finding yel-low caps on blue markers, and counting to five while each child takes a drink at the drinking fountain so that no kid hogs all the water.

Teacherhood is correcting papers while watching *Letterman,* calculating how many workdays are left till the middle of June, singing the "ABC Song" out loud when looking up a word in the dictionary, taking the 7:00 AM dentist appointment, asking the woman at the dry cleaners if she can get out glue stick, unrolling a brand-new package of paper towels because you need one more tube for an art project, taking your students out for free play and calling it PE, knowing that no matter how much food you have at the Thanksgiving feast—kids will just grab the popcorn, and calling your student three different names before finally getting it right.

Teacherhood is standing in the center of the dodgeball circle while twenty children try to get you out, counting kids' heads on a field trip, confiscating yardsticks that have magically turned into swords, snitching candy from your own goody jar, collecting abandoned bird nests, scooping goop out of pumpkins, understanding that cursive m is easier to write than cursive k, having ninety-seven items in your emergency preparedness backpack but not being able to find the Band-Aids, knowing all about Cabbage Patch Kids, Beanie Babies, Pokémon, Smurfs, Elmo, Tamagotchis, Webkinz, and Bakugan before they became hot, and sitting in the "barber's chair" on Colonial Day while getting a shave with a Popsicle stick and Cool Whip.

Teacherhood is writing "Do Not Touch!" on the tape dispenser then hunting for it the very next day, sweating over not being able to get the DVD player to work while twenty kids offer to "help," waiting out in front of Target the morning after Thanksgiving to save fifty cents on ribbon, making rain parkas out of Hefty bags when it starts pouring on the field trip, expecting more chase games on the blacktop in spring than in fall, explaining that a rock is a very important role in the school play, yanking so hard on the wall map that it shoots up and jumps off the metal hooks, having butterflies the night before school starts, and understanding that a child may forget what you taught her—but will always remember how you made her feel.

BACK TO SCHOOL

There is a moment in August when teachers everywhere experience the same migratory call. This tug is always followed by a sigh, or a shake of the head, or both. *Where did the summer go?* Eventually, we make that first trip back to our classrooms. The key turns. The door opens. Summer is officially over.

Inside, the tile floor around the sink shines with a new coat of wax. The room smells like carpet cleaner. It is time to rebuild our nests. So we unstack chairs, arrange desks, organize books, and decorate bulletin boards. We make copies, sort through files, and put a brand-new shoe-box house in the bunny cage. And best of all, we get to visit the supply room again.

Teachers love school supplies. We thrill in taking the cellophane off new boxes of markers, stacks of Post-it notes, and sticks of modeling clay. We get tingly all over when we see cans full of newly sharpened yellow pencils fanned out in a perfect circle. Squeezing brand-new bottles of glue—better than chocolate.

I don't know a single grade school teacher who can make it through the summer without checking out at least one Back to School sale. We can't resist. But teachers must exercise caution whenever entering any Back to School department. There is one very important rule that we must follow: *Do not let on that you are a teacher.* I made this mistake recently in Office Depot.

When I arrived, the parking lot was full. Signs on the doors posted extended hours. Lines at the registers stretched clear to the center of the store. The Back to School section was packed with dazed moms and dads with supply lists in hand hunting through shelves, rifling through boxes, and fighting over the last Hannah Montana pencil case. It looked like Toys R Us at Christmastime. A manager stood in the aisle directing traffic. His forehead was sweaty. "You should have a fast-track lane like they do at Disneyland," I joked. He wasn't amused.

One woman was standing in front of the shelves talking to herself. "What in the heck is a D-ring binder?" Another was trying to convince her daughter that her pocket folders did not have to match her notebooks. A third was holding up three backpacks while her darling sat in the shopping cart.

"Do you want Tinker Bell, Scooby-Doo, or Little Mermaid?" the mom asked.

The child slapped the handle on the cart. "I want Barbie."

As I made my way through the aisle, I spotted a mom staring blankly at the pens. Poor gal. She looked like she was about to cry.

"Excuse me," I said. "Do you need some help?"

She turned to me. "I don't know what kind of markers I'm supposed to get. The teacher just wrote *one pack of colored washable markers*." The woman pointed to the racks. "There are *twenty* different kinds of markers here. Do I get Bold, Classic, or Techno Brite?" She threw up her hands. "Do I get an eight-pack, ten-pack, or twelve-pack?"

"Well," I replied, pulling one of the boxes off the shelf, "I always ask my students to bring in Crayola Classics. Eight-count."

The woman's eyes grew big. "Are you a *teacher*?"

"Uh-huh."

She gasped and seized my arm. News spread like head lice that there was a *real live teacher* in the store. Within seconds I was surrounded by moms asking me questions:

"Is this the right paper for a first grader?"

"Does a kindergartner need a binder?"

"How many glue sticks should I buy?"

"What the heck is a protractor?"

I doled out advice on calculators and scissors, lunch bags and hand sanitizer, composition books and facial tissue. The mommies thanked me as they checked the items off their lists. Finally, after about half an hour, I said good-bye to my new friends, made my purchases, and left the store.

Every year, it seems like stores put their Back to School supplies out earlier and earlier. It's bad enough that I have to sift through Christmas wrap to get to the Halloween candy and that shelves are full of valentines before New Year's, but setting up Back to School displays in June is just plain wrong! Teachers haven't even had a chance to write thank-you cards for their end-of-the-year gifts. The class pets that we just took home to care for over vacation are still wondering why it's so quiet.

Other professions aren't taunted when *they* go shopping. Doctors don't walk into Walgreens and find displays full of tongue depressors at half off. Dentists don't have to listen to blue-light special announcements for toothbrushes and dental floss.

At the end of June, I was pushing my cart down an aisle in Wal-Mart looking for some flip-flops and sunscreen when I stopped dead in my tracks. "No!" I cried out loud. "It can't be. Not already!" There in the center of the aisle sat enormous bins full of Elmer's glue and Bic pens and Scotch tape and one-size-fits-all book covers. Immediately I whipped my cart around and raced away like I was being chased by the dinosaurs in *Jurassic Park*. I dodged into the Housewares Department. After catching my breath, I quickly slipped out.

So how can a teacher avoid this slap of reality in the middle of summer? The trick is knowing exactly where a store's Back to School aisle is located so that you do not suddenly find yourself surrounded by *High School Musical* backpacks. After careful investigation of three major retailers, here is what I discovered:

Wal-Mart's Back to School section begins exactly one hundred twenty-three steps from the front door (I paced it off). If you stay within one hundred twenty-*two* paces from the entrance, you'll be safe. *Warning:* If you step past the Home and Office Department, you have gone too far. I repeat—do *not* pass Home and Office. The school supplies are in the next aisle.

Target is trickier than Wal-Mart. When walking into Target, you will *feel* safe. You won't see any cardboard buses at the entrance loaded with binders and folders plastered with the Jonas Brothers. But don't be fooled. Above you hang dozens of giant banners with oversize smiling pencils and rulers and students. (There are never teachers in these posters.) These signs hang ten feet apart and lead the customers right to the Back to School aisle. Do not look up. Look straight ahead. Do *not* look up!

Safeway stores are sneaky, too. Be careful. Their Back to School items are always placed close to the front of the store. But the good thing is that you will only find them near *one* of their two entrances, behind Door Number 1 (by the meat section) or Door Number 2 (close to the produce). If you choose wisely, you will avoid their Back to School display completely.

One evening, I stopped at Safeway to pick up some food for dinner. Inside the store, I spotted a young woman stacking bags of Tootsie Rolls and Kit Kats and Starburst and Skittles on shelves by the entrance. *She's not putting Halloween candy out already,* I thought. *It's only August.* I walked up to the clerk and pointed to the display.

"Uh . . . Is this for Halloween?"

"Nope," she answered. "For Back to School."

She must be joking.

I half laughed. "You're pulling my leg."

"It's true."

I had never heard of Back to School candy before. "What's it for? Treats from the teachers?"

"No. For the kids' lunches."

My jaw dropped. "You . . . you mean to tell me that you're selling candy for kids' *lunches*?"

She nodded.

"How long has this been going on?" I asked, raising my voice.

"A couple of years. Everyone's doing it."

I rubbed my forehead in disbelief. "I'm surprised you don't have Back to School soda pop," I muttered.

She pointed. "Aisle four."

FLY ON THE WALL

Everyone knows that the person who really runs a school is the secretary. If you have questions, ask the secretary. If you lose something, see the secretary. If the copier is jammed, get the secretary. If a child throws up, send her to the secretary.

Ellen has been our school secretary for more than twenty years. Her computer is covered with Far Side cartoons and kids' photos and inspirational quotes to get her through the day. The sign over her desk says, "Ask not what your secretary can do for you, but what you can do for your secretary!"

The day before school begins, Ellen posts the class lists on the library windows at 3:00 PM. All the teachers try to be off campus when those lists go up. If they stay at school, they are sure to be bombarded by students and parents who just want to stop by and say hello. For three hours.

This year my friend Sandy, who also teaches third grade, stopped by my room at two forty-five.

"It's almost three," Sandy said. "You're leaving, aren't you?"

I sighed. "I can't. I have too much to do."

"Make sure you lock your door and shut the blinds," she warned.

I laughed. "I'm going to hide out in the library." I figured I'd be safe there.

"Whatever you do, don't let anyone see you."

"I won't. I'll stay out of sight."

Sandy glanced at her watch. It was two fifty. "I gotta run.

See you in the morning." Then she cracked open my door, looked both ways, and made a mad dash to the parking lot.

I grabbed my lesson plan book, hurried over to the library, and crept in the back door where I found a seat in the corner of the room. Parents and kids had gathered outside the front glass doors waiting for the lists to go up. I had a good view from where I was sitting. I kept the lights off so no one would see me. The windows above the doors were open so I could hear what was going on.

Ellen walked into the library at exactly three o'clock and spotted me.

"What are you doing here?" she asked.

"Hiding," I whispered.

She looked away quickly and pretended I wasn't there. Then she started taping the lists on the inside of the windows. The crowd swarmed around. After all the lists were up, Ellen turned around and darted to the back door.

"You're not staying?" I asked.

"Not for a million dollars."

I flashed a smile. "If anyone has any questions, I'll give them your home number."

She laughed. "And I'll make sure you have bus duty for the whole year."

As I sat hidden, I watched dozens of children run their fingers down the lists, hunting for their names. The search is always the same. When kids get the teacher they want, they scream. After finding their names they look for their friends' names. If their friends are in the same class, they scream again. Before leaving campus, they rush to their new classrooms, press their faces against the windows to get a peek inside, and declare, "No one's there."

As the crowd grew, I heard one child shout, "I got Mr. Done!" He was jumping up and down. That felt good. It was John. I knew him well. Last year when I was on cafeteria duty, I opened thirty-seven of his juice boxes.

A few minutes later, I heard a mom ask, "Who'd you get?"

"Mr. Done," a sad voice answered.

I craned my neck to see who it was. It was Sarah. I knew her, too. In fact, everyone knew Sarah. In second grade she wore leopard leotards, pink cowboy boots, a purple-fringed leather jacket studded with rhinestones, and a plastic purple Barbie watch. On Picture Makeup Day, she got confused and came to school wearing glittery lip gloss and eye shadow.

"What's wrong with Mr. Done?" Sarah's mom asked.

"He gives homework," Sarah grumped.

"They all give homework, honey."

Sarah looked horrified.

Soon I heard another voice. "I got him! I got him!" Since there are only two male teachers on my campus—Mr. Davis, who teaches fifth grade, and myself—there was a good chance that this was one of mine. It was. The voice belonged to Trevor. I'd had Trevor's brother Stephen two years earlier. In fact, Stephen was with Trevor at the library window. As the boys walked away, I heard Stephen say, "Mr. Done's nice. Laugh at his jokes. He likes that."

Over the next hour, more children came by and ran their fingers down the lists then left to go press their faces against the windows of their new classrooms. When the crowd began to die down, I gathered my things, sneaked out the back door, and returned to my room. I set my lesson plan book on my desk, took one last look around, and headed out. Just as I was locking the door, Stephen and Trevor rode by on their bikes.

"Well, look who's here," I said with a big smile. "How are you boys doing?"

"Great," Stephen replied.

I walked toward them. "Did you have a nice summer?"

"Yeah," they answered in unison.

"All ready for school to start?" I asked.

"Uh-huh," said Stephen.

I looked at Trevor and smiled. "So, do you know who your teacher is?"

Trevor grinned and nodded.

"I'm glad you're in my class," I said.

His grin grew.

Then I looked at Stephen. "Are you excited about fifth grade?"

"Sort of," Stephen responded.

"Who'd you get?" I asked.

"Mr. Davis."

"Ahhhh," I said. Then I lowered my voice to a playful whisper. "You want to know a secret about Mr. Davis?"

"Sure," Stephen answered. He stepped toward me.

"Well," I said, "Mr. Davis is nice. Laugh at his jokes. He likes that."

Trevor and Stephen snapped surprised looks at each other. I smirked and strolled away.

"See you two tomorrow," I sang. "And happy first day of school!"

WELCOME BACK

On the first day of school, I sit alone in my classroom and wait for the morning bell to ring. The room is ready. Everything is in its place — like a house just before company comes to visit. My company is coming to stay for 185 days.

After the bell rings, I take a deep breath, gulp down the rest of my coffee, then push the door open. Twenty third graders are lined up. Twenty moms and dads stand nearby, snapping pictures on their digital cameras and cell phones. Their last words to their children are *good luck, pay attention, be good, wear your hair back, you'll make new friends,* and *don't drive your new teacher crazy.*

I look out at their nervous faces. "Good morning, boys and girls."

"Good morning," they answer softly.

I know these soft voices will last only till the first recess; then I will spend the remaining 184.75 days trying to get them to quiet down.

I smile. "My name is Mr. Done. It rhymes with *phone*. Please come inside. You'll find your name tags on your desks."

One by one, the kids parade into their new classroom. In march twenty new backpacks, fifteen new pencil cases, ten new outfits, eighteen new binders, seventy-five new folders, sixteen new lunch sacks, nine pairs of new shoes, seven new haircuts, and 6,395 new markers.

I greet each child as he or she walks into the room.

"What's your name?" I ask.

"Emily."

"Nice to meet you, Emily."

She hands me a flower. The stem is wrapped in aluminum foil.

"Thank you, sweetheart."

The next student pulls her backpack behind her. It's on wheels. She looks like she is on her way to catch a flight.

I smile at her. "What's your name, honey?"

"Melanie."

"I like your backpack."

"Thanks. It has wheels."

"I see that."

Melanie rolls on in. A boy with a buzz cut steps on up.

"And what's your name?" I ask.

"Christopher," he answers brightly.

"Welcome to third grade, Christopher."

Immediately he leans way back and starts walking inside.

My eyes get big. "What are you doing?"

"The limbo!"

After all the kids are inside, I kick up the doorstop and start closing the door. I look out at the parents and smile reassuringly. "Don't worry. I'll take good care of them."

There are certain things that grade school teachers do on the first day of school. We read our students a story. We give them a tour of the campus. We play Name Bingo. We do all we can to make sure that the kids have a nice day. Why? So they go home and tell their moms that they like the teacher.

I give my students an All About Me Survey. It is a good way to get to know the children. Here are some of the responses to this year's questions:

When is your birthday? Gina: In six and a half days! *How many people are in your family?* Laura: Six including my dog. *What's your phone number?* Angela: Home or cell? *Where were you born?* Trevor: At Stanford, but I'm a Cal fan. *What is your favorite food?* David: Maraschino cherries. *What's the most difficult part of school?* Stacy: The monkey bars. *What is your favorite drink?* Christopher: Virgin Margaritas. No salt.

What are your favorite subjects in school? Sarah: Reading, writing, and imagining. *What would you like to study this year?* Danny: Taxidermy. *What would you like me to know about yourself?* Kevin: I eat paper.

What do you want to be when you grow up? Joshua: Jackie Chan. *Do you play any sports?* Brian: Soccer. My team is called the Barracuda Pirate Warrior Transformer Secret Agent Cone Heads. But everyone calls us the Cone Heads.

During the first week, teachers begin assessing their students. Sometimes this can be quite entertaining. One year I was checking Mark's understanding of geometry and set three blocks out in front of him—a triangle, a rectangle, and a pentagon.

I tapped the blocks with my pencil. "Could you please name the shapes."

Mark scrunched his nose.

"Just name the shapes," I repeated.

Mark looked at me with an *are you kidding me* sort of look and shrugged. "Okay." Then pointing to each block he said, "This one's Joe. This one's Frank. And this one's Bob."

Another year when I was sitting with Jacob, I drew some stick figures and cookies on a piece of paper.

"Okay, Jacob," I started, "if there are three students and six cookies, how many cookies does each child get?"

He shook his head. "Not enough."

Last year when checking Jessica's number sense, I said, "If I give you three hamsters one day, and four hamsters the next day, and five hamsters the third day—how many hamsters would you have altogether?"

She thought about it. "Thirteen."

"That's close," I responded. "Now think about it carefully. If I give you three hamsters the first day, four the next, and five the day after that, how many would you have?"

This time Jessica used her fingers.

"Thirteen," she answered again.

Hmm, I thought. *Let me try another approach.*

I grabbed some paper clips and arranged them on the table. *Maybe this will help.* "Look," I explained. "If I give you three paper clips, then four, then five—how many do you have?"

"Twelve."

"Then why did you say thirteen when I gave you hamsters?"

"Because I have one at home."

That same year I worked with Cindy on fractions.

"Cindy, let's say you're really hungry. Which would you rather eat—an eighth of a pizza or a fourth of a pizza?"

"What kind is it?"

I shrugged. "I don't know . . . pepperoni."

"With extra sauce?"

"Sure," I replied, smiling.

"And extra cheese?"

"Why not?"

"Are there olives?"

"Olives, too."

She shook her head. "I wouldn't eat it. I hate olives."

*　　*　　*

This year I began my reading assessments the second day of school. During silent reading, I called kids up one at a time to listen to them read. Each child read a selection entitled "All About Dogs."

Trevor was the first one up. Before he started reading the selection, I asked him some questions.

"Do you like dogs?" I asked.

"Uh-huh."

"Do you have a dog?"

"Yeah."

"What kind?"

"A golden retriever."

"What's its name?"

"Sparky."

"Is Sparky a nice dog?"

"No. He jumps on the furniture and drinks out of the toilet. He failed doggy school twice."

"Oh, I see."

"He can do tricks!" Trevor added.

"What kind of tricks?"

"Well, when we say, 'Sparky, do you like Paris Hilton?' he does this."

Trevor dived on the floor and played dead.

Next it was Melanie's turn.

"Melanie, do you have a dog?"

"No, a cat. She just had eight kittens."

"Wow, that's a lot."

"She was pregnant a long time." I held back a laugh. "Last week was her birthday."

"Did you celebrate?"

"No. She can't eat cake."

Christopher followed Melanie.

"Do you have a dog, Christopher?"

"Yep."

"What's your dog's name?"

"Bitsy."

"Is Bitsy a boy dog or a girl dog?"

"Well, she *thinks* she's a boy dog."

I look confused. "What do you mean?"

Christopher jumped off his chair, crouched down on all fours, and lifted his hind leg. "Now you understand?"

Teachers assess more than reading and math in the beginning of the year. We're also evaluating student behavior, sizing up the kids to see who the pistols are going to be. Over the years, I have developed several pistol assessments:

The Lunch Test: When the cafeteria serves hamburgers for lunch and she opens her ketchup packet by setting it on the picnic table and smashing one end with her fist.

The Sharing Test: When it is time for Show and Tell and he pulls out a bag of plastic tanks and Big Time Wrestling action figures.

The Cursive Test: When you ask everyone to make a cursive *a* in the air and he writes with his foot.

The Supply Test: When she punches thumbtacks into all the pink erasers to make little eraser men.

The Playground Test: If she tries to sell the little eraser men to the first graders.

The Seasons Test: When you ask him to name the order of the seasons and he answers baseball, football, and basketball.

The Math Test: When you're setting up a mock store during math time and he puts out a cup for tips.

The Entrance Test: When you open the classroom door in the morning and she shouts, "Trick-or-treat!" In August.

The Delivery Test: When you ask him to take a message to the office and he writes "UPS" on a sticky note and smacks it on his chest before dashing out the door.

The Color Test: When he tells you that his favorite color is camouflage.

The Clothing Test: When he walks in wearing a T-shirt that says, "Homework kills trees. Stop the madness."

The Science Test: When you ask her to tell you something about food chains and she says, "McDonald's is bigger than Burger King."

The Art Test: When drawing his self-portrait, he makes his eyes bloodshot.

The Interview Test: When you ask the kids to write down one question they have for the teacher and his is, "Do you have back hair?"

The Second-Grade Teacher Test: When you show the second-grade teachers your new class list and they cringe, gasp, cover their mouths, sit down quickly, shake their heads, cross themselves, grab their hearts, or ask if you're taking Prozac.

September

Well, remember the rules . . . no playing ball in
the house, no fighting, no answering the phone
"City Morgue."

The Cat in the Hat (the film)

KIDS

Pretty soon I will celebrate my twenty-fifth year in the class-room. I can't believe it's been that long. It seems like just yesterday I was a new teacher sneaking into the veteran's room and peeking in her lesson plan book to see what I should be teaching the next day. I calculated that I have spent three months of my life taking roll, five months passing out papers, and two years waiting for kids to finish grinding their pencils in the electric pencil sharpener.

Recently, someone asked me if kids today are different than the kids I taught when I first started. My answer is no. Kids are the same today as they always were. Yes, they have Xboxes and PlayStations and Game Boys and iPods and cell phones and computers now. But it's the gadgets that have changed, not the children. Kids are kids are kids.

Kids still get excited when you bring in a fossil or a magnet. They still get the giggles, and will giggle more when you tell them to stop giggling.

If a mom sends in milk with birthday cupcakes, one child will show you his milk mustache. Another will lap the milk up just like a kitty cat.

When throwing something away, they will always shoot a basket. When playing kickball, they will climb on the backstop while they're waiting for their turn. Someone's shoe will go fly-ing when he kicks the ball.

They cannot read *The Guinness Book of World Records*

during silent reading time without tapping the students next to them and pointing to the man with all the muscles.

When they can't find a paper, they will claim that they handed it in, then discover it in their desks two weeks later. When the bell rings at the end of recess, one boy will take the tetherball and give it one last whopping spin.

As soon as they spot their teacher coming to pick them up in line, they will shout, "Here he comes!" When they see him walking across the blacktop during lunch recess, they will wave at him and shout his name like they haven't seen him in five years.

If you spray cleaner on the overhead projector while the light is on, they will squeal as the ink spreads out on the glass. If you clean the projector glass with the light off, they will ask you to turn it on.

They will say "Yuck!" when licking the envelopes for their valentines. They will laugh when they squeeze the detergent bottle and it whistles. They will ask if they can write about Spider-Man for their animal report.

If you excuse them for lunch one second late, they will let you know. When they deliver something to the library, they will come back panting because they ran the whole way.

Just before you pass around photos, they will promise to touch only the edges. When you get the photos back, they will be covered with fingerprints.

If they get a new three-ring binder, they will proudly hold it up for you to see. If you hand them a piece of paper, they will stare at the three rings and ask how to put it in their binder. After you show them, they will open and close the rings until you tell them to stop.

When you bring in a box of Froot Loops to hand out as

treats, they will ask for the prize inside. When you finish hand-ing out the Froot Loops, one will ask if there are seconds.

If there are three staplers sitting on the counter and one of the staplers is smaller than the other two, they will call that one the baby. The other two will be Mommy and Daddy.

They will spend a week working on their Mother's Day cards then forget to take them home. If they have to leave for a dentist appointment at ten forty-five, they will remind you at eight thirty, nine thirty, ten thirty, ten forty, and ten forty-three.

If you ask them to pick a rhythm instrument out of the box, they will always fight over the drum. They will laugh every time you add a new body part to the poor guy in hangman.

When doing crosswords, one child will have no problem cramming seven letters into a five-letter word. When you hand out name tags with the sticky backs, somebody will immediately put the name tag over his mouth.

They will make gagging noises if you mention the words *kiss, hug, embrace,* or *smooch.* If you say *mistletoe,* they will scream. When you hold up a Hershey's Kiss and say, "Who wants a kiss?" they will scream also.

When they are almost at the end of a piano piece, they will forget the music and ask if they can start over. When they clean the whiteboard with erasers, they will pretend they're playing air hockey. When a child stands in front of the classroom shar-ing her family photo album, she will hold the album so that only she can see it.

They will always ask the teacher what kind of car he drives. If you show them your car in the parking lot, they will look in-side and announce how messy it is.

When a visitor speaks to the class and you ask the children for questions, one will launch into a story. If you say, "Let's give a round of applause," they will clap while moving their hands in a circle.

If you light a candle in science class, they will ask if they can blow it out. When you pass around a conch shell, they will always listen for the sea.

When you're taking a vote, some wise guy will raise two hands. When you ask one child a question, another will blurt out the answer.

After they sing "I've Been Workin' on the Railroad," someone will always ask, "Who's Dinah?" If they sing "You're a Grand Old Flag" at the school assembly, kids in the front of the multipurpose room will end up finishing before kids in the back.

They can't talk to you without fiddling with something on your desk. Most can't speak to you without turning back and forth like the inside of a washing machine or standing on one leg like a flamingo.

When the grass is frosty, they will pretend to ice skate on it. When playing Red Light, Green Light, one child will always take an extra flying leap after the teacher shouts, "Red light!"

If they were in your classroom last year and come by to visit, they will look to see whose name tags are on *their* desks. If they see that you're doing something new this year, they will always say, "Why didn't we do that?"

When they tear the wrapper off a Band-Aid, they will never throw it away. If you say, "Open your book to page fifty-seven," and a child opens her book right up to page fifty-seven, she will announce it and show you.

They will ask for an ice pack when they don't really need it. They will always ask if they can return the ice pack to the office during class time.

When you give a child a Dixie cup, he will put it over his mouth and suck in all the air so that the sides of the cup cave in.

When they're turning the knobs on the microscope and the crystal that they're examining comes into focus, they will shout, "Whoa!"

If you explain that soon they will get to work with a partner, they will reach for their best friend before you finish giving directions. They will ask why coffee cake is called coffee cake if there is no coffee in it.

When your stomach growls, they will tell you. When you cut open a pumpkin to count the number of seeds, one child will shout, "You're killing it!" When they run to tell you that they just kicked the ball over the fence, they will always smile when they announce it.

They will not think that bringing in eight My Little Ponies, twenty-seven polished rocks, and an entire snow globe collection is too much for one afternoon of Show and Tell. In their minds, there are only two types of teachers—nice ones and mean ones.

When solving problems using the greater-than and less-than signs, they will turn the > and < signs into fish, alligators, and Pac-Men. They will have a favorite multiplication problem. It will *never* be 8 × 7.

Hand them a straw and they'll blow off the wrapper. Pass out animal crackers in the red circus box and they'll always tell you which animal they got.

When you go on a field trip to the theater and hand them their tickets, they will pretend the tickets are razors and shave with them. When they're watching the play and the soloist sings a ballad, they will squirm. When you leave the theater, someone will slip her hand into yours.

Would I trade this life of giggles and stories and songs and runny noses and glitter and chairs that are too small to sit in? Not in a million years. Life with kids is a rich one. And though there are days when I'd rather not deal with spilled paint and the missing books and sick betta fish, I'm sure that someday when I'm retired I will look back on all this and itch to clean out a backpack, pump up a ball, and hear a good knock-knock joke.

TEACHING 101

This month, my niece Amanda began her first year at a local university. I took her out to dinner to celebrate.

"So, Amanda," I said, "do you know what you want to study?"

A smile spread across her face. "I'm thinking of going into teaching."

That warmed me up inside. "That's great. What grade do you want to teach?"

"Well, maybe first or second. Or maybe third. I'm not really sure. Definitely the little ones."

"Just like me," I said, smiling.

Amanda leaned in. "Uncle Phil, why did you decide to teach elementary?"

I chuckled. "They can't drive yet. I wanted to find a parking space."

As I drove home from dinner that night, I thought about how I could help Amanda and other aspiring teachers. And so I decided to write down a few pointers — a few essentials I've learned along the way.

THE PRIMARY TEACHER'S SURVIVAL GUIDE

CHAPTER ONE — PREPARATION

So you want to be a teacher? Well, you don't have to wait until you have a classroom to get ready. There are lots of things you can do right now to help you prepare.

Practice cutting apples, pumpkins, hearts, and shamrocks out of construction paper. Learn to double-knot shoelaces, read upside down, peel bananas with no stems, and make bumblebees, caterpillars, butterflies, ants, spiders, alligators, and the centers of daffodils out of egg cartons. Start drinking five cups of coffee at the beginning of each day. Hold until lunchtime. Look cheerful.

Begin saving cottage cheese containers, Clorox bottles, oatmeal boxes, Styrofoam meat trays, orange juice cans, plastic butter tubs, mayonnaise jars, and the tubes in wrapping paper, paper towels, and toilet paper. Stuff all this into a closet along with Halloween costumes, cowboy hats, tambourines, maracas, sombreros, plastic leis, and copies of the Declaration of Independence and the Gettysburg Address on crinkled yellow paper.

Whenever you go to a restaurant, point out all spelling mistakes on menus, move all water glasses from the edge of the table, call food servers "sweetie," and ask if you may keep the crayons that come with the child's menu. If you order pizza, give whomever you are with a lesson in fractions. Gulp down meal in three minutes.

Relearn everything that you forgot since you finished grade school, including the parts of speech, the order of planets, the original thirteen colonies, large Roman numerals, all the state capitals, the names of the presidents, how to make a cursive $\mathcal{Q}$, and the second verse to "This Land Is Your Land." Memorize the following sayings: "I love that book, too," "Thank you. I'll hang it right here," "Please stop bouncing that ball," and "Get your collar out of your mouth. Lunch is in five minutes."

Practice opening Tupperware containers, potato chip bags, milk cartons, and Go-GURT tubes. Fill your pockets with rubber bands, marbles, trading cards, finger skateboards, and anything with *Hello Kitty* on it. Before you go to bed, empty all of this onto your nightstand. Repeat daily.

Not sure if you are up for the messes? There are several things you can do to prepare:

1. Squeeze paint on paper plate. Turn paper plate upside down. Drop on carpet. Let dry.
2. Pour apple juice in Styrofoam cup. Set on desk. Knock cup over.
3. Make peanut butter sandwich. Take one bite. Hide remainder in desk. Leave for five months.
4. Go outside. Walk in mud. Walk back inside. Do not step on mat. Walk directly on carpet. Repeat twenty times.

Never visit the BMW dealership, read *Town and Country,* or walk into any store carrying Gucci, Hermès, Ferragamo, Louis Vuitton, Tiffany, Rolex, Cartier, or Mont Blanc. You cannot afford it.

Chapter Two — Which Grade Should I Teach?

Once you are ready to teach, you must now decide which age you would like to work with. Since you already know that you want to be with little ones, here is a guide to make your decision easier:

Kindergartners

Kindergartners love to be read to. They will ask you to read the same book five hundred times. When you are reading, they will want to sit very close to you on the carpet so that they can touch your shoes and rub your legs. For kindergartners, snack time is playtime. When they sit down to eat, their bananas will turn into guns, their pretzels will become helicopters, and their carrot sticks will morph into World War II fighter jets. Kindergartners take their classroom jobs seriously. Two attendance monitors will carry the roll sheet with four hands all the way to the office. The picker-uppers will make vacuum noises when they clean the floor. Kindergarten boys often miss the toilet completely when going to the bathroom. *Advice for new teachers:* Emphasize the second step in Using the Restroom Speech: (1) Ready; (2) *Aim;* (3) Fire.

First Graders

First graders like to be the first in line. They will stand by the classroom door during the entire recess so they can be at the head of the line when the bell rings. First graders love to use big words like *infinity* and *bazillion.* They will know more dinosaur names than you do. First graders are obsessed with Velcro. During Story Hour they will strap and unstrap the Velcro on their shoes. If the teacher has Velcro on his shoes, they will strap and unstrap his, too. First graders like to bring the conversation back to them. If you're talking about crocodile teeth, they will open their mouths and show you where they lost theirs. If you talk about fish, they will tell you how long they can hold their breath underwater. First graders also love to glue. Whenever they glue something, they will use enough to cement a skyscraper. *Advice for new teachers:* Hide Elmer's.

Second Graders

Second graders are crazy about erasers. They will use the entire pink tip of a pencil to erase one word. The more they erase, the more little eraser droppings they can blow off their desks. Second graders love their teachers almost as much as they love their erasers. They will bring their teacher daisy chains and dandelions and worms that they found at recess. Second graders enjoy bringing things in from home, too. Show and Tell items may include dead mice and dentures. *Advice for new teachers:* Check each sharing item *before* it is pulled from the bag.

Third Graders

Third graders are obsessed with money. They will tell you how much they have in their bank accounts. Do not be surprised if they have more than you. Third graders have very strong opinions. If you mention a food that they do not like, they will grab their throats. Third graders enjoy learning about history. When you teach them about Vincent Van Gogh, they will remember that he cut his ear off. When learning about the Pilgrims, they will remember that they drank beer. Third graders also love routine. If the class changes the calendar together every day then sings the weather song, but the substitute sings the weather song before changing the calendar, the children will tell the sub that she did it wrong. If the substitute writes the date on the whiteboard with a blue marker when the teacher normally uses a red marker, the students will report this to their teacher as soon as he returns. They will recall this incident thirty-seven more times throughout the year. *Advice for new teachers:* Do not be absent.

Chapter Three — Nuts and Bolts

Congratulations! You have been offered your first job. You got the grade level you hoped for. You have been given the keys to your very first classroom. The school year is about to start. Now what? Here's a list of everything you need to know to make your rookie year a success.

How to Prepare a Bulletin Board

Go to workroom. Pull paper off large roll. Return to classroom. Starting at one end of bulletin board, begin stapling paper onto board. Smash out air bubbles as you go. If there is a fire extinguisher or a thermostat on the wall, cover it with paper. (Cut out fire extinguisher and thermostat later.) When you get to end of paper and discover that you still have two feet of bulletin board left because you did not measure board or paper when you started, go back to supply room and get more paper. Patch wall. Trim with scalloped border.

How to Set Up Your Classroom

Plaster walls with posters of the water cycle, rocks and minerals, volcanoes, the layers of the earth, the parts of speech, and a birthday chart. Prop wooden apples and *Teachers Are Special* books on desk. Put Little League photos of students on file cabinet, magnets on whiteboard, and origami on top of computer. Hang number line over whiteboard, lunch menu by entrance, and sign on front door that says, "Sorry I missed you. Either I am on a field trip, on yard duty, at PE, or I ran away."

How to Fill in Your Lesson Plan Book

Open your planner. Look at blank squares. Block out all recess times. Pencil in all lunch periods. Draw big smiley faces in boxes when students go to PE and library and when the art teacher comes in. Make giant X's in all holidays.

How to Greet Children in the Morning

Open classroom door. As your students walk inside say, "Hello," "Good morning," "Nice to see you," "Show me what's in your hand," "Leave the caterpillar outside," and "You can visit him at recess."

How to Get Kids to Read

Sit at your computer. Let student stand behind you. Start typing e-mail.

How to Survive Back to School Night

When standing up in front of the classroom, find one parent who is smiling and direct entire presentation to her. Talk all the way till the end of the hour so that you do not have time for questions.

How to Get Students to Quiet Down Immediately

If your cell phone rings during class, answer it.

CHAPTER FOUR — SIZING UP YOUR STUDENTS

Once your room is set up and your procedures are in place, it is time to get to know your students and determine their learning styles. Musical learners will sing "The Funeral March" when the tadpole dies. Spatial learners will take apart the pencil sharpener for you if it's not working. Verbal learners will point out the spot on your chin where you missed shaving. Kinesthetic learners will show you their double-jointed body parts, will press down so hard on their pencils that you can read their writing clear through to the other side of the paper, and—when making landform maps out of flour, salt, and water—will taste the volcano.

When I finished writing my *Survival Guide,* I slipped it into an envelope and wrote Amanda a note:

> My Dear Amanda,
>   I thought this might come in handy someday. I won't lie to you: The kids will keep you on your toes. But you'll find no other profession as rewarding. I

promise you that. Nor as entertaining. This morning one of my students asked me if I was free to babysit on Friday night. Another wants me to get a disco ball for the classroom. And all day long my kids applauded every time I took a sip of coffee. You'll make a wonderful teacher. I'm proud of you.

Love,
Uncle Phil

PHOTOS

Recently I was hunting in my closet at home when I came across my box of old school photos—not photos of me as a kid, but as a teacher. I've saved them all. Every year when the pictures arrive at school, I pull them out of the envelope, check my hairline, then tuck them back. Eventually, I toss the photographs into my picture box. I never give any of them away. What am I supposed to do—mail them with my Christmas card and write on the back: "Phil in third grade"?

Looking through my box of photos reminded me of a night at the Oscars. In one, I sported a mustache (Tom Selleck phase). In a second, my hair was greased back (Antonio Banderas). In a third, I looked like I had just woken up (Sean Penn). And in another, I had a buzz cut that was so short I appeared to be bald (Bruce Willis).

As I neared the bottom of the box, I pulled out a photo of me with a goatee. I laughed when I saw it. That goatee certainly didn't last long.

"What's that?" Julie asked from her desk one day, pointing to my chin.

"It's a toupee," Anthony announced across the classroom.

"It's *not* a toupee," I corrected. "It's a *goatee*."

"A *what*?" Julie demanded.

"A goatee," I repeated, rubbing my new whiskers. "It's a beard but just around my chin."

I lifted my jaw for Julie to see. She examined it.

"You've got a lot of gray," Julie pointed out.

That night, I bought one of those boxes of hair dye for men. After I mixed it up and brushed it into my whiskers, I noticed that some of the dye was getting on my skin. *Uh-oh. Is this stuff permanent? What if it stays on my skin?* Panicked, I grabbed a razor and shaved the goatee. The next day when Julie saw me, she said, "Your mustache looks good off."

Since I started teaching, there are certain things about school photos that have never changed. First is the envelope they arrive in. It always has a window in it. Through this window you get to see a third of your face, the top of your head, and one ear. There is only one reason the envelopes have this window: to ease the shock. The background in school photos hasn't changed, either. For as long as I've been teaching, all school pictures have had that same light blue background. In fact, if *Jeopardy!* ever posted "School Photos" as a category, I wouldn't be surprised if the winning answer were "What is blue?"

Look at any teacher's individual photos and you'll see that most look preoccupied. Some appear dazed. If they're smiling at all, the smile seems fake. Why? Do you know what grade school teachers have been doing just before sitting down to have their individual photos taken? They have been smashing down bed hair, tucking in shirts, keeping children in line, straightening collars, tying bows, fixing buttons that are in the wrong holes, blotting sweaty after-recess foreheads, handing Kleenex to kids with runny noses, standing behind the photographer trying to get kids to smile, and searching in the Lost and Found box in the corner of the multi for a shirt for Danny to wear because his mom will not be happy if she sees half the soccer field all over his new shirt.

One of my jobs on Picture Day is to pass out the plastic combs while the children wait in line. Before I start handing them out,

I always give the Comb Speech: Do *not* share your combs. Hold on to them. Please take them out of your hair before having your picture taken.

Normally, the little plastic combs are black. But this year they were red, green, blue, and yellow.

I handed Melanie a blue one.

"Can I have red?" she asked.

I gave her red.

Sarah was next. "Green, please."

I felt like I was handing out Otter Pops.

Gina studied the combs in my hand as if she were deciding on which cupcake had the most frosting. "Mmm . . . can I have yellow?"

"Honey, they're all the same."

She pointed to Emily. "*She* got yellow."

I let out a sigh and handed her a yellow. Then I made an announcement. "Okay, class, no more choosing colors. Take the ones I give you."

"Then can we trade?" asked Brian.

"No!"

By the time the teacher gets to sit down for his own photo, he is completely wiped out. But the fun has just begun. Now the teacher must take a seat on the photographer's stool. This is similar to sitting in the dentist's chair while he performs a root canal. The teacher can't move. He must sit perfectly still with hands folded, knees together, back straight, chin up, and feet planted on the masking tape while his students stand on the sidelines unsupervised.

Our school photographer's name is Charlie. He has been taking school photos for thirty-seven years. Charlie loves taking kids' pictures—except when the cafeteria is serving pizza. If Picture Day takes place on Pizza Day, Charlie says kids will have ear-to-ear sauce stains and look like clowns.

This year while I was sitting helplessly on the stool and Charlie was tilting my chin, Christopher was demonstrating for his classmates how to slide across the multi floor as if he were stealing second base. Trevor was making farting noises as he emptied his gel bottle onto Kevin's head. And John was trying to see if he could turn his plastic comb into a boomerang.

Every year before I take a seat on Charlie's stool, I say the same thing: "Listen you guys—when I sit down I don't want anyone to fool around. I mean it. I'm serious." But do you think my students listen? Absolutely not. They stand behind the lights and point and giggle and make faces at me because few things are more fun than trying to make your teacher laugh when he is having his photo taken on Picture Day.

VANILLA WAFERS

We have a new teacher at our school. Her name is Carrie. Carrie teaches third grade a few doors down from me. At the end of the first week, I went to check on her. She was sitting at her desk sorting through some papers.

"Well," I said, clapping my hands together, "you made it through week one. Congratulations!"

"Yeah!" Carrie cheered.

"Only 180 more days to go."

"Ahhhhhh!" she cried.

I sat down in a kid chair. "So how's it going?"

"Well," she sighed, "between today's fire drill, a birthday party, and the school assembly that I forgot about until the last minute, I don't know if my kids learned anything."

I laughed. "That's normal." I leaned back in my chair and crossed my legs. "So can you relax this weekend?"

She held up her lesson plan book and grinned. "It's empty."

"Ah yes," I said with a nod. "I remember. Don't worry. The second year is easier. Trust me."

"I hope so," she breathed out.

"Hey," I said, "mind if I give you some advice from an old vet?"

"Please."

I uncrossed my legs and leaned in. "Don't try to do it all your first year."

Carrie gave an understanding nod.

"You'll want to make everything perfect," I continued. "Like you were trained to do in teacher school. But you can't." Carrie nodded some more. "And cut yourself a lot of slack. Learning to teach is like learning a new language."

"Uh-oh," she squeaked.

"What?"

"I didn't do so well in French."

We both laughed.

"May I tell you something else?" I added.

"Absolutely."

I paused for a moment. "Sometime in the next few weeks you'll have such a bad day that you will wonder why you even went into this profession. Expect it. We all have those days."

Her eyes got big. "Even *you*?"

"Absolutely. But the funny thing is that every time I have a really bad day, it's soon followed by a wonderful one that reminds me of why I became a teacher in the first place." Carrie listened closely. "In all my years of teaching, it has never failed. Never."

Her face broke into a smile. "I'll try to remember that."

I turned and looked around the room. Her students' self-portraits filled one board. Their autobiographies were up on another. Giant tempera-painted sunflowers mounted on black paper hung over the sink. "It looks great in here. You're ahead of me. I don't have all my kids' work up yet."

"Thanks," Carrie said. Then she put her elbows on a stack of papers, rested her chin in her hands, and looked out at the desks. "Phil, I *think* everything is going well, but I'm not sure that I'm . . . I'm not sure that I'm reaching them."

"Ahh," I said, nodding my head. "Vanilla wafers."

"Huh?"

"Vanilla wafers," I mused aloud. "When I was a new teacher, I had the same thought. I wondered if I was making an impact.

Then one morning I walked to the front of the room and found a Ziploc bag with three vanilla wafers resting on my desk. I figured someone had dropped it on the floor and the custodian picked it up. I held up the bag and asked if anyone had lost them. No one answered. Then a soft voice in the first row whispered, 'They're for you.'"

A smile crossed Carrie's face.

"*That* was my sign," I said, holding up one finger.

My eyes shifted to the wall behind her. Taped on the whiteboard was a colored-pencil drawing of a woman with rosy cheeks, long eyelashes, and a Marlo Thomas hairdo. A bright sun wearing glasses smiled in the corner. A rainbow swooped through the words *To Miss Baxter.*

I pointed to the drawing. "Is that from one of your students?"

Carrie turned and looked at it. "Yes."

"There's your sign," I said with a smile. "You're doing great."

LETTERS

They say that the art of letter writing is dying. Well, this simply is not true. Ask any elementary school teacher if you don't believe me. Teachers help kids write friendly letters all the time—letters to pen pals, cards for Grandparent's Day, thank-yous to our field trip drivers. When a child writes a letter that is really cute, sometimes I'll pull in his mom and share it. Last year after we wrote valentines to the veterans, I showed Martin's mom. Martin wrote, "Dear Vet, Happy Veteran's Day. Thanks for taking care of my cat. She's all better now."

Writing a friendly letter is not easy for a third grader. There is *so* much to think about—which words to capitalize, where to put the commas, what to indent, and whether to sign off with *Sincerely, Love,* or *From.* It's a lot for a child to wrap his head around. But letter writing isn't just difficult for the kids. It's not easy to teach, either.

This year on the morning of Back to School Night, I handed out paper to each child. Then I drew a giant piece of paper with lines and margins on the whiteboard.

"Okay, everyone," I began, "today we are going to start writing letters to our parents welcoming them to Back to School Night. We'll leave them out on our desks so that your moms and dads will see them when they walk into the classroom tonight."

Dylan looked worried. "*On* our desks or *in* our desks?"

"On *top*," I answered.

He sighed loudly. "Good."

I continued the lesson. "Now boys and girls, there are five

parts to a friendly letter. The first part is the *Date*." I tapped the large paper that I had drawn on the board and pointed to the place for the date. "In a friendly letter, the date goes on the upper right side of your paper. But try not to write in the margin."

"What's a margin?" Gina asked.

"The space on the side of your paper." I grabbed a sheet of binder paper off my desk and pointed to the left margin. "*This* is the left margin. See the pink line." Everyone looked down at the pink lines on their papers. I moved my finger to the other side. "And *this* is the right margin. There's a pink line there, too, but it's harder to see. Can you all see it?" Everyone leaned in.

"I see it!" John shouted.

"I see it!" Kevin echoed.

"Me, too!" Emily burst out.

I went on. "The reason the pink line is so light is because it's on the other side of the paper."

As soon as I said this, the entire class turned their papers over at the same time and started chattering.

THIRD-GRADE FACT: Finding the pink line on the back of a piece of binder paper is a very important discovery.

"Okay," I said, "now we are all going to write the date."

I wrote it on the board: *September 10, 2008.*

"Make sure you put a comma after the *10*," I instructed. "A comma *always* goes after the day."

"Can we write . . ." John cringed as he tried to think of the right word. "Can we . . . you know . . . make it smaller?"

I helped him out. "You mean—may you *abbreviate*?"

THIRD-GRADE FACT: Abbreviating is more fun than writing the whole word out.

I shook my head. "Sorry. I'd like you to practice writing the whole word."

"Can we write 9 slash 10?" Laura asked, making a hand movement for the slash.

THIRD-GRADE FACT: Making slashes is even more fun than abbreviating.

"Not today," I answered. "I want you all to practice writing the date out entirely."

I moved on. "Okay now, I'd like all of you to write today's date on the top line. And try to not write in the margin."

I knew exactly what would happen next. When kids first write the date on the top line of their letters, they *never* allow themselves enough room. An eight-year-old will begin writing the date in his normal penmanship. But when he is about half-way through, he will realize that he is quickly approaching THE PINK LINE. Determined to not cross it, he will start to write smaller and smaller, eventually stacking letters one on top of the other. When he is finished writing the whole date, it will look like it just crashed into a pink wall. Unhappy with the way that this has turned out, the child will then begin erasing his paper with the same force that one uses to clean a dirty pan with an S.O.S pad. The paper will tear. He will ask for a second piece, upon which he will start writing the date in the exact same place he did on the first one.

After my students wrote the date (and I handed out more paper), I continued with the lesson.

"The next part of our letter," I explained, "is the *Greeting*. The greeting is where you write *Dear Mom and Dad*." I pointed to the left side of my large letter. "The greeting begins on *this* side of the paper. It goes on the next line after the date." I wrote *Dear Mom and Dad* on the board. "Does anyone know what mark follows the greeting?"

"A comma," Laura answered.

"Very good. In a friendly letter, the greeting is always followed by a comma." I drew a gigantic comma after *Dad*. It was bigger than my head. The kids burst out laughing. "This is our second comma." I pointed to both of them. "See?" Then, putting my cap back on my marker, I turned and faced the kids. "Okay, next I'd like you all to write *Dear Mom and Dad* on your papers. And . . ." I paused. "Don't forget the comma."

Now, you'd think that writing *Dear Mom and Dad* would be easy. It's only four words plus one little comma, right? Wrong. Do you know how many variations there are on these four words? Thirty-three! And *that's* if the children know how to spell *dear* (which they don't). Every year I see all thirty-three variations:

dear mom and dad
dear mom and Dad
dear mom And dad
dear Mom and dad
Dear mom and dad
dear mom and dad,
dear mom and Dad,
dear mom And dad,
dear Mom and dad,
Dear mom and dad,
dear mom And Dad
dear Mom And dad
Dear Mom and dad
dear Mom and Dad
Dear mom And dad
Dear mom and Dad
dear mom And Dad,

dear Mom And dad,
Dear Mom and dad,
dear Mom and Dad,
Dear mom And dad,
Dear mom and Dad,
Dear Mom And dad
Dear Mom and Dad
Dear mom And Dad
dear Mom And Dad
Dear Mom And Dad
Dear Mom And dad,
Dear Mom and Dad,
Dear mom And Dad,
dear Mom And Dad,
Dear Mom And Dad,
And my favorite: *Dear Mom and Dad Comma*

After the children finished their greetings, I tapped my pen on the board. "Okay class, look here. What I'm about to say is *very* important." I waited until everyone's eyes were on me. "You do *not* write under the word *Dear*. This is where we indent."

Melanie looked puzzled. "What's *that*?"

I looked around the room. "Who here knows what an indent is?"

"My mom has one on the side of her car," Laura chipped in.

"Well," I laughed, "that's *sort* of an indent. An indent in a letter is where you leave a space." I walked to the board and put my finger under the word *Dear*. "You do *not* write there."

"Why?" Dylan called out.

I shrugged. "That's just how you do it." I pounded the same spot on the board with my fist. "DO. NOT. WRITE. THERE."

There was a good reason that I was making such a big production of this. No matter how many times teachers say, "Do not write under the word *Dear*," half the class will. I don't know why, but children just do *not* want to leave a space under that word. I've tried having them put a finger under it, but that doesn't work. They'll spend five minutes coloring their fingernails. I've told them that there's "hot lava" under that *Dear*, and they can't touch it. But the hot lava idea backfired. As soon as I said it, everyone wanted to write in the lava spot and scream that their words were burning up. I know I shouldn't say this, but I hate that indent.

I forged ahead.

"Okay, boys and girls, the next part of our letter is called the *Body*. It is the main part of your letter. It is *not* to be confused with this kind of body." I posed like Arnold Schwarzenegger. Giggles. "In the body you should welcome your parents and thank them for coming to Back to School Night. Ask them to look around the room at your work."

It is at this point in every letter writing lesson that one of your students will say, "I don't know what to write." To avoid this I always write a sample on the board. I began writing.

> *Dear Mom and Dad,*
>   *Welcome to Back to School Night! Thank you*
> *for coming to my classroom. Please look around*
> *the room at my work. You will see . . .*

"Mr. Done?" Christopher interrupted.

"What?" I said, continuing to write.

"Can we tell our parents that they have to listen to the teacher?"

I smiled. "Sure."

Trevor grinned. "Can we tell them that if they don't listen they have to go to the principal's office?"

Melanie giggled.

"Uh . . . I think that's going a little too far."

Stacy raised her hand as I finished writing the example.

"Yes, Stacy?"

"How long does the letter have to be?"

"Mmm . . . I'd say about half a page. You're big third graders now. Third graders can write at least half a page."

Stacy's jaw fell open. David threw his head on his desk. Gina made a high-pitched squeal. You'd think I had just asked them to write *Moby-Dick*.

"Can we copy that?" Rebecca asked.

"Yes."

Brian's hand was up next.

"Yes, Brian?"

"I don't know what to write."

I was almost finished with the lesson. "Okay, kids, the last part of the letter is called the *Closing*. Watch closely." I put my finger up on the date. "Place your finger on the beginning of the date like this." The children copied me. "Now drag it down your paper in a straight line." I slid my finger down the board. They did the same. "Pretend there is an imaginary dotted line here." I drew a thick dotted line so they would understand what I meant. I tapped the bottom of it. "This is where you write *Sincerely* or *Best Regards* or *Love*. Since you're writing to your parents, you should write *Love*."

"Ewww!" David shouted.

I gave him a look then wrote *Love*. "Now you make your third comma." I drew another giant comma. This one was even bigger than the last. Laughter swept the room. "Finally, you sign your name under *Love*—indenting it just a little—and you're all done." To finish it off, I signed Trevor's name. More titters. Trevor's face lit up.

THIRD-GRADE FACT: Whenever you use a child's name in an example, he will beam.

After I reviewed where to put the commas and where to make the indent one last time, the children began writing their own letters. When they were finished, several lined up at my desk for me to check what they had written.

Gina was first. She indented in the correct place but also indented every line after that.

I rubbed my forehead. "Gina, next time you only need one indent, okay?"

"Okay." She handed it in.

Dylan was next. He signed his letter *Love From Your Favorite Son*.

Smiling, I turned to him. "What will your brothers say about this?"

He giggled then played with the stapler on my desk as I read more.

"Dylan, how many commas in a letter?"

"Three."

"Good. But I don't see any in yours."

He leaned over his paper and stared at it. "Oh yeah." He snatched it back and ran off to fix it.

David was third in line. My lips scrunched into a pucker when I started reading. He had only written *Welcome to Back to School Night!*

"Uh . . . what happened to writing at least half a page?"

"It *is*!" He pointed to the words *Love, David* in the center of the paper. "See!" Between *Welcome to Back to School Night* and his signature, there were six inches of blank space. I gave it back.

Sarah stepped up and set her letter on my desk. I smiled when I saw it. A thick dotted line ran from the date to the closing. In her margins, she had drawn pixies and butterflies.

"Honey, your letter is beautiful, but this dotted line is supposed to be *imaginary*, not real."

"Ohhhh!"

She picked up the paper and skipped back to her desk. A couple of minutes later she returned and handed it to me. The dotted line had been transformed into a giant beanstalk. Fairies hid in the leaves. More butterflies and pixies flew all around it.

"Well, honey," I said, fighting back a laugh, "that's the best imaginary dotted line I have *ever* seen."

CURSIVE

Apparently, fewer and fewer people are using cursive these days. On a recent SAT exam, only 15 percent of teens used cursive. The rest wrote in block letters. Could this mean that handwriting may someday end up the way of filmstrip projectors, record players, and hairnets on the cafeteria ladies? I hope not.

If my school got rid of cursive, I'd have to start going to the gym. Teaching handwriting is my daily workout. I get my stretching in by forming giant loops and curlicues in the air. I lean to the right like Jack LaLanne so my kids will slant their letters. I work up a good sweat racing around to each desk turning pieces of newsprint at an angle, correcting pencil grips, checking that feet are on the floor, and making sure that their lowercase *m*'s go all the way up to the dotted line and only have three bumps. Not seven.

For children, learning cursive is right up there with trick-or-treating, getting a new hamster, or writing "Clean Me!" on the teacher's car. They love it. Kids' first handwriting lessons are like losing the first tooth, taking off the training wheels, or getting bedtime extended half an hour. It's a rite of passage from being a little kid to a big one. Few things make children feel more grown up than writing *man* for the first time without picking up their pencils.

You should hear my students when they learn new cursive letters. They squeal. They ooh and aah. They laugh when I show them that capital *2* in cursive looks like a 2. When I point out that the only difference between a capital *I* and a capital *F* is that little line in the middle, you'd think a flower just popped out of the tip of my overhead marker. When I showed this year's group that g is just a lowercase a with a tail, they applauded.

Whenever I introduce the letter formations, my students always tell me what they think the letters look like. Gina thinks a looks like a Hershey's Kiss. To Chloe, a row of c's resembles waves. David says the bottom of a B looks like a banana. Laura claims that the loop inside the H looks like a fish. Dylan thinks it looks like a corn dog.

The one letter that I get a bit nervous about teaching is p. It's a tricky one. If I say, "And now we are going to make p." I might as well cancel school for the rest of the day because half my class will be rolling on the floor. It is always best when introducing p to say, "We are now going to learn the LETTER p." By saying *letter* really loudly you will cut down considerably on all rolling.

If schools wiped out cursive, what would children look at in the front of the classroom? Every third-, fourth-, and fifth-grade teacher in the universe puts the cursive alphabet over the whiteboard in the front of the room. It belongs up there. Just like the clock and the overhead screen and the American flag! And what would kids do without the laminated strips of manuscript letters that are taped across the top of their desks below their name tags? What would they fiddle with and pick at and scribble on while the teacher is talking? What would they blow their pink erasures on? Where would they put their stickers?

Just like children have a favorite color and sport and ice cream, kids have their favorite cursive letters, too. Lowercase e is popular because it looks like a roller coaster. Capital M is always well liked because it begins with a candy cane. D is a big hit because it looks like a big belly if you draw a belly button in it. Poor *Z*. I feel sorry for that little guy. No one ever picks *Z* as his favorite. It's just too dang hard.

One day when the children were practicing their letters, I overheard a couple of my girls talking.

"*L* is my specialty," Jennifer declared, admiring how beautiful it looked on her paper. "What's your favorite?"

"*G*," answered Gina.

"Why?" Jennifer asked.

"It's my first initial."

"Mine's lowercase *l*," Sarah chimed in.

"How come?" Jennifer said.

"It's easy," Sarah replied.

Chloe joined the others. "I like little *f* and big *J*."

"Why?" said Gina.

"They're loopy. I like loopy letters."

Jennifer turned to Sarah. "What's your second place?"

"*O*," Sarah answered.

"Me, too," said Jennifer. "I'm really fast at it."

Some children become very attached to their own ways of writing those letters. Just this week, I noticed that Rebecca was forming her *W*'s incorrectly.

"Rebecca, let me help you with that." I wrote a *W* properly on her paper. "There. You see?"

She pulled the paper back. "I do it differently than you."

It's not just students who take pride in their cursive. Teachers do, too. Bankers and lawyers and engineers have their fancy homes and Lexuses and stock options. Teachers have their perfect slanted writing. It's our badge. It's how we're identified. I know the one thing I have that my doctor doesn't is my nice cursive.

A few days ago I was in the grocery store and found a yellow sticky note in a shopping cart. When I picked it up, I knew immediately that it had been written by a teacher. Her $\mathcal{E}$'s were not backward. Her t's were crossed. The slash in her x was not slanted the wrong way. The top of her f was not collapsing. Her ℓ wasn't too fat. And her $\mathcal{L}$ did not look pregnant. Of course I could have identified the list as a teacher's even if it had been written in print. It said: Excedrin, graham crackers, and beer.

October

I've just decided to switch our Friday schedule to Monday, which means that the test we take each Friday on what we learned during the week will now take place on Monday before we've learned it. But since today is Tuesday, it doesn't matter in the slightest.

—*Charlie and the Chocolate Factory*

WHAT IS A TEACHER?

Mark Twain once wrote that teaching is like trying to hold thirty-five corks underwater all at once. But what I'd like to know is—*who* drank those thirty-five bottles of wine in the first place? My bet's on the teacher.

What exactly is a teacher anyway? A lot of different things. Teachers are like puppeteers. We keep the show in motion. When we help children discover abilities that they don't know they have, we are like talent scouts. When we herd kids off the play structure at the end of recess, we are like shepherds.

Teachers are like conductors. We try to get everyone to play together nicely. Some years it's like leading the entire navy band. When I take the lunch count, I feel like a waiter. Once in a while, I feel like the dust jacket on a popular book in my classroom library—well worn, rarely untouched, more wrinkled than last year, close to falling apart.

When my students are tapping on me, I feel like a tree trunk that a flock of woodpeckers has just landed on. When the kids are buzzing around the room in all directions, I feel like a bee-keeper. When we're walking in line, I feel like Daddy Duck leading his chicks.

When I have two minutes to finish my lunch, I look just like a squirrel eating in fast motion. When someone leaves treats in the staff lounge, I turn into a hyena. When a lesson tanks, I feel like a gutter ball.

Teachers are like birds. We use a variety of flight strategies.

Sometimes we glide. Some days we soar. Most of the time we flap our wings furiously trying not to crash-land.

Teachers are like farmers. We sow the seeds — not too close together or they'll talk too much. We check on them every day and monitor their progress. We think about our crop all the time. When we see growth — we get excited.

Teachers are like doctors. Both have lots of tongue depressors and cotton balls. Both own human body charts and stethoscopes, and use white butcher paper. Both put on Band-Aids, hold bloody noses, and take care of kids with tummyaches. Doctors, however, don't see twenty patients at a time. And they only see kids *after* they've thrown up on the teacher's carpet.

Teachers are like actors. We work in front of an audience. We project our voices to the back of the room. We sing, dance, do our own stunts, and make jokes about pencils coming from Pennsylvania, ants living in Antarctica, and fractions being invented by Henry the $1/8$th. For five hours a day, five days a week, we try to hold our audience's attention. Come rain or shine, the show must go on. If it's bad, the audience tunes out.

When I blow my whistle, I feel like Captain von Trapp in *The Sound of Music*. When I hand out certificates for good deeds, I might as well be the Wizard of Oz. When I pass out percussion instruments for music time, I feel like Harold Hill in *The Music Man*. And when my students are absolutely bonkers because it has rained all day and they've been cooped up inside for six hours, I know *exactly* how Captain Hook must have felt at the end of *Peter Pan* when he jumped off his own ship.

Teachers are memory makers, too. We know that the stories, paintings, and plaster of paris handprints that children make at school will someday become family treasures. Each day we create experiences in our classrooms that our students will someday look back on and laugh over and talk about and perhaps even try to re-create in their own children's lives. We understand that kids are like wet canvases. We help paint the backgrounds.

And so we collect the field trip notes and throw the parties and play the piano and pitch the balls and wear our shirts inside out on Backward Day. We set up the experiments and buy the pets and run to the store and clean the spills and fill the bird feeders. And when it is time to send our students' artwork and craft projects home, we *always* make sure that their names and the date are written clearly on the back.

SPELLING

When I first started teaching, there were several things I did not expect. I did not know that Show and Tell would be the most important hour of the week. I never thought I'd have class rules about where children *shouldn't* put their feet. I never imagined that the doorknob in the staff bathroom would have hand lotion on it every time I tried to get out. And I did not expect that I would become the dictionary.

"Mr. Done, how do you spell *every?*"

"Mr. Done, how do you spell *special?*"

"Mr. Done, how do you spell *SpongeBob?*"

"Mr. Done, how do you spell *ponna?*"

"*Ponna?*" I said, confused. "Use it in a sentence."

"You know . . . like 'once a *ponna* time.'"

My students think I'm the spelling genie. All day long they ask, "Mr. Done, do I drop the *y?*" "Mr. Done, does that word start with a capital?" "Mr. Done, is that a drop-the-*e*-add-*ing*-word?"

And all day long I sing: "*I* before *e* except after *c*." "An *e* at the end of a word makes the vowel say its name." "When two vowels go walking, the first one does the talking."

I repeat my spelling tricks, too: *Eat* is in the word *great*. *Here* is inside of *there*. *Ear* is in *hear*. *Lie* is in *believe*. *Ant* is in *restaurant*. *Bus* is in *busy*. And the *principal* is my *pal*.

Swimming has M&M's in the middle of it. *Tomorrow* contains three little words: *Tom, or,* and *row*. *Together* has three words in it, too. If you draw spokes on the *c*'s in *bicycle,* they look like wheels. And if you put circles around the *e*'s in *eye*, it looks like the word is wearing glasses.

You know those circus performers who spin plates on long sticks and try to keep them up in the air? Well, sometimes that's how I feel. Just this week I juggled three words at once.

"Mr. Done, how do you spell *great?*" Laura shouted out.

I began spelling: "*G—*"

"Mr. Done, how do you spell *swimming?*" Kevin interrupted.

I looked at him. "*S-W-I—*"

Back to Laura: "*R—*"

Back to Kevin: "Double *M.*"

Melanie jumped in. "Mr. Done, how do you spell *with?*"

To Melanie: "*W—*"

To Laura: "*E-A-T.*"

To Melanie: "*I—*"

To Kevin: "*I-N-G.*"

To Melanie: "*T-H.*"

"Wait!" Laura broke in. "What was after the first letter again?"

I started over.

Every year there are certain words that I am *sure* my kids will ask me to spell. These include: *pirate, treasure, castle, blood, sword, chocolate, army, pizza, en garde, dinosaur, warrior, underwear, Frankenstein, fairy, lava, princess, guillotine,* and *Godzilla.* Rarely am I ever asked how to spell *Mississippi.* I am convinced that most children are born knowing how to spell this word.

Sometimes the kids want help with words I can't spell. I hate that.

"Mr. Done, how do you spell *Philippines?*" Dylan asked.

"Uh . . . go look at the map."

"Mr. Done, how do you spell *Ouija*?" John wanted to know.

My eyebrows scrunched together. "*Ouija*? Why do you need to know that?"

"It's on my birthday list."

"Ask for something else."

Stacy walked up to my desk. "Mr. Done, how do you spell *piranha*?"

"Look it up in the dictionary."

"I did. It's not there."

"Bring it here."

Stacy fetched the dictionary, and I watched her flip through the pages to the end then flip back through the pages to the front. *This could take years.*

I offered to help. Finally, we found it.

"Why is it spelled like *that*?" Stacy asked.

"Beats me."

Danny raised his head. "Mr. Done, how do you spell *croissant*."

"WHAT?" I said, eyebrows arched.

"How do you spell *croissant*?"

I took a deep breath. "Why do you guys always ask me such hard words? Why don't you ask me something easy once in a while?" I started spelling it out. "C-R-O . . ." I stopped. "Ahh . . . just write *roll*."

I have also become an expert at spelling every conceivable sound.

"Mr. Done, how do you spell the sound pirates make?"

"*A-R-R-G-H-H.*"

"Mr. Done, how do you spell when a car brakes?"

"*E-R-R-R-R.*"

"Mr. Done, how do you spell when a lion roars?"

"G-R-R-R-R."

One day Christopher shouted out, "Mr. Done, how do you spell the sound that bombs make?"

I squinted at him. "You mean like *kaboom?*"

"No." He made an exploding noise. "Like that."

The other kids looked up.

"Uh . . . I'm not sure," I replied.

"I know!" Trevor announced, jumping up. "It's *P-U-H-H-H-H-H!*"

"No, it's not!" John piped up. "It's *C-H-H-G-R-H-H!*"

Pretty soon every boy in the room was impersonating bombs and grenades and volcanoes. Trevor could only make the sounds while diving on the beanbag chair. Finally, the class settled on *"pchhhhh!"* and *"ppPCHHchhh!!"* for a really loud one.

Kids' spelling mistakes never change: *they* will be *thay, grandpa* will be *grampa, different* will be *difrent, every* will be *evry, goes* will be *gose, improve* will be *inprove, kind of* will be *kindov,* and *sandwich* will be *sandwitch.* In December, *ornaments* will be spelled *ordaments,* and *candy canes* will be *candy cans.* Santa's name can give kids trouble, too. After the movie *Santa Clause* came out, some children added an *e* to the end of his name. (I hate when moviemakers do that. Don't they know I'm trying to teach spelling here!) Sometimes it's Santa *Claws.* Last year when Abigail wrote in her journal that she visited Santa at the mall, she got her letters a little mixed up and wrote that she sat on "Satan's lap."

Over the years I've encountered pretty much every misspelling imaginable. I've seen *insects* spelled as *insex, garbage* as *garbitch, tutor* as *tooter, peninsula* as *penisula,* and our sixteenth president written as *Ape Lincoln.* I've read *littel, speshl, butaful, grat, frist, rember, probly,* and *whith* so many times that the misspelled versions look correct. I've received secret notes on my desk saying, "Mr. Done, you are the *beast*." And once when the kids had to answer "Who discovered the New World?" Rachel wrote *Colombo*.

Grade school teachers are master code breakers. As a matter of fact, I wouldn't be surprised if the guy who figured out the hieroglyphic mystery on the Rosetta stone wasn't at one time a third-grade teacher. When a child writes *uperd*, I don't have to think twice. He means *appeared*. I know immediately that *ine* is *any*, *doter* is *daughter*, *exited* is *excited*, *fell* is *feel*, and *turd* is *third*. Yesterday Brian wrote *bowenairo*. That was an easy one: *bow and arrow*.

There is always one student who keeps me entertained with her spelling. This year it is Melanie. Melanie is a darling little girl. She loves art and singing. But she can't spell a lick. When we made cards for the art teacher who was going on maternity leave, Melanie wrote, "I'm very sad you are living." In this week's creative writing assignment, the mom in her story woke the child up with, "Good morning, sweaty."

Once Melanie came running up to me at recess. I was on yard duty.

"Mr. Done," she tattled, "Joshua said the G word."

What's the G word?

I bent down and whispered. "What did he say?"

Melanie whispered back. "Jerk."

I stood up, biting my lip. "Josh, come here." He walked over. "Did you call Melanie a jerk?"

"No."

"Yes, you did," Melanie protested.

I gave him my best teacher look. "Josh, did you say it or didn't you?"

He thought for a moment. "I opened my mouth and it just fell out."

Melanie often leaves letters out of her words. Once she wrote me a card that said, "Mr. Done, you are god." I didn't know if she meant I was a good teacher, or she really had a high opinion of me. Another day I stopped at her desk and glanced over her shoulder while she was writing. "Uh . . ." I pointed to one of the words. "What's this word?"

"*Shirt.*"

"That's what I thought you meant. You left out the *r,* honey."

After our trip to the nature reserve, Melanie wrote an elaborate story all about the food chain. She named all the shorebirds and snails and crabs and microorganisms.

"Melanie, could you come up here please?"

She skipped on up.

"I love your story, sweetheart. You did such a good job." I pointed to one of the words. "Can you read this for me, please?"

"Organism."

"You left out the *n* and the *i,* honey."

"Ohhhhhh!"

"You *have* to put the *n* and *i* in that word. It's *very* important."

I'm not the only spelling teacher in class. My students like to teach me about spelling, too.

"Mr. Done," Christopher said one day, "spell *pig* backward. Then say 'different colors' real fast."

I didn't think about it. (*Warning:* Never spell something out loud when a child asks you to without thinking it through.) "Okay," I replied. "*G-I-P* different colors."

Hoots of laughter shot up to the ceiling. I stood there, staring at them all. Mouth apart. *Hold on please while I bang my head against a wall.* Finally, I spoke. "What is so funny?"

"You . . . you pee in different colors!" Christopher declared, still cracking up.

There went the ceiling again.

I narrowed my eyes. "Where did you guys learn this?"

"Everyone knows *that*!" Laura decreed in between laughs.

Christopher leapt to his feet. "Mr. Done, spell *icup*."

I cast a sidelong glance and made a face. "I know this one."

"Please!" Christopher begged.

I shook my head. I knew what would happen if I spelled it. There'd be complete chaos—utter pandemonium.

"Please!" he pressed.

"No."

"PLEASE!"

"NO!"

Everyone joined in. "PLEEEEEEEASE."

I looked out at their twenty upturned faces then let out a giant sigh. There are certain moments in teaching when the teacher's best option is to just give in.

"Okay," I conceded. *"I-C-U-P."*

Well, I was right. As soon as I said it, the class went into convulsions. A third of the kids jumped out of their chairs. Peals of uproarious laughter echoed in the room. It sounded like one giant tickle fight.

"Okay, okay," I said, trying to reel them back. "I hope you're happy. Christopher, get back in your chair. Trevor, get off the floor. Kevin, breathe." Then I walked to the board and wrote *htam*. "Christopher, spell this backward."

He spelled it out loud. *"M-A-T-H."*

"Good," I said. "Now everyone get your math books out. Spelling is over."

THE TEACHER'S DESK

On Columbus Day, I tell my students about the discovery of America. Everyone knows the story, of course—how Christopher Columbus sailed the *Niña*, *Pinta*, and *Santa Maria* in 1492 in search of a shorter route to the Indies. Columbus kept a log during his voyage. He reported that when the wind was strong, his ships made a lot of progress. When it wasn't, they made very little. As the weeks went on, the crew grew restless. Storms brought trouble. Supplies became limited. Some of the food went bad.

I can't help but think how much Columbus's famous voyage parallels life in the classroom. In the beginning of the school year, teachers set their course. Some days we make a lot of progress. Some days we don't. Our crews complain, too. Rain spoils recess plans. We run out of supplies. The food in the cafeteria isn't very good, either.

As I sat in the reading corner pointing out Columbus's route on a map, Bob my principal walked in carrying a form for me to sign. When he saw that I was busy with the children, he pointed and whispered, "I'll just put it on your desk."

Uh-oh. Not the desk.

I followed him with my eyes as he walked to the front of the room. When he reached my desk, Bob stopped and scratched his head, hunting for a place to set the form. I considered telling him that I was in the middle of spring cleaning, but since it was only October, I decided against it. Instead, I cringed and watched him set the form down as if he were adding to a tower of playing cards.

My poor desk. It looks like the floor of a snow globe after all the flakes have settled to the bottom. It is covered with stacks of papers, overhead transparencies, lesson plans, teachers' manuals, construction paper, sticky notes, permission slips, library passes, spelling lists, answer keys, clipboards, grade books, and my attendance folder. That's just the top layer.

My coffee cup has never rested on a flat surface. My elbows have never leaned on wood. When Christopher set his hamster on my desk, it took us five minutes to find her.

My students tease me about my desk all the time.

"Mr. Done," Stacy said one day, "you need to clean Oscar."

"Who's Oscar?" I asked, tilting my head.

"Your desk."

I blinked hard. "You named my desk *Oscar*?"

"That's only one of his names."

"You have *more*?"

"Yeah. Want to hear them?"

"No."

Actually, my students have only seen Oscar clean twice—once on the first day of school when everything looked perfect and again on the morning after Back to School Night. When the kids walked in and saw that my desk was clean, they started clapping.

Bob's desk does not look like mine. It does not resemble the return counter at Macy's the day after Christmas. His stapler looks polished. The little plastic circle that sits in his tape dispenser always has tape on it. (I'm sure he has never had to hunt for the end of the tape on the little roll then scrape it off with his fingernail.) Bob's planner sits perfectly in the center of his desk. His to do list is color-coded. All the pens in his pencil can have caps on them. His pencils do not have masking tape flags on them that say, "THIS IS NOT YOURS!" His paper clips are not all globbed onto a magnet that someone pulled off the whiteboard. There are no trolls or plastic toys taped to the top of his computer. The little brush inside his bottle of Wite-Out does not look like it just had a seizure.

Of course, I'm not the only teacher with a messy desk. There are lots of us out there. Teachers with messy desks know who all the other teachers with messy desks are. It's like a secret club. We even sit together at lunch. But we don't talk about our desks—especially around the teachers whose desks are not messy.

I'm convinced that there really are only two types of people in the world—those with neat desks like my boss's and those with messy desks like mine. *Tidys* and *Messys,* I call them. It really is a Mars-and-Venus sort of thing. The two groups do not understand each other. *Tidys* roll their eyes at *Messys* and make jokes about us waiting for the File Fairy to come clean up our piles. *Messys* long to be accepted by *Tidys.* That's why you will occasionally see *Messys* shaking their doormats wildly out in front of their classrooms. We want *Tidys* to see us cleaning.

You know those decorating magazines that show cluttered rooms transformed into organized ones? Well, the "before" photos are always taken at a *Messy*'s place. *Tidys* do the make-overs. Sometimes in those magazines there are quizzes to see how organized you are. You answer questions like: Do you leave your keys in the same place? Do you keep your desk neat and organized? Can you find your stapler today?

But *Messys* understand something that *Tidys* do not: A cluttered work space can serve as an invaluable teaching tool. Take our planet, for example. A messy desk provides the perfect illustration for teaching students about the layers of the earth. On every messy desk you'll find the December dittos stacked on top of November's grades, which are piled on October's correcting basket, covering September's lesson plans. Just like the layers of our planet, the older layers are on the bottom and the newer ones are on the top. I wouldn't be surprised if hole punches and scissors lodged between the piles eventually began to fossilize.

A desk like mine can also be used to simulate a multitude of forces in nature. When a child bumps into my desk and disrupts one of the piles, students observe the seismic shift of an earthquake. If one of the piles collapses, children witness firsthand how landslides move. When the teacher sweeps everything on top of his desk into a large box the day before Open House, children see just how quickly deforestation can wipe out an entire rain forest.

With a messy desk—who needs a social studies text? For my geography unit, I have used the stacks and piles on my desk to illustrate mountains, hills, caves, caverns, highlands, lowlands, canyons, peaks, valleys, plateaus, crevasses, wilderness territory, and badlands. When the piles spread onto nearby counters and tables, students understand urban sprawl.

And don't forget about Mr. Columbus. Digging through a messy desk also provides the perfect metaphor for Columbus's voyage. In fact, it is a metaphor for *any* exploration. All of the great explorers faced disappointment, experienced hardships, adjusted their courses, and overcame adversity. Last week when I realized my keys were missing, I started searching the corner of my desk (*embarked on my quest*). I lifted piles and dug under papers but couldn't find them anywhere (*disappointment*). After no success, I switched to the other side of the desk (*changed my course*). Suddenly my coffee cup spilled all over the desk (*hardship*). The kids began to laugh (*further hardship*). I ran to the back of the room to get paper towels and mopped up the spill (*overcame adversity*). Then I continued my search (*forged ahead*). Finally, I spotted the end of the key chain, pulled it out from under a stack of books, and shouted, "I found them!" (*joy of discovery*).

This morning after I finished reading to my students, I excused them back to their seats and tossed the Columbus book on my desk. All of a sudden the tallest pile on the edge came tumbling down into the wastebasket. There was a loud crash. The basket tipped over. Papers spilled out all over the floor. Everyone stopped and stared at the mess.

"It's an avalanche!" Trevor shrieked.

What did I tell you? They learn so much.

THE MESSY OR TIDY QUIZ

Not sure if you're a *Messy* or a *Tidy*? Take the following test and find out.

1. Do you have shoe boxes stacked on the top shelf in your bedroom closet for diorama projects? If yes, give yourself 1 point. Under your bed? 2 points.
2. Do you have enough pie tins, glass jars, and plastic cottage cheese tubs under your sink at school to start a recycling center? 1 point.
3. When you look at the wilted celery in the vegetable bin in your refrigerator, do you think, *Good. Bunny food*? If yes, 1 point.
4. Have you ever worn a sweater to work over your shirt even though it was a hot day because nothing at home was ironed? 1 point.
5. Does your laundry basket look like the Lost and Found box at school? If so, 1 point.

6. Do you find White Elephant gifts easily in your home? If yes, 1 point.
7. Are all the alphabet letters on your refrigerator in alphabetical order? If not, 1 point.
8. When describing your classroom, do you prefer the words *relaxed, comfortable,* and *lived-in*? 1 point.
9. Do you have school stuff in the passenger seat of your car? 1 point. In the passenger seat *and* the backseat? 2 points. Is your trunk full, too? 3 points.
10. Can your students write their spelling words in the dust on your TV? 1 point.

Score of 0:   My principal will love you.
Score of 1–5:   You cheated.
Score of 6 or more: You can eat lunch with me.

THE TOOTH FAIRY

Third graders look like little jack-o'-lanterns. Half my kids are missing some of their front teeth. The other half have their hands in their mouths trying to pull their teeth out.

I can always tell when a child is close to losing one. She speaks to me while turning and twisting and yanking on some poor little baby tooth. "Don't pull it out at school!" I cry. But they don't listen to me. They keep tugging away. There is money at stake here.

By third grade some children don't believe in Santa anymore, and some have their doubts about the Easter Bunny. But more than 90 percent of them still believe in the Tooth Fairy. I'm not sure why exactly. Maybe it's because she is the only one who brings cash.

Have you seen what the Tooth Fairy is bringing these days? When I was a kid, she usually brought nickels and dimes. Nowadays some kids get a dollar a tooth. This year when Emily lost a molar, she got ten bucks! At that rate I'm tempted to pull out a few of my own.

The kindergarten and first-grade teachers on my campus are always prepared. If their kids lose a tooth at school, they get to take it home in a Tooth Taxi. Tooth Taxis are black plastic film containers decorated with pictures of Tommy the Tooth driving in a yellow cab. These containers are coveted. In fact, parents have reported that their children will do all they can to *not* lose their teeth at home just so they can get one.

I don't send teeth home with Tommy the Tooth. When my students come to me with a bloody, newly pulled tooth, I just say,

"Grab an envelope. Right-hand desk drawer. I don't need to see it."

I should probably carry envelopes with me. Once we were on a field trip watching a play when Emily screamed, "I lost my tooth!" Everyone turned around. Emily got up in the middle of the show, crawled over twenty kids, and handed me the tooth. *What am I supposed to do with this?* For some reason, all children deliver their newly pulled teeth to their teachers. It is automatic—like handing over every staple they find in the carpet during story time. I dropped Emily's tooth in my shirt pocket.

When I was in my tooth-losing years, I was always afraid that the Tooth Fairy would not find my room—or worse yet would mistake my brother's room for mine and give him the money instead of me! So I'd make signs with arrows pointing to my bedroom and plaster the whole house. She always found me.

There was that one terrible time when the Tooth Fairy forgot to come. I was devastated. Then my dad explained the Tooth Fairy's rules. She likes the open end of the pillowcase facing out so she does not get tangled up when putting the money under the pillow. The next night I made sure to have the case open on the correct side. She came. I got double my normal rate.

In third grade, I was determined to catch the Tooth Fairy. One night I heard the bedroom door open slowly and pretended to be asleep. *That's her,* I thought. *She's here!* I didn't move. I kept my eyes shut. Then all of a sudden there was a loud noise. Everything I had barricaded behind the door came tumbling down.

"What the . . . ," I heard a voice cry.

I sat bolt upright and pointed my flashlight at the door.

"Dad! What are you doing here?"

"Uh, well, I...I came to see if the Tooth Fairy had come yet."

"No! Get out! She won't come if she sees you!"

Last year, my mom handed me a shoe box with all the letters I ever wrote to the Tooth Fairy, Santa Claus, and the Easter Bunny. When I lifted the lid, I pretended to be shocked. "How did *you* get these?" She laughed. I pulled out a few letters and read them. My baby teeth were still inside the envelopes.

Dear Tooth Fairy,

This is my third tooth. Last year I got a dime. This year I would like a quarter. My dad says there is inflation.

Dear Tooth Fairy,

I have another loose tooth. It's the same tooth as last time but on the other side. Please send me a picture of you. I want to bring it in for Show and Tell. Everyone says you are not real but I believe in you. My bedtime is 8 o'clock so you can come by anytime after that.

Dear Tooth Fairy,

Instead of money could you please bring a guinea pig?

It seems like every month one of my third graders is losing a tooth. Earlier in the year, David was pushing a loose one back and forth with his tongue.

"I hope it's not your sweet tooth," I joked, trying to sound serious. "Then you can't taste any more candy."

He looked worried.

One day after I had just handed Chloe an envelope, she said, "Mr. Done, how does the Tooth Fairy find all the children?"

I started to answer. "Well . . ."

"I know," Trevor interjected. "My mom says she uses GPS."

The day after Christopher lost a tooth, I asked, "How much did you get for it?"

"A dollar."

"That's a lot."

"It had a filling. They're more valuable."

Melanie's Tooth Fairy is high tech.

"Melanie, did the Tooth Fairy come last night?" I inquired the morning after she lost a tooth.

"No. But she e-mailed my mom and said she'd be by tonight."

I smiled. "Why didn't she come last night?"

"She had to go to the bank."

Recently Robbie was in at recess to finish his homework but preferred working on his loose tooth instead.

"Mr. Done," Robbie said, pulling his finger out of his mouth, "I'm sure I'll lose this tooth tonight and the Tooth Fairy will give me a dollar. Maybe even five dollars."

I didn't look up. "Get to work."

"I'll give you five dollars if you let me go out to recess."

"No deal."

This week, Stacy came up to me and asked if I believe in the Tooth Fairy.

"Yep," I answered.

"I don't," she said, emphatically. "And I'm going to do a test to find out."

"What sort of a test?"

"Well, my tooth came out yesterday. See." She opened her jaw wide, pulled back her lip, and pointed the hole out with her tongue. I examined it. "I didn't tell my parents. And I'm going to put it under my pillow tonight and see if there is any money under it. If there isn't, I'll know that the Tooth Fairy isn't real."

I nodded my head. "Sounds like you've got a plan."

The minute school was over, I called Stacy's mom and told her all about Stacy's scheme. That night the Tooth Fairy passed the test.

SCHOOLS

Remember writing a report about a foreign country in grade school? After choosing the country, you copied everything out of the encyclopedia onto your mom's blank recipe cards, then wrote the final copy in your nicest handwriting. The paper was divided into sections: geography, economy, climate, culture, food, history, and population. Well, I've come to the conclusion that all schools are just like those reports. Following is the "country report" for any school:

Geography: A set of buildings with rubber balls kicked proudly on their roofs at recess.

Economy: In one year produces 475 book reports, 4,500 spelling tests, 220 science fair projects, and 75,000,000 multiplication flash cards.

Climate: If the principal is away—breezy.

Culture: Major cultural events throughout the year include Talent Show, Pajama Day, Bicycle Rodeo, Hoe Down, Watermelon Eating Contest, School Carnival, and end-of-the-year baseball game where the whole school gets to watch twenty teachers get whipped by the entire fifth-grade class.

Food: For teachers: coffee, microwavable lunches, leftover candy corn, conversation hearts, and birthday cake. For students: anything that turns their tongues a different color and makes slurping noises through the straw when they reach the bottom of the box.

History: In 1950, if it rained outside children played Heads Up 7-up. Today, if it rains outside children play Heads Up 7-up.

Population: Several hundred kids, twice as many parents, and a menagerie of bunnies, guinea pigs, hamsters, snakes, and tarantulas. Staff consists of the following: The Mom Teacher (owns a rocking chair; reminds other teachers to put the lid down on the copier), The Veteran Teacher (has forty-five million book order points; doesn't think twice about walking into the boys' bathroom), and The New Teacher (works every weekend, sick all year). Population may include Man Teacher.

The Man Teacher does not eat Lean Cuisines or count Weight Watcher points, does not lick his fingers before turning the page, attends baby showers against his will, does not use chimes to get his students' attention, and knows all about Britney Spears, Jennifer Aniston, and Angelina Jolie because the only reading material in the staff bathroom is *People*.

TRICK-OR-TREAT!

There are certain triggers that *always* wind children up: rain clouds, wind, a close game in PE, and—the week before Halloween. The closer the calendar gets to that day, the more bonkers children become. The last week of October is when teachers start using all sorts of names to describe their students—squirrels, monkeys, livewires, spitfires, rascals, firecrackers, and sparkplugs. Mine are Doan's Pills.

To be perfectly fair, it's not completely the kids' fault that they can't stay focused. Teachers are partly to blame. We tell ghost stories by candlelight, stuff scarecrows, carve jack-o'-lanterns, and play Pin the Wart on the Witch. We sing "pumpkin carols," draw haunted houses, and graph candy corn. We serve caramel apples and cupcakes topped with Gummi worms while we walk around wearing our Official Halloween Candy Taste Tester buttons.

On the morning of Halloween, I lock my classroom door, pull the blinds shut, and put on my costume (I refuse to drive to work in it). As the kids line up outside, I can hear them chattering and trying to guess what I will be wearing. This year when the bell rang, I did not open up right away. I wanted to make them wait. A couple of them started banging on the window. Finally, I pushed the door open. When the children saw me, they screamed and shouted and pointed and laughed. (You'd think they'd never seen a white sheet before.)

The kids were all dressed in their costumes for our morning Halloween parade. Into the room walked Spider-Man, a clown, an angel, Scooby-Doo, two devils, Pocahontas, an astronaut, one fortune-teller, a pack of Ninjas, Mr. Peanut, a giant whoopie cushion, and three iPhones. Just as I was about to close the door, one of my room moms handed me a Starbucks Grande.

"What's this for?" I asked.

She smiled. "I figured you'd need it today."

Smart mom.

Our PTA holds a giant auction the Saturday before Halloween. It's one of our best fund-raisers. Traditionally, each teacher donates something. This year when Michele, the PTA president, came by my room to ask what I'd like to donate, I had no idea.

"Well," Michele proposed, "how would you like to offer yourself as a chaperone on Halloween night?"

I laughed.

"I'm serious. Trick-or-treating with Mr. Done. I'll bet it would bring a lot of money."

I thought about it for a second. The truth was that I didn't particularly want to stay at home all night on Halloween and open my door for three hours saying, "Aren't you getting a little old for this?" and "Hey you, just take one!" Besides, it had been a long time since I had gone trick-or-treating. It might be fun. I agreed.

The night of the auction, the multi was packed with parents and students. Some of the parents came in costume. Michele stood on stage auctioning off the items from the podium. She was dressed as a giant rubber chicken. I was one of the last items up for bid.

"Okay, everyone," Michele announced, holding a gavel in her hand. "Next on our list is trick-or-treating with Mr. Done."

The room erupted with laughter. Michele waved for me to come on stage. I walked up the stairs, stood beside her, and felt my face turn red as I tried to look like standing on an auction block is something I do all the time. Michele pounded several times on her gavel.

"Okay, parents," she began, "here's your chance to have Halloween night off. Do I hear twenty dollars?"

"Twenty!"

"Thirty!"

"Forty!"

"Fifty!"

"Sixty!"

"A hundred!" someone shouted from the back.

Everyone turned around. It was Trevor's dad. Trevor was standing by his side. He caught my eye and grinned.

"Do I hear one hundred ten?" Michele announced.

"One hundred ten!"

"One hundred twenty."

"One hundred fifty."

It can't go any higher than this.

"Do I hear one hundred sixty?" Michele coaxed. "Anyone want to bid one hundred sixty?"

"Two hundred!" a voice boomed from the back of the room.

There was a great in-drawing of breath as every head snapped to the opposite corner of the room. It was Christopher's dad. Christopher stood beside him, beaming.

Michele pointed at him. "We have two hundred. Do I hear two hundred ten?"

"Two hundred ten," Trevor's dad called out.

Christopher's dad raised it. "Two hundred twenty!"

"Two hundred thirty," cried Trevor's dad.

Christopher's father cupped his hands over his mouth and bellowed, "Two hundred forty!"

The noise in the hall escalated. Never in the history of our school auction had a teacher gone for so much money.

Michele stared at Trevor's dad. She looked at Christopher's. Then back to Trevor's. "Do I hear two hundred fifty?"

Everyone watched Trevor's father. He was thinking. Trevor tugged on his dad's arm.

"Going . . . ," Michele said, slowly.

Trevor's dad scratched his head.

The room grew quiet.

"Going . . . ," Michele repeated, stretching out the word even more.

Trevor continued to pull.

Finally, Trevor's dad shook his head.

"GONE!" Michele shouted, pounding her gavel. "To Christopher's family!"

The room exploded. As I walked down the stairs, people I didn't know patted me on the back. Several of my students raced up to the stage, giggling. Christopher ran up to me and jumped up and down. I leaned over the railing. "You know what this means, don't you?" I paused and grinned. "On Halloween night I get half your candy."

The day after the auction, I told Christopher that he could bring along a friend. He invited Trevor. I thought that was nice of him. On Halloween night, I picked the boys up at Christopher's house just before it started to get dark. They were all ready to go. Christopher was dressed up as Darth Vader. Trevor was a pirate. As we walked out of the door, Christopher zapped me with his lightsaber. I turned to Christopher's father and said, "Three hundred if you reconsider." He laughed.

With their pillowcases in hand, Christopher and Trevor tore out the door, ran to the first house, and rang the doorbell. I waited on the sidewalk with my flashlight. A woman wearing a witch's hat answered the door. The boys shouted, "Trick-or-treat," grabbed their candy, and flew off the porch.

"What did you guys get?" I asked as they raced across the lawn.

They didn't hear me. They were already halfway to house number two. I walked quickly to keep up. At the second house, a small boy in a Piglet costume was waiting at the door. His mom was standing next to me on the sidewalk. When the door opened, Piglet stepped inside. His mother rushed in the house to fetch him.

After Piglet was out, Christopher and Trevor reached into the bowl and dashed down the steps.

"Did you two say thank you?" I yelled.

"Thank youuuuuu!" they both hollered over their shoulders. And they flew to house number three.

The third house was all decked out. Styrofoam tombstones stood on the lawn, cobwebs covered the bushes, jack-o'-lanterns sat on steps, and yellow caution tape wrapped around the porch. The *Addams Family* theme song was playing in the window.

"Come on!" Trevor called back to Christopher as he ran up the driveway. "They had Skittles last year!"

My eyebrows went up. "You remember what they had last year?"

"Yeah!" he shouted.

At that moment, I realized that I was out with two trick-or-treating aficionados. Christopher and Trevor had this candy-collecting business down to a science. For the next two hours the boys slid through hedges, flew up walkways, jumped over gutters, dodged strollers, and raced down sidewalks. They hit hundreds of houses. They knew every shortcut. That night I got an education in trick-or-treating. Here are some of the things I learned from the experts:

TRICK-OR-TREATING LESSONS

Run outside at the first sign of dusk.

Banging on the door and ringing the doorbell at the same time make the people in the house open the door faster.

After saying "Trick-or-treat!" ask "How many can I have?"

Good candy: Tootsie Rolls, Kit Kats, Nerds, Twizzlers, Jolly Ranchers, Starburst, Skittles, Snickers, and Whoppers. Bad candy: toothbrushes.

Third graders do *not* need flashlights.

Pillowcases hold twice as much as plastic grocery bags and three times as much as plastic orange pumpkins.

After being handed a piece of candy, always look back in the bowl to see what you did not get.

When presented with a bowl of ten different candies, a third grader can decide which candy to take faster than he can answer $18 \div 3$.

The best candy is often on the bottom of the bowl.

If a group of children gathers at the door, sometimes it is best to be in the front so you do not have to wait and can run immediately to the next house. But sometimes it is better to be the last one because you might get two pieces of candy for being patient.

Do not get stuck behind a little kid at the door. Little kids take *forever* to decide.

Old people either are very generous or give you one peanut. There is no in between.

Handing out candy is like serving wine at a party. People serve the good stuff first and save the not-so-good stuff for later. The longer you stay out on Halloween night, the worse the candy gets.

Lots of decorations in the front yard means good candy. They spend a lot on Halloween.

Men don't care what they're handing out. Women give raisins.

It is always better to choose your candy than to have someone else choose it for you.

When parents chaperone, moms say, "Be careful" and "Remember your manners." Dads say, "Wha'd ya get?"

The later you stay out, the better chance the person at the door will give you a handful of candy instead of just one piece because she doesn't think she will have many more visitors.

Raid the candy bowl at your own house before you go trick-or-treating and again when you get home.

Cute costumes = more candy.

Dads stay out later than moms.

Do not show your teacher what you have in your lunch bag the day after Halloween or he'll point to the Official Halloween Candy Taste Tester button that he's wearing and ask for all your Reese's Peanut Butter Cups.

November

Judge each day not by the harvest you reap
but by the seeds you plant.

— Robert Louis Stevenson

REBECCA

All teachers have their "pillow students"—students we worry about before we fall asleep at night. How can we help them? What will happen to them when they leave our classes? Will they succeed in school? This year one of my pillow students is Rebecca.

Rebecca's mom is in jail—again. She is expecting her fourth child; each one is from a different father. Rebecca and her siblings are being raised by their grandmother, but unfortunately she doesn't have a lot of time for Rebecca, either. Oftentimes, Rebecca is late for school. Occasionally, she doesn't even show up at all. When she does come, she complains that she's not feeling well. Sometimes she gets into fights at recess with her friends. In class, she cries because she misses her mom.

Rebecca struggles with her schoolwork, too. Math is difficult. So is writing. She reads two years below grade level. When she reads with me, it takes her a long time just to get through the shortest page. I work with Rebecca on her reading as much as I can, but her progress is slow. I doubt that she has ever finished a whole book.

Once in a while when the class is reading together and all the children have copies of the same book, I'll ask Rebecca if she'd like to take a turn reading aloud, but she always refuses. She knows that she is behind the other children.

One night as I was thinking about how to help her, I had a brainstorm. *What about Max? What if Rebecca could read with Max?* Max is a golden Lab. He belongs to Ellen, our school secretary. Two or three times a week, Ellen brings Max to school after lunch, and he lies calmly behind her desk with a red bandanna tied around his neck. Max has a wonderful disposition—calm, friendly. Everyone loves Max. He has become our unofficial school mascot.

When a child comes into the office for a Band-Aid or an ice pack, Ellen always lets him come around the counter and pet the dog. Max pounds his tail on the carpet and soon the child forgets about why he came into the office in the first place. *If Rebecca could read to Max*, I thought, *maybe she would forget how difficult reading is for her.* Max wouldn't correct her. He wouldn't make fun of her. He'd just listen.

The following day, I discussed my plan with Ellen. She thought it was a great idea. I knew that Max couldn't come into the classroom. It would be too distracting. So Ellen and I decided that Rebecca would visit Max in the office. Things are pretty quiet there after lunch. Ellen volunteered to keep an eye on Rebecca.

When I first told Rebecca about the idea, I thought she'd be excited, but she wasn't. Rebecca knew Max, of course, but said that she didn't want to leave the classroom. I could tell that she was nervous. But I also had a hunch that after one visit with Max, she'd be hooked.

I knelt down beside her desk. "Rebecca, Max likes to be read to, but Ellen is too busy."

She hesitated.

"You'll be helping Max. And if you don't like it, you don't have to go back. Will you give it a try?"

She nodded.

"That's a girl."

The next day, I sent Rebecca to the office with a book. Ellen introduced her to Max. He raised his paw and shook Rebecca's hand. Then she sat down next to Max, opened her book, and started reading. Max hunkered down beside her. Ellen went about her work, pretending not to listen. After a few minutes Rebecca was petting Max with one hand while she followed the words in her book with the other. Max never moved. He never interrupted. He was the perfect audience.

After about twenty minutes, Ellen said it was time to go. She let Rebecca give Max a treat from her bottom desk drawer then sent her back to the classroom.

"How'd it go?" I asked Rebecca when she returned.

"Great!" she replied, enthusiastically. "Can I go again tomorrow?"

"Well," I said, smiling, "I was thinking that you could read to Max once or twice a week."

"But I think I should see him soon."

"Why?"

"I didn't finish the story."

From then on, Rebecca visited Max every Monday and Wednesday. She never needed to be reminded. When we had a Monday holiday, she asked if she could make up the time.

Rebecca became Max's teacher. She picked out books that she thought he would like—often about dogs. When we studied rocks, she took a book about rocks. Since we were just past Halloween, she taught Max all about bones. Once when she couldn't find the right book, I grabbed one off the shelf titled *The Christmas Cat*. "How 'bout this?"

Rebecca put her hands on her hips. "Mr. Done, Max is a *dog*!"

Ellen took good care of Rebecca. For each book Rebecca read to her new student, Ellen gave her a dog sticker. And for every ten stickers, Rebecca received a new book that Max autographed with his paw. If Ellen heard Rebecca struggling to read a word, she'd help her pronounce it. If Rebecca came to a word that Ellen thought she didn't understand, Ellen would say, "I don't think Max knows that word." Then Ellen would tell Max what it meant.

One afternoon while Rebecca was reading, Max fell asleep.

"His eyes are closed," Rebecca pouted.

Ellen swiveled around in her chair. Sure enough, Max was sound asleep. Ellen set her hands on her knees and said, "Oh, he's just concentrating so he can understand better."

As the weeks went by, I started to notice small changes in Rebecca. Her attendance improved. She wasn't tardy as often. She complained less about other children, and she got into less trouble on the blacktop. She smiled more.

One day I was sitting in the classroom with all my students reading *The Story of Helen Keller*. Every child held a copy of the book, including Rebecca. I walked to the whiteboard and wrote the word *obstacle* in large letters. I knew it was a new word for the children.

"Helen Keller faced enormous obstacles," I explained, tapping the new word on the board as I said it. "An obstacle is something that gets in our way." I grabbed the back of my chair and rolled it into the aisle. "See this chair. If I want to walk down the aisle, this chair is in my way. It's an obstacle. It's preventing me from getting to the other side of the room."

I took a few steps and purposefully ran into the chair. The kids laughed. I took a seat in the chair and continued.

"Helen Keller wanted to read and write just like you and I do, but she faced enormous obstacles. Who can tell me what some of them were?"

"She was blind," said David.

I pointed at him. "Yes."

"And she was deaf," Jennifer added.

"That's correct," I answered. Then I popped up and wrote *overcame* on the board. I pointed to the word. "Boys and girls, Helen *overcame* her obstacles. That means that even though she couldn't see or hear, she still accomplished what she wanted to do." I stepped out among the students. "Do you think it was easy for her to overcome her obstacles?"

"No," several answered.

The kids turned in their chairs as I walked down the center aisle.

"Do you think she got frustrated?" I asked.

"Yeah," most responded.

"Sure she got frustrated," I said, leaning on the table in the back of the room. "I'm sure there were times when she wanted to give up. But she didn't. She learned to read and write *despite* her obstacles. When Helen got older, she went to college. And she even wrote a book."

"She did?" Chloe blurted out, surprised.

"Yes," I replied. "She was a courageous young woman." I walked back to my desk, picked up the book, and flipped through the pages to find where we had left off. Rebecca raised her hand halfway.

"Rebecca, do you have a question?"

She nodded as her eyes studied the page in front of her. My heart made a little flip. Suddenly I realized why her hand was up. Rebecca wanted to read. She was volunteering to read aloud.

"Would you like to read for the class, honey?" I asked, gently. She nodded again.

At that moment, I wanted to jump up and wrap my arms around her and give her a hug and announce, "Yes, yes, yes!!" But of course I didn't. The best thing to do when a child is taking a risk is to act like what she is about to do is the most normal thing in the world. I looked into her nervous eyes and smiled encouragingly. "Okay, sweetheart. Why don't you start at the top of the page."

Soon the classroom was quiet except for one soft voice sounding out words—carefully, one word at a time. Her index finger moved slowly from left to right down the page.

I helped her when she stumbled or stopped in front of an unknown word or came to one that I knew she'd have trouble getting through. I praised her under my breath. Each word read was a victory. Each sentence completed was a win.

Rebecca flipped the page. Twenty pages turned along with her. No one read ahead. No one giggled. No one said hurry up. Robbie helped her pronounce a word. Melanie jumped in to help, too. They knew what was going on. Children can tell when something important is happening.

Finally, Rebecca reached the end of the paragraph. She stopped reading and looked up at me. A huge smile stretched between her cheeks. She had made it. She had overcome her obstacle. Some of the other children looked up at me and smiled, too. I reached over and squeezed Rebecca's arm. "Nice job." Then I pretended to rub my eyes, but really I was wiping away a tear.

Later that day when Rebecca went to see Max, he got up and wagged his tail. While Ellen typed on her computer, Rebecca curled up beside him and opened her book. "Oh, Max," she said excitedly, "I have a story that you are just going to *love*. Have you ever heard of Helen Keller?"

YARD DUTY

Ask any kid what his favorite subject in school is and he'll say recess. Ask any teacher what his *least* favorite subject is and he'll say recess—especially when he has yard duty. Yard duty is right up there with rainy days, writing report cards, and being serenaded by three boys singing "A Hundred Bottles of Beer on the Wall" while driving on a field trip.

The first recess at our school begins at ten o'clock. When the bell rings, five hundred children run outside at the same time with rubber balls and ropes and snacks. Three or four teachers patrol the blacktop, where they dodge basketballs that missed the hoop and spatula first-grade girls off their legs who have decided that the grown-up is base. At ten twenty the five hundred children run back inside their classrooms with dew and sand and dirt and gravel and mud and tanbark and half the grass from the newly mowed lawn on their shoes. The playground and field are cluttered with forgotten sweaters and abandoned balls all carefully labeled with permanent marker.

I have yard duty twice a week. That means on Tuesdays and Thursdays, I have no chance to use the bathroom from 8:00 AM till lunch. That means on these days, if I don't want to explode, I limit my liquids.

One Tuesday at the beginning of recess, I grab my whistle and my coffee and walk outside. I start at the corner of the blacktop. Joshua and Kevin are standing ten feet apart. They have just stuffed red rubber balls into their shirts.

"Hey, you two," I say. "What are you doing?"

"We're playing Sumo!" Joshua shouts. "Watch!"

Kevin counts off. "On your mark. Get set. Go!" The two boys run at full speed toward each other. *Bam!* Their stomachs collide. They go flying. It is bumper cars without the cars.

Joshua gets up first. "Mr. Done, watch again!"

"No," I reply, shaking my head. "I have to do yard duty."

I walk on. Soon I stop at a group of kids digging a hole next to the bike racks. Brian and five other boys have been working on this hole for a week.

"Have you hit water yet?" I ask.

"No," one of them answers without looking up.

"Mr. Done," Brian says excitedly, "we're digging a tunnel!"

"Where to?"

"Under the fence."

My eyes survey the dirt. "Just like Alcatraz."

"Yeah!" the boys cheer. They dig faster.

I leave the great escape and am nearly run over by three girls walking backward. I almost spill my coffee.

"Hey, be careful!"

"Mr. Done," one of them proclaims, happily. "We're in reverse!"

"I can see that. Watch the speed limit."

Moments later I stop at a basketball pole. Angela and Emily are just finishing up tying Michael with a jump rope.

"Hey, Mr. Done, you want to play?" asks Laura.

"No, thanks."

Nearby, I spot a group of children hopping around in a circle. "What are you all up to?"

"We're doing a rain dance," one of them answers.

I look up. There isn't a cloud in the sky. "Keep dancing."

As I make my way down the blacktop, I come to a game of Helicopter. You remember Helicopter? One person holds the jump rope and twirls it around in a circle on the cement while everyone else jumps over it. The person holding the rope keeps spinning until it hits someone's feet.

"Mr. Done, will you play with us?" Jennifer begs. "Will you play?"

"Yeah!" the others join her. "Play!"

I look at the kids. I look at the rope. I look back at them.

"Please!" Jennifer cajoles.

I think about it. Seven faces look up at me waiting for an answer: chins ducked, heads tilted, eyes wide, and pouty lips out.

"Oh, all right."

"Yeah!" they scream.

I set my coffee mug down on the picnic table, and Dylan hands me the rope. I begin twirling it around on the blacktop.

"Boys!" I call first.

All the boys jump in.

I continue to spin.

"Girls!" I holler next.

The girls join them.

Pretty soon the children are all a blur and I feel like I am in one of those circular carnival rides that spins one hundred miles per hour and everyone is pressed against the wall trying not to throw up. I stop.

"That's enough," I stammer, trying not to fall over.

"No!" they shout.

"Yes . . . that's all."

I hand the rope to Jennifer and stagger off.

As I walk away, several kids come running over to me. One little girl is in a panic.

"Mr. Done! Mr. Done!" she pants out. "Sam is hurt. Hurry!"

I follow her quickly over to the edge of the tanbark where students are standing in a huddle.

"Okay," I say, breaking through. "Let me in. Let me in."

I reach the center of the crowd. And there is Sam.

"This is Sam?" I ask, raising my eyebrows. Sam is a caterpillar.

"Yeah," someone answers. "He's dying!"

Everyone starts chattering at once.

"He fell out of the tree."

"He'll get squashed!"

"What do we do?"

"Okay. Okay. Don't worry," I say as I crouch down and scoop Sam up with a leaf. "I've got it under control." I hand the caterpillar off to one of the kids. "Here. Take Sam over to the bushes. He'll be safe there. Got it?"

"Got it!" they answer. And they all scurry off. The boy in the back wails like an ambulance siren.

As I stand up, Robbie and Dylan sprint up to me.

"Mr. Done! Mr. Done!" they shout.

"What?"

"Why did the chicken cross the playground?" Robbie asks, out of breath. Both look like they are nanoseconds from exploding.

I scratch my head, pretending to be stumped. "I give up. Why did the chicken cross the playground?"

They explode. "To get to the other slide!"

I laugh as though I've never heard it. "That's pretty good." Before they can tell me another one, I point to the yard duty teacher at the other end of the play structure. "Hey, go tell Mrs. Wilson. She loves jokes."

After they bolt off, I look around the yard. All looks normal. The fifth-grade boys are playing basketball. Several girls are turning cartwheels on the grass. Others are hanging upside down from the monkey bars. The picnic tables are crowded with children eating snacks. Three kids are writing words on the blacktop with their water bottles. Two are scaling the basketball poles. A couple of my students are walking around with banana peels on their heads. (Chloe started The Banana Peel Club.) And a line of second-grade boys is crouched down as low as possible with their shirts stretched over their knees following one another along the grass quacking. I put my hand up like a crossing guard and wave them on. "Make way for ducklings!" They waddle by.

As soon as the ducks pass, Peter runs up to me. He is in the other third-grade class.

"Mr. Done," he says, "can I take my shoes off?"

"Why?"

"They're all wet."

I look down. His shoes are drenched.

"How'd they get wet?"

"I poured water on them."

"Why'd you do that?"

"It's hot."

I just stare at him.

"Can I take them off?"

"Ask your teacher."

Just then I notice a first grader crying in the corner of the field. I walk over to him.

"What's wrong?" I ask.

He points to two other boys. "They won't throw the football to me."

I glance over at his two friends. Neither one is holding anything. I turn back to the one who's crying. "*What* football?" The boy's bottom lip quivers. "Now calm down. I don't see any ball. What ball are you talking about?"

"It's . . ." He wipes his nose with his sleeve. "It's pretend."

I make a face. "Pretend?"

"They won't throw it to me." He sniffs.

I wave the two over. "You boys come here." They look scared. Clearly, this is the first time they have ever gotten in trouble with a big mean third-grade teacher. "You need to share that football or I'm taking it away. Do you understand?"

Both nod.

"Okay now, you three shake hands."

They stare at me.

"You heard me. Shake hands."

They all look confused.

"Come on," I say.

The boys look at each other then turn back to me. Together they stick their hands up in the air like they're being held up and start shaking.

THE INTERCOM

A classroom is like a home. Both have cupboards and closets full of clutter. Both have pets and cages with water bottles that need to be filled up. Both have stashes of candy. Come to think of it, there isn't much of a difference between the two. I guess this is why teachers and parents say the same things to their kids: "Don't talk with your mouth full." "Do you think that jacket is going to pick itself up?" "Let me see your homework." "I'm not the cleaning lady." "What do you mean you're hungry. You just ate an hour ago!"

But one thing classrooms have that you will not find in most homes is the intercom. The intercom system has been around in schools for a long time. Before telephones were installed in classrooms, the intercom was the main way with which the office communicated with the teachers. The secretary or principal would stand in front of a big metal machine, press a button, and call students to the office for dentist appointments, doctor checkups, and visits to the orthodontist so that the rubber bands on their new braces could be changed.

Today the intercom is used mainly to announce special assemblies, hearing tests, and other all-school news. Just this week Bob, our principal, came on the intercom to talk to the whole school. It was a special day on campus. The Dairy Council was bringing Ellie the cow to our assembly. "Teachers," he said, "please excuse the interruption." All the kids stopped working and looked up at the speaker on the wall. Bob continued. "Ellie will be late. She is stuck in traffic."

Once when I was in third grade, the secretary forgot to flick off the switch after making an all-school announcement. More than five hundred children listened to the office staff chattering away until one honest teacher called in and told her. We all heard the secretary scream. Then the intercom went dead.

This year in the middle of November, my class visited our kindergarten buddies. Each class at my school is teamed up with another. We get together once a month and share an activity. My buddy teacher is Gail. I like being Gail's buddy. She cooks a lot with her students, and I get to taste-test. But I have to be careful. Last year I snatched what I thought was a cookie off a paper plate and just about gagged. They had just made doggy biscuits.

So there we all were in Gail's classroom getting ready for our big Thanksgiving Feast. Forty kids sat around the room at different stations making vests out of brown paper bags, decorating oatmeal box drums, and tracing turkeys around small hands on brown construction paper.

In one corner of the room, a volunteer mom was helping kindergartners write what they were thankful for on a piece of yellow butcher paper. I started reading the list:

"I am thankful that my dad changed my sandwich from peanut butter and jelly to bologna."

"I am thankful I am not a turkey."

"I am thankful for my brain for making new dreams every day."

"I am thankful for dogs when they lick me."

"I am thankful for Comcast because now I can tape my shows."

The mom gave me a grin. I smirked back and walked on. In another corner of the room, Gail's aide, Robyn, sat with the kindergartners taking dictation. They were making a class book entitled *How to Cook a Thanksgiving Turkey*. I stopped and listened as Robyn interviewed one little girl. She wore a white paper Pilgrim bonnet tied with fat black school yarn.

"How heavy is the turkey?" Robyn asked.

"A hundred pounds," the girl answered.

Robyn tried not to laugh as she wrote down the answer. "And how long do you cook it?"

"An hour."

"At what temperature?"

"Hot."

"Then what?"

"You put a lot of oil on it."

"How much?"

"About ten gallons."

I smiled, gave Robyn a wink, then walked on. A few minutes later I crouched down beside one of the kindergartners. His name was Scotty. He had just moved to our school. Scotty was wearing an orange headband covered with thunderbirds and some serious warrior paint on his cheeks. He was stringing a macaroni necklace.

"Hi, Scotty," I said. "Nice hat."

"Thanks."

"That's a mighty nice necklace. Are you going to give that to your mom?"

"No. She doesn't wear macaroni. She only wears diamonds."

I smiled. "I see."

All of a sudden the principal's voice came on the intercom. "Teachers, please excuse the interruption."

Gail clapped her hands in a rhythmic pattern. The children stopped what they were doing and clapped back. The classroom grew quiet.

"Okay, listen up everyone," Gail called out.

Scotty stared intently at the round speaker on the wall.

"Well," the principal continued, "it looks like it is going to rain. So teachers, we will have recess inside today. Thank you."

When the announcement was over, the children got back to their projects. Scotty continued staring at the speaker.

"Everything okay, Scotty?" I asked.

He didn't respond.

I set my hand on his shoulder. "What's the matter?"

Then with huge eyes he turned to me and whispered, "Was that God?"

LISTENING

This week in class we made our family trees. When I asked the students about their heritage, Joshua reported that he's half cowboy, Christopher claimed that he is one-fourth pirate, and Kevin (who is Irish) declared that he is 100 percent leprechaun. When Trevor told me that he was named after his grandfather, he looked disappointed.

"Why the long face?" I asked.

He sighed. "I'd rather be named after a football player."

Art Linkletter was absolutely right. Kids do say the darndest things. But that's only the half of it. When kids say the darndest things—their teachers have the darndest responses. Here are some of the most popular:

The Fake Listen

This response is used when you're pretending to listen to a child but actually aren't. I implement The Fake Listen when being followed around the blacktop at recess by a child who wants to explain every one of the tricks he can do on his new skateboard, or during Show and Tell when Laura is sharing her 50th foreign coin and has another 250 to go. The Fake Listen is similar to The Fake Applause. The Fake Applause is commonly utilized when a teacher is whispering with one of his colleagues during the school assembly and suddenly realizes that everyone is applauding so he starts clapping his hands, too, but really has no idea why.

The Buying Time

Teachers employ The Buying Time when asked questions that they are not exactly sure how to answer. When John, for example, asked me in the middle of the math lesson, "Why do women crave sardines when they're pregnant?" I used it. When Lisa asked me what *in heat* meant, I used it. And when Laura asked me why they called it a booby trap if there were no boobies in it—I used it, too. The best way to implement The Buying Time is simply to respond to the child's question with another question. Buying Time responses include, "*What* did you just say?" and "Where did you hear *that*?"

The Teacher Dodge

Unlike The Buying Time in which teachers are not sure just how to respond, The Teacher Dodge is implemented when they absolutely do *not* want to answer a child's question. This year when Dylan asked me if Santa knows God, when Gina shouted out, "Why is that frog on top of the other frog?" and when David wanted to know what the difference is between a steer and a bull, I sidestepped with The Teacher Dodge. To do it, simply change the subject as quickly as possible in order to avoid answering the student's question. Successful Teacher Dodges include: "Oh sorry, out of time," and "Never mind that. Get back to work."

The Frozen Teacher

This response is accompanied by a state of surprise, shock, bewilderment, speechlessness, and utter disbelief. Since the new school year began, I have already used The Frozen Teacher on multiple occasions. The first time was when my students and I were playing charades. It was Trevor's turn. He ran around the room, crashed into the wall, fell over, got up, and fell over again. I was dumbfounded. After a couple of seconds, I spoke.

"Uh . . . I give up. What are you supposed to be?"

The corners of Trevor's lips stretched upward. "A chicken with my head cut off."

The second time I responded with The Frozen Teacher, I was searching for something on my desk when Kevin and Danny walked up to me.

"Mr. Done," Kevin said, "do you know how to French-kiss?"

I spun around, eyes bulging. Kevin kissed Danny on one cheek and then on the other. Then Kevin turned to me and smiled. "That's how the French kiss."

Me: *Blank. Completely blank.*

A few months ago, I was in the middle of a lesson when Emily stood up in the back of the classroom, stretched to the ceiling, and let out a huge yawn. I stopped teaching and stared at her, immobilized. When she finished yawning, Emily sat down, crossed her hands on her desk, and gave me her complete attention.

Finally, I came to. "Emily, *what* was that?"

"Seventh-Inning Stretch."

Last week I pulled my latest Frozen Teacher. We were talking about cats when Christopher volunteered, "I've eaten cat food."

Full-freeze frame.

"You . . . you *what*?" I asked, shaking myself back to reality.

"It tastes good," he admitted, proudly.

I should *not* have asked the next question.

"How many of you have tasted cat food?"

Half the class raised their hands.

The Teacher Fib

Now I know it sounds bad, but there are times when employing The Teacher Fib is absolutely necessary. It is not a lie, per se. It is more of a survival tool. I only use it when I'm in a really tight spot. This year's Teacher Fibs include:

1. Telling Robbie that I was allergic to the birthday cupcakes he brought in after I noticed that most of the frosting had been licked off.
2. Telling Sarah that I left my grade book at home after she asked me what her spelling test score was when in actuality I couldn't find my grade book.
3. Telling Rebecca that I couldn't attend her birthday party because I already had other plans.
4. Telling Brian that the fire detector in the classroom is really a hidden camera and that if he didn't sit down immediately I was going to show the tape to his mother. He sat.

Sometimes one teacher response is not enough. This was the case just last week when Stacy asked me her big question. It was a peaceful Monday afternoon. We were reviewing our new spelling list for the week. The words were all in past tense using *-ed* endings.

Stacy looked up from her paper. "Mr. Done, what's E.D.?"

Eyes bulging, I snapped into The Frozen Teacher. My eyebrows felt like they were locked in too tight a face-lift. *Did I hear her correctly? I think she just asked me what E.D. is. What do I say? Try a Buying Time.* I adopted a calm expression. "What did you say, honey?"

She repeated the question.

She did *just ask me what E.D. is! Oh my gosh! I don't want to answer I don't want to answer I don't want to answer!* I could feel the blood rushing out of my head. *Deep breath. Deep breath. Close your mouth. Go for second Buying Time.*

I feigned a relaxed smile. "Why do you ask?"

"It was on TV."

As I opened my mouth to speak, I noticed that the rest of the class was now listening to our conversation. I looked back at Stacy. *She's still waiting. Now what? Try Teacher Dodge.*

"I think you should ask your parents."

"I did. They won't tell me."

Alarm bells began going off in my head. I could hear the little *Lost in Space* robot voice sounding off: *Warning. Warning. Danger, Phil Done. Leave topic immediately!*

I glanced up at the clock. *Attempt Dodge Number Two.*

"Oh my! It's time for recess. Okay, everyone, put your spelling lists away. Time to clean up."

"It's not time for recess," Laura pointed out. "We still have seven minutes."

She was right. I couldn't send them out this early. I looked over at Stacy. She was still waiting for an answer. Sweat started soaking through my shirt. As I ran my finger under my collar, I pictured Wile E. Coyote waiting helplessly for the burning fuse to reach the dynamite. I had no other choice but to pull out The Teacher Fib. I looked down at my watch, glanced up at the clock, then shook my head.

"That dang clock," I said. "It's slow again. I better call maintenance." I turned to the kids. "You're excused."

Everyone sprang out of their chairs and ran out of the room. *Whew.*

WORDS

Teachers are word warriors. All day long we explain, correct, examine, define, recite, check, decipher, sound out, spell, clap, sing, clarify, write, and act out words. We teach spelling words and history words and science words and geography words. We teach describing words and compound words. We teach synonyms and antonyms and homonyms, too.

The other day when I was reviewing homonyms with my students, I wrote the word *hair* on the whiteboard and touched the top of my head.

"Can anyone give me another kind of *hair*?" I asked. (I was looking for *hare*.)

Stacy raised her hand.

"Yes, Stacy."

"Chest hair."

In my class we collect words. Each week my kids bring in their Wonderful Word of the Week. It can be any word—one they overheard their parents say, one they discovered in a book, one they'd like to learn, or one they just like the sound of. They don't have to know what the words mean. They don't even have to know how to pronounce them.

"Okay, class," I said one morning, "get out your Wonderful Words." The children pulled out their papers. "Who'd like to go first?" Several raised their hands. I called on Rebecca.

"*Exquisite*," she shared.

"Ah yes," I said, nodding, "*exquisite* is a beautiful word. It means wonderful, fabulous. The princess wore an *exquisite* piece of jewelry. I love that word, too." I wrote it in big letters on the board. "Who's next?" More raised hands. I called on Robbie.

He looked down at his paper. "*Ram-bunc-tious,*" he read, slowly. "Is that right?"

"Yes. That's correct. *Rambunctious.* Another excellent word. Where did you hear that?"

"My mom said it to me."

I let out a laugh.

"What does it mean?" Chloe asked.

"It means rowdy." I gave an example. "The kids were running around the room making a lot of noise. They were *rambunctious.*"

"Like us!" Christopher boasted.

"You got that right," I replied as I wrote *rambunctious* on the board. I turned and looked back at Robbie. "Robbie, that's a five-dollar word."

"What's *that*?" he said, sitting up straight.

I inhaled as if I were smelling something wonderfully delicious. "Well . . . five-dollar words are nice, *juicy* words. There are also ten-dollar words and twenty-dollar words. There are even a few hundred-dollar words."

"Whoa!" several called out.

I put the cap back on the marker. "Okay, who's next?"

Trevor shot up his hand. I called on him.

He pressed his lips together in a devious little grin. "*Rocks.*"

Christopher snickered.

"Trevor, come on now," I said, one eyebrow raised. "Be serious."

"I *am* serious. Not like rocks in the ground. Rocks in a drink. Like a Martini on the rocks."

There's always one.

"Is that a five-dollar word?" Trevor asked.

"No!"

One day I gathered my kids on the carpet in the corner of the room and wrote *said* on the board. I drew a big circle around the word then crossed it out with a red marker like one of those No Smoking signs. The children waited to see what would happen next.

"Boys and girls, we are not allowed to use the word *said* today, so I've crossed it out."

"Said is dead!" Dylan shouted out, delighted with himself.

I smiled at him. "For this morning, yes." Then I faced the class. "Today we are going to learn about synonyms for *said*."

I took the cap off my dry erase pen and wrote *Mr. Done said, "Hi, Kevin."* on the small whiteboard. Everyone turned and looked at Kevin. He beamed. I pointed to the word *said* in my sentence. "Now, I could write *Mr. Done screamed, 'Hi, Kevin.'*"

They giggled.

"Or I could write *Mr. Done whispered, 'Hi, Kevin.'*"

They chuckled.

"I could even write *Mr. Done sang, 'Hi, Kevin.'*" I cleared my throat and sang, "Hi, Kevin," in my best Pavarotti.

Giddiness traveled around the carpet.

"You see," I continued, "the words *screamed, whispered,* and *sang* are all what we call synonyms. You've heard of synonyms before, right?"

"Yeah," they answered together.

"Can anybody give me another synonym for *said?*"

John sat up on his knees. *"Shouted!"*

"Exclaimed!" Angela added.

Laura jumped in. *"Yelled!"*

"Very good," I praised. "You got it. Now, today we are going to see how many synonyms you can come up with for the word *said*. And you may work with a buddy." Immediately the kids turned to their friends and linked arms like the barrel of plastic monkeys. "Not yet. Not yet. Trevor, let go of Christopher." They unhooked themselves.

Then I flopped back in my chair and gave a big, loud sigh. "Of course, I don't think you could possibly beat the *world record*."

Joshua jumped up. "There's a world record?"

"Of course," I responded with a straight face.

"What is it?" Sarah demanded.

"Oh, it doesn't matter," I sighed again. "You'll never beat it."

Jennifer seized my knee. "WHAT'S THE WORLD RECORD?"

I put on a surprised expression. "You really want to know?"

"YEAH!" everyone chanted. Jennifer shook my leg.

"Well . . . ," I continued, thumping my temple with my finger for dramatic effect, "if I'm not mistaken . . . I believe that the world record for the most synonyms ever brainstormed for *said* is fifty."

Trevor sprang to his feet. "I'm going to beat it!"

Dylan shot up next. "So am I!"

Christopher jumped up with them. "Can we start now?"

I pretended that I hadn't planned on it. "Now?"

"YEAH!" the class chirruped.

I glanced at the clock then shrugged. "Okay. Off you go."

Immediately everyone grabbed their buddies, collected their paper and pencils, spread out around the room, and started making their lists. The noise in the room began to bubble. I walked around to lend a hand. Synonyms were popping up everywhere.

"Laughed!"

"*Hollered!*"

"*Stuttered!*"

"*Cheered!*"

"*Yelled!*"

"Think of animals," I called out as I circled the room. "What if animals could talk?"

"*Roared!*"

"*Squeaked!*"

"*Growled!*"

"*Croaked!*"

"*Hissed!*"

"*Barked!*"

Kevin leapt up from behind the piano. "Is *tweeted* a word? Like Tweety Bird tweeted?"

I thought about it for a second. "I'll accept it."

Kevin popped back down. Gina ran up next.

"Is this one?" she asked, pointing to her paper. It said *soft*.

"Not quite, honey. That's the *way* you can talk. You wouldn't say, 'Gigi soft, Hello.' Understand?"

"Ohhhhh," she said. "I get it." She dashed off.

Christopher skidded up to me.

"How many words do you have?" I asked.

"Seventeen. Is this one?" He cupped his hand over my ear. "*Sneezed.*"

"Hmm," I said, pursing my lips. "Can you *sneeze* a word?"

Right away he let out a huge "Ah-choo!" like he was auditioning for a Claritin commercial. "See! *Ah-choo*'s a word!"

I couldn't help but smile. "Well, there you go. Sure, *sneezed* works."

He sped off.

I walked over to the door and flicked off the lights. Everyone stopped writing. "Think of monsters and ghosts," I prompted. "How do ghosts talk?"

"*Moaned,*" Emily whispered to her partner.

"*Howled!*" Danny exclaimed. "Like a werewolf."

Melanie raced up to me next. She was shaking her paper. "Mr. Done, what sound does a witch make when she laughs?"

"*Cackled.*"

"Thanks." She started to leave.

"Hey, Melanie." She turned around. I was smiling. "*Cackled* is a five-dollar word."

She smiled broadly then darted off. I sat down on the arm of the couch. Christopher ran up to me again.

"I got one! I got one! Does this count?" He waved for me to bend near then whispered loudly, "*Gargled.*"

I gave him a teacher face: head cocked, lips pursed, chin down, eyebrows up.

"My dad can gargle and talk at the same time," he argued.

I had to laugh. "Okay."

"Don't tell anyone," he ordered. And he shot off.

Around the room children buzzed, pencils scribbled, and arms held clipboards close to the chest like poker cards so no one would steal their synonyms.

"Think of kings and queens," I directed. "What does a king do?"

"Chop people's heads off," Trevor announced, happily.

I shot him a look.

"*Ordered!*" David spewed.

"*Commanded!*" Brian shouted.

"*Proclaimed!*" Laura squealed.

I eyed the clock. "It's almost time for recess." Everyone looked above the pull-down screen. The big hand was on the 11.

Five minutes left. Suddenly the room became more animated. Christopher ran over a third time and tapped me on the shoulder. He was practically hyperventilating.

"I got another one! I got another one!" Then he stood on his tiptoes. I cupped my ear. *"Burped."*

"No way," I said, pulling away.

"Why *not*?"

"Because, you cannot *burp* and *talk* at the same time."

"Yes you can. Yes you can," he asserted, tapping my arm. "Listen." Then Christopher cleared his throat, took a giant gulp of air, and started burping the alphabet. *"A . . . B . . . C . . ."*

Immediately the room fell silent.

"D . . . E . . . F . . ."

All eyes were glued to the burping boy. The class was entranced. Christopher looked triumphant. I was speechless.

"Does it count?" Dylan yelled.

"G . . . H . . ."

"Mr. Done," Dylan repeated, *"does it count?"*

"I . . . J . . ."

I threw up my hands. "You win."

DRAMA

This morning I walked out of the staff room with my coffee mug in hand to meet my students. It had just started to rain. When I got to my door, the kids were pretending to pass something down the line.

"What are you doing?" I asked, patting my pocket for my keys.

"Playing Pass-It-On," Angela replied.

"What are you passing?"

"The imaginary sausage," Brian answered, happily.

I took a gulp of coffee. *This is going to be a long day.*

As I started unlocking the door, Angela tossed the sausage to Brian. Brian tossed the sausage to Jay.

"Mr. Done," Joshua said, "catch!"

"Sorry," I replied, swinging the door open. "My hands are full. No more sausage. Time to come in now. Wipe your feet."

It started to rain a little harder. The children hurried inside. After the last one was in, I shut the door. I pictured Noah when he closed the door on the Ark, trapped inside with a bunch of wild animals.

When I walked into the classroom, all of the kids were waving their hands and shouting, "Me! Me! Me!" Brian was standing on his chair looking for someone to catch his pass.

I teacher-pointed him. "I told you to put that sausage away!"

"I *did*," he stated. "This is the imaginary pickle."

Brian tossed the pickle to James. I took another gulp of coffee.

*   *   *

Kids love pretend. When we're studying Antarctica, they all want to jump off the desks and act like they're penguins diving off glaciers. When we're learning about the rain forest, all the boys want to play boa constrictor and squeeze the life out of one another. When we're learning the difference between *predator* and *prey,* everyone in the class wants to be the tiger. They beg *me* to be the hurt little antelope.

Children never need to be taught how to pretend. They're natural performers. In all my years of teaching I have never had to instruct a child in how to faint, yawn, die, snore, trip, beg, fly, move in slow motion, or sing like an opera star. Send them up on the jungle gym and they're on the *Santa Maria* searching for land. Push a few desks together, and they're climbing the Sierras in a covered wagon. Spray them with a little water and those wagons are crossing the Platte River. One smart aleck will always fall out, yell he can't swim, and drown.

Kids love costumes, too. Sheets are capes. Rolls of masking tape are halos. Give a boy an eye patch and he'll say, "Ahoy there, matey!" Put a paper crown on a girl and she'll order, "Off with his head." Hand a kid a bandanna and he'll turn into a bandit. Let him have two black staplers and he'll twirl them like revolvers.

No child ever needs help handling a prop. Chairs are thrones, desks are caves, paper towel rolls are spyglasses, trash cans are treasure chests, pull-down screens are magic mirrors, jump ropes are lassos, tennis balls are poisoned apples, and my coffee mug is a bottle of rum.

Nothing makes a better prop than a yardstick. Yardsticks can double as swords, bows, arrows, canes, spears, javelins, axes, brooms, machetes, branches, flagpoles, rifles, hockey sticks, bayonets, lightsabers, and magic wands.

Third graders are also sound effects experts. In fact, I have yet to meet a child who wasn't able to re-create the following sounds on command: frog, motorcycle, bird, ghost, witch, phone, cat, doorbell, chicken, thunderstorm, siren, breeze, dog, snore, creaky stairs, and the jingle from *Jeopardy!*

The kids' enthusiasm comes out at our annual school play. As soon as I assign parts, they will search their scripts and count how many lines they have. When I say it's time for play practice, they'll start moving the furniture around the classroom faster than the guys on *Extreme Makeover: Home Edition*. When we start rehearsing, they will say their lines with their backs to the audience. On opening night, one child will search the folding chairs for his mom until he finds her. Children will giggle on stage when they're supposed to freeze, and fix their hair when they're supposed to be asleep. When they take their bows, their hats will fall off.

When I was a kid, I loved doing plays. I wrote shows for the neighborhood kids. We performed them in Jennifer King's garage. I directed and starred in them, too. All the neighbor ladies came and paid a quarter to get in—even Mrs. King. For scenery I raided our garage. For props I raided my house.

"Where's the rug?" my mom called out one day, walking into the entryway.

"In the show!" I replied. "You'll get it back in a couple of days. We close Sunday."

This year I have a bunch of budding thespians in my classroom. When Trevor didn't like the game we were playing in PE, he started limping. When he didn't want to write, he tied his arm up in a sweatshirt and said he broke it. This week as I was walking around the room helping kids with their math, I stopped at his desk. His eyes were shut.

"What's wrong with you?" I asked.

"I can't do my math."

"Why?"

"I'm blind."

"Oh, that's too bad," I said, placing my hand on his shoulder. "Guess you'll have to miss the movie we're watching after lunch."

Trevor sat up straight. "We're watching a movie?"

"We might."

His eyes popped open. "I'm healed!"

Not long ago, I was walking across the playground and noticed a group of kids on the lawn. They were lined up in three rows in a triangular formation. Another child stood about ten feet away with a red rubber ball. He rolled the ball toward the triangle. When the ball hit the kids, they went diving and flying in all directions. After they fell on the grass, they all jumped up and returned to their three lines.

I stopped. "What are you guys playing?"

"Bowling Alley!" John announced. "We're pins!"

Another day we were out for free play and I spotted half my class lying frozen on the grass. Kevin was standing over them with his hands outstretched. I walked on over.

"What's going on here?" I asked.

"Shhh," Kevin said.

I whispered, "What's going on here?"

Kevin leaned in. "I hypnotized them."

"Oh."

All of a sudden the bell rang. No one moved.

"Okay, Kevin, time to *un*hypnotize them."

"I can't."

"Why?"

"I forgot the magic words."

I looked out at the comatose children. Then I raised my arms slowly, circled them in the air, and spoke in a low, Harry Houdini voice.

"Ooooone . . ."

No one moved.

"Twooooooo . . ."

Still hypnotized.

"TWO AND A HALF."

The kids popped up and ran back to the classroom. I turned to Kevin and winked. "It's all in the wrist."

One rainy-day recess, my students were spread out all around the classroom. Dylan, Melanie, and Rebecca were in the corner acting something out. They had moved some desks. On them lay stacks of papers and books. Dylan was wearing a pair of plastic glasses and a tie from the costume box.

"Are you playing school?" I asked.

"Yeah," said Rebecca.

I looked at Dylan. "Who are you?"

A giant smile was plastered on his face. "I'm Mr. Done."

I laughed, shook my head, and rubbed my forehead all at the same time. Then Dylan started madly searching through the stacks on his desk and throwing papers on the floor. "Where are my keys?" he cried out loud. Suddenly the room grew quiet and everyone stared at Dylan. Aware of his new audience, Dylan stood on his chair, squeezed his skull, and shouted, "HAS ANYONE SEEN MY CAR KEYS?"

December

My first copies of *Treasure Island* and *Huckleberry Finn*
still have some blue spruce needles scattered in the pages.
They smell of Christmas still.

—Charlton Heston

HOLIDAY HOTLINE

I'm amazed at how many hotlines there are for stressed-out cooks at the holidays. Crisco has one. So do Campbell's and Ocean Spray. Libby's, Hershey's, and Betty Crocker all have them as well. At the Butterball Turkey Talk-Line, anyone can call up twenty-four hours a day and get answers to their questions: "Do I roast the turkey with or without the plastic netting?" "Can I pop popcorn in the turkey's cavity during the roasting process?" "How do I thaw a fresh turkey?" "Where does the meat thermometer go?" "I can't find the turkey I buried in the snowbank. Can you help?"

Teachers could definitely use a hotline to get them through December, too. The week before winter break at any school feels like blending a pitcher full of Margaritas and forgetting to put the lid on. This week I have already twisted dozens of red pipe cleaners around candy canes to make reindeer antlers, spray-painted oodles of walnuts gold, rolled out miles of gingerbread dough, and glued twenty Happy Meal Toys in the bottom of baby food jars to make snow globes for parents' holiday gifts then ended up wrapping them all myself. (Have you seen third-grade boys wrap?)

The Holiday Hotline for Teachers would offer harried educators—not recorded tips—but live assistance from veteran colleagues on everything from what to bring to the White Elephant exchange to recipe suggestions for the staff Christmas party potluck.

HOTLINE: Holiday Hotline. May I help you?
TEACHER: Hi. Do I have to get my boss a Christmas present?
HOTLINE: Have you had your evaluation yet this year?
TEACHER: It's next month.
HOTLINE: Buy him something expensive.

HOTLINE: Holiday Hotline. May I help you?
TEACHER: My first graders and I disagree on the echo part in "Rudolph the Red-Nosed Reindeer." I say that after singing "They never let poor Rudolph join in any reindeer games," you shout "Like Monopoly." They insist that it's "Like Poker." Which one is it?
HOTLINE: (*pause*) What grade did you say you teach again?

HOTLINE: Holiday Hotline. May I help you?
TEACHER: I'm calling from the staff lounge. I just burned a batch of gingerbread men.
HOTLINE: How old are your kids?
TEACHER: They're kindergartners.
HOTLINE: Are any of your students with you right now?
TEACHER: Yes.
HOTLINE: Do not let them see the cookies.
TEACHER: Why?
HOTLINE: Last year we had a kindergarten teacher call. She burned a batch of gingerbread men just like you. When she pulled them out, one of her kids picked up the phone and started dialing 911 to save them.

HOTLINE: Holiday Hotline. May I help you?
CALLER: I'm sitting here naked and . . .
HOTLINE: Sorry. We're not that kind of hotline.

*　　*　　*

HOTLINE: Holiday Hotline. May I help you?

TEACHER: Yes. I'm dying here. My kids are bonkers. They won't work. They won't sit still. Help!

HOTLINE: Have you shown the *Santa Claus Is Coming to Town* video?

TEACHER: Yes.

HOTLINE: Have you shown *How The Grinch Stole Christmas*?

TEACHER: Yes.

HOTLINE: Have you shown *Frosty the Snowman*?

TEACHER: Yes.

HOTLINE: What other videos do you have?

TEACHER: Only *Barney's Valentine Adventure*.

HOTLINE: Show it.

HOTLINE: Holiday Hotline. May I help you?

TEACHER: Are LEGOs toxic?

HOTLINE: Why do you ask?

TEACHER: Well, I was making cranberry bread for my Secret Santa. My son was playing with his LEGOs on the counter. When I had my back turned he put the LEGOs in the batter.

HOTLINE: Did you bake the bread yet?

TEACHER: No.

HOTLINE: Good. Fish them out. You should be fine.

ESTHER

The December I was in third grade, my mom bought my grandmother a navy-blue coat with a fur collar at Macy's. I was with her when she purchased it. On Christmas morning when my family opened their presents, Mom handed my grandmother a box. The tag said, "To: Grandma. From: Santa." Grandma unwrapped her gift and pulled out the blue coat. She loved it. But I was very concerned about that tag. *There must be a mixup,* I thought. *Now my grandmother will never know that Mom was the one who really bought the coat.*

In third grade, there are three camps when it comes to Santa Claus: Those who believe. Those who don't. And those who are on the fence. When I was a kid, I was in the Believer Group. This made sense, of course. Heck, I thought the Jolly Green Giant and Chef Boyardee were real. I believed that Betty Crocker looked just like the drawing on the front of her cookbook and that Sara Lee made her own cheesecakes, too.

In every primary classroom—sometime in December—the question of Santa's existence always comes up. And every year there is always at least one student whose mission it is to convince his classmates that Santa Claus is not real. Whenever the Santa Claus debate begins in class, teachers must act quickly to nip it in the bud. If there is one thing that children are passionate about—it's Santa.

One day I was helping a student at my desk when I heard the word *Santa* coming from the second row. My teacher antennae perked up.

"He isn't real," Danny insisted.

"Yes he is!" Laura protested.

Uh-oh. Trouble.

"Santa Claus is just your dad," Danny ruled.

"No, he isn't!" Laura countered.

I'd better intervene.

"Danny," I said, stretching out his name, "are you working?"

The two stopped talking and looked down at their work. Seconds later, Laura continued.

"I *know* he's real," she snarled.

"How do you know?" Danny snapped back.

"*Okay, you two,*" I said, raising my voice. "That's enough."

But Laura wasn't finished yet. "Because Santa Claus drives a sleigh, and my dad doesn't know how."

You go, girl.

The week before winter break, my class makes its annual trip to the local senior center. It's just down the street from our school, so we walk over. The children sing "Frosty the Snowman," "Santa Claus Is Coming to Town," and "Jingle Bells" for the center's holiday luncheon. After the concert, the hostesses give each child a candy cane. The children hand out Christmas cards that they made at school. It's a lovely morning.

This year after the children received their candy canes, they walked out into the audience to pass out their cards. John approached a little old lady sitting in the front row. She was sitting in a wheelchair. The woman wore a red dress. A gold Christmas tree brooch covered with colored glass stones was pinned to her collar. Her hair was the color of snow. It smelled like Aqua Net.

John handed her his card.

"Oh, thank you," said the woman. Her eyes twinkled like Christmas lights.

I stood behind John as the woman examined the cover. John had colored Rudolph pulling Santa in his sleigh. Santa was shouting, "Ho! Ho! Ho!" Rudolph's nose was as large as his body.

The woman looked up at John. "You got Santa's beard just right. A lot of people don't get his beard right, you know. It really is longer than most people think."

John's eyes grew as big as saucers. "You know *Santa Claus*?"

She sat up, slapping both hands on her knees. "Of course I know him."

John took a step back then turned to the students standing beside him. "Hey," he announced, "she knows Santa Claus."

Word spread like a game of Hot Potato that the old lady in the wheelchair knew Santa. Quickly she was wreathed by children. All ears waited to hear what she had to say. Including Danny's.

"What's your name?" the woman asked John.

He answered.

"Nice to meet you, John. I'm Esther."

John regarded her steadily. "How do you know Santa Claus?"

Esther laughed. "Oh, I've known him for years."

"Honest?" Laura asked, moving in closer.

Esther turned to her. "Honest. Of course, I haven't seen him in quite some time, but I talk with him every year."

Melanie leaned on Esther's knee. "You *do*?"

"Oh yes," Esther replied. "He used to call me on the telephone every December to ask me if my children had been good. Then after my kids grew up, he'd call and ask if my grandchildren had been good."

"Does he still call you?" Chloe chimed in, eagerly.

Esther looked at Chloe. "Yes. But my grandchildren are all grown up now, too. So he asks me about all the other children I know." She turned back to John with a warm smile. "Or have met recently."

"Has he called you yet this year?" Kevin piped in.

"Not yet," Esther answered. "But I suppose he'll be calling me any day now." Then Esther leaned into John and looked straight into his eyes. She held them with her own. "Have you been good?"

John didn't speak. Only nodded.

Esther grinned. "I'll let Santa know."

I glanced down at my watch. It was time to go. "Okay, kids, I'm afraid it's time we start heading back. Say good-bye." The room was filled with good-byes and waves as the children lined up to leave. The moms collected the kids' coats and hats, and we walked out of the hall. As we gathered in the lobby, I counted heads to make sure everyone was there. I was short one child.

"Who's missing?" I asked the class.

The kids looked around.

"Danny," several answered.

I walked back into the hall. Danny was talking to Esther.

"Hey, Danny, come on," I called. "We're leaving."

Smiles were exchanged. Esther's gaze followed Danny up the aisle as he raced to join the rest of us. Danny met me in the lobby.

"What were you two talking about?" I asked.

"I told her what I wanted for Christmas," he replied, breathing heavily.

"Why?"

"Mr. Done, didn't you *hear*? . . . She knows Santa Claus!"

THE BELL

A small silver bell sits on my desk at school. It's nothing fancy. But it means a lot to me. It was a gift from my Grandma Vie when I first started teaching. She said that every teacher should have one. My students call it Grandma Vie's bell. Occasionally when the bell is looking tarnished, I'll pull out some silver cream and clean it up in front of my students. And when I do, I make the same speech: "School is a lot like silver cream. It polishes us up."

Sometimes I'll let a child ring Grandma Vie's bell. This afternoon when it was time for Show and Tell, I chose Joshua to give the bell a shake, then asked everyone to get ready for sharing.

As Joshua set the bell back on my desk, I asked him if he had ever seen *It's a Wonderful Life*.

He shook his head.

"You should see it," I suggested. "There's a famous line in the film." I paused to remember it just right. "'Teacher says every time a bell rings—an angel gets his wings.'"

Joshua thought about this for a moment. "What does he have to do to get 'em?"

"Well," I said, "I imagine that the angel has to do something good—to prove that he is worthy of earning his new wings."

Then we started Show and Tell. After Angela shared a miniature Statue of Liberty that her dad had brought her from New York, Kevin showed us his molted rattlesnake skin, and Robbie played "Chopsticks" on the piano, I called on Joshua. He reached under his desk, pulled out a shoe box, and walked up to the front of the classroom.

I cleared a spot on my desk. "What do you have for us today?"

Joshua set the box down. As he lifted the lid, the children leaned forward to get a better look. The kids in the back row stood.

The box was full of small bundles wrapped in paper towels. Joshua pulled one of them out, unwrapped it, and set a ceramic figurine on my desk. It was a lamb, no more than two inches high. Then he unwrapped a wise man.

My eyes widened. *Uh-oh. He brought a Nativity set to school.*

Soon the desk was covered with sheep and camels and donkeys and two more wise men. Baby Jesus and his family sat on my desk, too. I shifted in my seat. I had read about teachers getting into trouble for such things. When he finished unwrapping all the pieces, I said, "Thank you for bringing these in, Joshua. It's very nice." Then I turned to the class. "Okay. Who's next?"

"Wait," Joshua stopped me. "I'm not done yet."

I felt my jaw clench.

Then like Linus in *A Charlie Brown Christmas,* Joshua began telling the Christmas story. He picked up Mary and Joseph and moved them across my correcting basket to Bethlehem. The shepherds marched on top of my piles to the inn. He led the wise men over my lesson plan book to the manger. His classmates listened closely. Joshua knew the story well.

As he spoke, I sat quietly in my chair with my arms crossed, nibbling the end of my pen. Thoughts were firing in my head. *What if my boss walks in? What if one of my students goes home and says that I taught the Christmas story in class? Didn't teachers go to court for this?* Finally, Joshua started collecting the figurines. I helped him gather them up.

"Thank you for bringing this in," I told him.

Then Joshua turned to me. "Can I pass them around?"

I inhaled sharply. *Pass them around? At school? Now?* Of course I had to let him. I always let my students pass around their sharing. I've never said no—not even when Alisha brought in her tarantula. I took a deep breath and let it out like a leaky balloon. "Sure."

Soon Mary, Joseph, and all the rest were being passed down the rows. Brian made sheep sounds each time he handed one off. I kept an eye on the door as my fingers drummed on my desk. After everyone had a chance to hold the pieces, Joshua collected them in his box and walked to the back of the room. He started arranging the figures on the back counter.

"Joshua," I called out, "what are you doing?"

"I'm Student of the Week."

I stared at him—unable to blink. He was right. He *was* Student of the Week. And the Student of the Week gets to display whatever he brings from home on the counter in front of the Student of the Week bulletin board. And these things stay on the counter for five days. *What if a parent sees the Nativity? How will I explain this?*

"Can I share next?" Rebecca shouted.

I turned to her. "Huh? . . . oh yes . . . of course."

Rebecca walked up to the front with a photo album. As she turned the pages, my eyes shifted to the back of the room. Josh was almost finished setting up the crèche. I heaved another sigh. *You know,* I thought, *this is* his *sharing. This boy is entitled to share* whatever *he wants. He's not doing anything wrong here. Phil, calm down.*

Soon Rebecca finished and Joshua walked up to me. "Can I go outside and get some grass?"

"Why?"

"For the sheep."

"What for?"

"To sit in."

I rubbed the back of my neck and smiled. "Why not?"

After Show and Tell was over, it was time for math. The kids took out their practice books and began solving the problems I had put on the board. I glanced over at the crèche spread out on the counter in full view for all to see. Then I looked over at Joshua. He was quite a kid. I respected him—his faith, his honesty, his innocence, his lack of fear. Hopefully, he would never lose these qualities. Maybe someday, privately, I would tell him that the shepherds in my own crèche at home look like his.

Just then I spotted the silver bell sitting on my desk beside the pencil can. I picked it up, walked over to Joshua's desk, and knelt down beside him. Softly, I tinkled the bell next to his ear. He turned toward me with a surprised expression.

"Why are you ringing Grandma Vie's bell?" he whispered.

I looked into his eyes and smiled. "Remember that line from the movie I told you about? 'Teacher says every time a bell rings— an angel gets its wings.'" He nodded. "Well . . ." I tapped him on the nose. ". . . I know one little angel who just earned his."

GIFTS

At my school the teachers affectionately call the week before winter break—Mug Week. This is when we all add to our World's Greatest Teacher coffee cup collections. At last count I think I have thirty-seven. I figure by the time I retire, I will have a different mug for each day of the year.

One Mug Week, I was sitting around the table in the staff room eating lunch with my colleagues.

"Lisa, what are you doing this weekend?" I asked.

She sighed. "Unwrapping Christmas presents."

"*Un*wrapping?" I said, confused. "What do you mean?"

Lisa gave a fake smile. "Well, I have to remove the packaging from my kids' presents before I wrap them. If I don't, they'll be crying on Christmas morning because Mommy can't get Barbie's car out of the box."

I laughed.

"I know just what you mean," Sandy chipped in. "I spent twenty minutes at my son's birthday party trying to free his Deluxe Tool Kit. By the time I got it all out, my camera batteries were dead."

Just then Kim walked in and put her hands on her hips. "Guess what I just got from one of my kids."

"A mug rack?" Lisa guessed.

"Nope," Kim said. She held up her new gift. "One earring."

"Ha!" I whooped. "Just *one*?"

Kim smiled. "My aide got the other one."

Everyone laughed.

"I can top that," Dawn added. "I got a box of cereal once."

We all stopped eating. *"Cereal?"*

"Why did you get *that*?" Joan asked.

Dawn shrugged. "They said they liked the recipe on the box."

Kim let out a loud guffaw.

"That's it!" Lisa declared. "I'm getting my son's teacher a box of Grape-Nuts."

Sniggers followed. Sandy had to breathe deeply through her nose because her mouth was full of sandwich.

"You all know my Sanjeev, right?" Joan said, unscrewing the lid on her thermos. "His parents are both from India. Well, he gave me a pretty little wooden box. I said to him, 'Sanjeev, is this from India?' He said, 'No, it's from The Dollar Store.'"

I cut through the chuckles. "Men are lucky. We don't get wooden boxes and jewelry." I reached down and held up my Rudolph tie. "We get designer ties like this instead." I pushed his nose. Burl Ives started singing.

"Okay, you guys," Kim began while opening her lunch bag, "what is the most *memorable* teacher gift you ever received?"

Sandy spoke first. "Mine was a bottle of perfume. From Donald."

"That's nice," Lisa said.

Sandy made an exaggerated grin. "When I thanked him he said, 'It's free. My mom works at Avon.'"

"Mine was a mug," Dawn tossed out.

"What else did you expect?" I said.

Dawn turned to me and smiled. "It said 'Happy St. Patrick's Day.'"

We enjoyed another laugh. Then Kim raised her Diet Pepsi and announced, "To Mug Week!" We all raised whatever we were drinking and cheered along with her. "To Mug Week!"

*　　*　　*

I remember the very first teacher gift I ever gave. I was in kinder-garten. My teacher's name was Miss Brooks—just like the TV show. My mom had decorated a white lunch bag and filled it with goodies for the teacher: pens, rubber stamps, an inkpad, and some candy. Well, I added some goodies of my own to the bag when my mom wasn't looking. The next day when Miss Brooks opened her present, she found two snowman candles with their heads melted off, half a can of mixed nuts, and a pork chop wrapped in aluminum foil.

Starting in first grade, I always gave my teacher a box of Whitman's chocolates. (Mom was done with goody bags.) I'd wrap the yellow box up all by myself. The week before break, I'd slip it on my teacher's desk when she wasn't looking and wait for her to open it up at the Christmas party. Whenever she reached for a present, I'd hold my breath, hoping it would be mine. At last, she'd select my gift, read the tag, and look for me among the stu-dents. One of the best parts of giving a present is when the per-son you love smiles at you just before opening your gift.

Every teacher I ever had in elementary school opened up Christmas presents the exact same way. First, she'd set the gift in her lap and admire the wrapping paper. Next, she'd ask if I wrapped it myself and, if I did, tell me what a nice job I had done. Then she'd untie the ribbon, remove the bow, and set them in a bow-and-ribbon pile. (Teachers love to sort.) After that she'd turn the package upside down and run her fingernail under the tape so as not to rip the paper. (Teachers do not rip paper.) Sometimes she'd do all this while talking to the class. (Teachers do not like dead space.) And sometimes she'd make silly guesses so we would laugh. Of course she would *always* open her gifts slowly.

Teachers know that the slower they unwrap their presents—the longer a child feels the reward of giving.

Eventually, she would pull the paper away in one piece, put her hand on her chest, and say, "Chocolates!" in such a way that I knew a box of Whitman's was *exactly* what she was hoping to get for Christmas. Finally, she'd smile and say, "Phillip, are you trying to make me fat?" Everyone would giggle. The other kids would beg her to share the candies. But she wouldn't. She'd hug the box and say, "No, they're all mine."

Some of my most memorable gifts revolve around candy, too. Once I had a student named Andrea who gave me a box of See's candy. I didn't open it. When I got home, I put the white box in the freezer. I already had enough sweets around the house. A couple of months later, I was looking for something to eat. I opened the freezer and spotted the box of See's. So I pulled it out and opened it up. Inside was a tie.

Another year I received a fancy box of chocolates from a student named Patty. I decided to share them with my students, so I walked around the room and let each child take a piece. After a few moments, I heard a child shout, "Yuck!" "These are rotten!" another screamed. Pretty soon everyone was spitting out the chocolates. Quickly I grabbed the lid and read it. They were *full* of cognac.

If I had to pick one Christmas gift that touched me the most, it would have to be Henry's. I hang it on my Christmas tree every year. On a high branch. In the front.

It was the day before winter break several years ago. All

week long, the kids had been begging me to unwrap my gifts. I wasn't planning to open them at school, but they persisted. So at the Christmas party, I gathered my students around my desk and opened their presents. I unwrapped each gift slowly. I made one pile for wrapping paper and another for ribbons and bows.

After the party it was time for lunch. I was on lunch duty in the cafeteria. As I walked down the center aisle, I stopped at the table where my students were sitting. The girls sat with the girls. The boys sat with the boys. I spotted Henry sitting quietly at the end of the table. He didn't have a lunch.

"Why aren't you eating lunch today?" I asked.

Henry lowered his head.

"Did you forget to bring it?"

He didn't answer.

I whispered in his ear. "Would you like the cafeteria lady to make you a peanut butter sandwich?"

He shook his head.

"Are you sure?"

He nodded.

"Okay." Then I patted his buzz cut and walked on.

As I stepped away I glanced back. Henry was generally a lively child—but today he looked like something was on his mind. Perhaps my opening the gifts had made him sad. Henry hadn't given me one. Of course I didn't expect anything. I felt bad for opening them.

After lunch we began silent reading. The children grabbed their books and scattered around the room to read. All was quiet except for the sound of the bunny drinking from the water bottle. As I circled the room, I noticed Henry hiding behind the piano. A pair of scissors and the tape dispenser lay on the floor beside him. When Henry saw me, he put his hands behind his back. I pretended not to notice and walked on. He was probably making me something for Christmas. *Cute.* I let silent reading time go a little longer than usual to give him time to finish. Finally, I clapped my hands. "Okay, boys and girls, nice reading. Please put your books away. Back to your seats."

As the children moved to their chairs, Henry walked up to mine and placed a thin package on my desk. It was wrapped with binder paper, decorated with Magic Marker, and sealed with masking tape.

"What's this?" I said, acting surprised.

He looked down. I could see him smiling. Then I set the gift on my lap.

"Did you wrap this yourself?" I asked.

"Yeah," he said softly.

"You're a really good wrapper."

His dimples grew deeper.

Carefully, I untaped the binder paper and pulled out a card. It was made of red construction paper. The fold was creased multiple times where he had tried to get it just right. On the cover it said, "Merry Crismas Mr. Done" in his best cursive. He had drawn a smiley face in the *o*.

"It's beautiful!" I gushed. "Thank you."

Then I opened it. A surge of warmth filled my chest. Taped on the inside were eight quarters, four dimes, four nickels, and fifteen pennies—$2.75—the price of one school lunch.

WRAPPING PAPER

We all have Christmas memories that are forever imprinted in our minds. We just need close our eyes and instantly we're back in time. I have many such memories: reading all the tags with a flashlight on Christmas morning while my grandma snored on the couch, singing Christmas carols to my mom at my own front door then asking for a quarter when I was finished, listening to my dad climb the roof on Christmas Eve to be Santa and hearing him swear when he slipped, and playing the innkeeper in the Christmas pageant at church. I wanted to be Joseph, but my Sunday school teacher wouldn't trust me with the part. At one rehearsal when Mary and Joseph arrived at the inn, I said, "We have lots of room. Come on in!" Now you see why I wasn't Joseph.

Of all my Christmas memories, there is one that stands out among the rest. It happened in Hungary. I was on leave from my job in the States teaching at the American International School in Budapest. The week before Christmas vacation, the Boy Scouts from my school were going to throw a party at an orphanage where the children were all preschool age and had hearing disabilities. My colleague Hank asked me to help him chaperone. Hank was the Scout leader. Since several of my own students were in the troop, I agreed to go along.

As we drove to the orphanage, Hank explained that our visiting was a big deal. Because the children were so young and hearing-impaired, the orphanage didn't let just anyone visit. In fact, our Scouts were one of the first groups of foreigners the orphans would meet. When we arrived, Hank drove the van through a rusted iron gate into a large courtyard. Gravel and snow crunched under our tires. Giant pines weighted down with snow hid the sky. The building was large and gray. It looked unloved. There were no lights on save for one bulb without its shade illuminating three broken steps at the entrance.

The director greeted us at the door. Her name was Elizabeth. When we stepped inside, we removed our hats and scarves and kicked the snow off our shoes. Tall white iron radiators crackled as we walked down the hall. Elizabeth escorted us into a room where twenty-five young children sat waiting on crowded wooden benches. Their feet didn't reach the floor.

As we gathered in the room, the orphans chattered and pointed and wiggled in their seats as children do whenever a visitor whom they have been waiting for walks in. One little girl waved then hid herself quickly in her neighbor's lap. Their teachers sat close by against the wall. An old black upright piano stood in the corner. Its lacquered finish was worn in spots like an old teddy bear.

Elizabeth walked in front of the children and introduced us.

"Jo estét," the little ones said in unison. Good evening.

"Jo estét," we said back.

Soon we began our party, and the Scouts started unloading their bags. We had brought cookies and juice, but Elizabeth asked us to just serve the cookies. It was too close to bedtime for juice. The Scouts passed out the treats and the teachers told the little ones to say *köszönöm* (thank you). I gave an understanding smile. Telling a child to say thank you after taking a cookie is universal.

Music came next. The Scouts sang Christmas carols in English for the Hungarian children. I plunked out the tunes on the piano and chuckled as I played. Surely, this was the first time that this instrument had ever played "Frosty the Snowman." The orphans and their teachers smiled as we sang. Christmas music needs no translation.

After we finished, the young ones stood up and sang a song for us. Their hearty voices warmed the small room like heat from the radiators. They reminded me of little drummer boys: Their only gift was their music. I wondered—would Santa even visit the orphanage? Would the children find anything under the tree on Christmas morning? Was there even a tree? I hadn't seen one.

When they finished singing, the Scouts started handing out the gifts they had brought. The orphans squealed and held them up and ran their fingers over the shiny paper and played with the bows. They hugged their presents and showed their friends and giggled when they spotted Mickey Mouse and Donald Duck and Goofy on their wrapping paper.

Suddenly Elizabeth drew in her breath sharply.

"What's the matter?" I asked.

She closed her eyes and shook her head. Then, biting her lip, she looked down at the floor.

"What's wrong?" I asked again.

Covering her mouth, Elizabeth leaned over to me and whispered. Her voice was shaky. "They don't know that there is anything inside the packages."

I snapped my gaze at the children. They were all laughing and pointing and playing with their presents. But none was opening a single gift. A lump shot up in my throat. *The wrapping is present enough.*

I looked over at the teachers. A few were dabbing their eyes with handkerchiefs. They realized what was happening, too. Then Elizabeth took a deep breath and walked over to the children. With watery eyes, she smiled and clapped her hands. The children looked up at her and stopped talking. Elizabeth cleared her throat then very gently began to speak.

"Gyerekek, a csomagban van valami." Boys and girls, there is something under the paper, she told them. The older ones' eyes widened. But the little ones did not understand. Elizabeth picked up one of the presents and pointed to the inside. "Nézzetek csak, ebben van valami," she repeated. "There is something *under* the paper."

Gasps filled the room as the children looked down at the presents. I expected the kids to immediately start ripping open their packages, but none did. *They must be waiting for permission to open them,* I thought. But no one was speaking. Then Elizabeth knelt down beside one little girl and started helping her unwrap her gift. The girl and those sitting beside her looked on. My lips parted but no words came out. *They don't know what to do with the paper.*

For a second I stood there motionless. Then I wiped my eyes, and together with the other teachers and the Scouts I got down on my knees and helped the children unwrap their gifts.

Merriment swirled around the room as the children pulled out puzzles and jump ropes and coloring books and bright pink and blue bottles of bubbles. The Scouts showed them how to dip their plastic wands in the soapy water and blow. It was a magic moment.

Ever since then—sometime during the holidays—the memory of these children in that faraway land draws a chair up to the hearth of my heart and pays a visit. And when it does I smile, close my eyes to pull the chair closer, and hear the laughter.

SANTA CAUSE

One of my favorite scenes in *Miracle on 34th Street* is when attorney John Payne proves that his client, Mr. Kringle, is in fact Santa Claus. Mail carriers from the United States Postal Service march into the courthouse carrying thousands of children's letters addressed to Santa. By delivering these letters to Mr. Kringle, Payne argues that the Post Office Department—a branch of the federal government—recognizes Kris Kringle to be Santa Claus. The judge announces that his court will not dispute it. Santa is saved by the Post Office.

Every holiday season the US Postal Service receives tens of thousands of letters addressed merely to *Santa Claus, North Pole*. What happens to them? Many are collected by Operation Santa, a program sponsored by the Post Office Department that recruits volunteers to answer the letters. I joined the operation several years ago.

Early in December, I pick up a batch of letters from Betty. She has been heading the program at my branch for years. Every year, Betty is decked out in a Christmas tree sweatshirt and red and green ornament bulb earrings. (She looks like she should be teaching first grade.) When I get the letters, they have already been opened and sorted. The envelopes are stapled on the back.

"Wow," I said, looking through this year's box. "You already have a lot."

"Each year we seem to get more than the year before," Betty said. "In a week or so, they'll really start to pour in."

I pulled out an envelope with hay in it. "What's this?"

Betty smiled. "For the reindeer."

This year I enlisted my teacher friends Kim, Lisa, and Dawn to join me in answering the letters. There is nothing like reading a child's wish list for Santa written in crayon and filled with hay to get you into the holiday spirit. In our replies, we wrote that Santa was busily preparing his sleigh and getting the reindeer ready. Of course we never made any promises to the kids. We didn't sign off from Santa, either—only as his helpers. This keeps the big guy more mystical. When we're finished, I'll send the letters off to be stamped with a North Pole cancellation. Betty says that a stamp from Santa's home can turn a doubter into a believer for at least another year. Our letters don't actually go to the North Pole for the cancellation though. They go to Arkansas.

"What do *you* want from Santa?" I asked Lisa as we were working on our replies.

She sighed. "A paper cutter that cuts straight."

Kim started laughing.

"Good idea," Dawn said.

"I'd ask for a pair of teacher scissors with a homing device," Kim volunteered. "And a take-a-number machine like they have at the deli."

"Me, too," I said.

Dawn joined in. "What's that machine at the bowling alley that drops down and takes all the pins away? I need one of those to drop down in my room and snatch up a few seven-year-olds."

This brought a laugh.

Kim looked at me. "What would you ask for?"

I didn't even have to think about it. "Three straitjackets. Boys' medium."

At the end of the evening, the four of us picked our favorite letters. Dawn's was from Linnea. She wrote: "Please deliver a Lincoln Navigator. In pink." Lisa's favorite said, "Dear Santa, I'd like real glass slippers. Size three." Kim's number one: "Bring any toy. It doesn't matter. I know that everything is so *spencive*." Mine was from Adam: "Dear Santa, if you are real can you please give me a science kit? If you aren't real can somebody else get me a science kit?"

Kids' letters to Santa are pretty darn cute. When a child really wants something badly, he'll write in capital letters then go crazy with the exclamation marks. ("PLEEEEEASE BRING ME A TURTLE!!!!!!!!!!!!!!") Sometimes the papers are just lines and scribbles. Fortunately, their moms "translate" at the bottom of the page. If a child has moved recently, he'll leave detailed directions to his new home or even a map. Once in a while, a child will reprimand St. Nick. ("Santa, last year I asked for an alligator and all I got was a hamster! I hope you'll do better next time.") Rarely will a child sign his last name. ("Hey Santa. Matthew here.") There's no reason to, of course. Santa knows who he is.

Some of the kids' requests are pretty offbeat: "Please replace my younger brother with a dolphin." "Can you send a spaceship?" "I'd like my own planet. Mars would be nice. It's close to Earth." Other letters come with pretty tall orders: "I want to meet Batman." "I'd like an igloo." "If you give me an elf, I promise not to let my cat near it." This season, Monica requested a flat-screen TV, a new laptop, a pogo stick, an iPhone, a camera, an iPod Nano, and a helicopter. Monica is six. Oftentimes children will put in requests for their parents and siblings. This year's top requests for moms: jewelry, maids, Hummers, and panini makers. For dads: socks.

The kids' letters are also good indicators of what's hot and what isn't. LEGOs, Barbies, PlayStations, stuffed animals, and new baby brothers are always popular. So is money. (They never ask for less than a billion.) Real animals are consistently at the top of the list, too. This year's letters included requests for puppies, kittens, ponies, monkeys, penguins, pandas, baby hippos, and the killer whale at SeaWorld.

There are always lots of questions for the man up north: "How's Rudolph?" "How's Mrs. Claus?" "Do reindeer really fly?" "Was I nice or *notty*?" "If I'm on the naughty list, what can I do to get off of it?" "How do you fit down the chimney?" "Do you know the Easter Bunny?" "How many elves do you have in your workshop?" "Are you older than Jesus?" and "Could we set up a Web cam?"

Kids are smart. They bring up Santa's snack *before* they make their requests: "Santa, how many cookies do you want?" "Please feel free to raid the fridge when you're here." "What do you like—milk, juice, or whiskey?"

I'm always surprised at how many children tell Santa that they *love* him. I never wrote that I loved him when I was a kid. I was too busy listing what I wanted. In fact, one year after writing my thirty-seventh request, my mom warned me that Santa might think I was being greedy and take me off his good list. Concerned, I crossed out half the items and asked for world peace.

GIVING

My school participates in a charity program that provides food and toys for families in need. Our PTA sponsors about fifty families. Each receives a bag of groceries for Christmas dinner, a gift certificate to Safeway for a turkey, and toys for the children.

This year on bag-filling day, the volunteers gathered in the multipurpose room after school. I had invited two of my students, Robbie and Stacy, to help. When we walked into the room, stacks of cans and baking goods were piled on long cafeteria tables. Two tables piled with toys—one marked "Girls" and another "Boys"—stretched against the wall.

One of the PTA moms handed me a list of food items and some cards. Each card had the number of children in the family and their ages. All the families were assigned numbers. No names were used.

Soon Robbie, Stacy, and I started filling bags. The kids ran around the room collecting cranberry sauce and green beans and bags of tangerines. I checked them off the list.

"Okay," I said, "all we need is one box of stuffing mix and we're done with the food." I pointed to the stuffing. Both children ran and picked it up. Together they placed it into the bag.

"Great! Now we need to get the presents." Robbie and Stacy fixed their eyes on the toys as I started reading the card. "We need gifts for an eight-year-old girl and a nine-year-old boy." I looked at Stacy. "You be in charge of finding something for the girl." Stacy ran to the girl table. I turned to Robbie. "You're nine, right?"

"Uh-huh."

"Find a gift for a nine-year-old boy."

Robbie dashed off to the boy table. In a few moments, Stacy returned with an art set and held it up.

"Would an eight-year-old girl like that?" I asked.

"Definitely!"

"Great."

She set it into the bag.

Robbie ran back. He was holding a basketball.

"Are you *sure* about this?" I said, smiling.

"Oh, *yeah*!" he exclaimed. "This is the *best* present for a nine-year-old boy."

"Well," I laughed, "you're the expert."

I held the bag open as he put it inside.

For the next hour, the kids and I filled several more bags. Other volunteers came by and wrapped the gifts that we had selected then covered the bags with cellophane and ribbon. The family's card was tied on each one.

The next day, I volunteered to help deliver the bags. The PTA gave me a list of addresses matched with the number assigned to each family. The families knew that we would be dropping by. After school I loaded my car, put on my Santy Claus hat, and dropped off bags all over town. Everyone I spoke with was grateful. Several invited me in. Most wanted to give me something in return. One woman wouldn't let me go until I filled a bag with persimmons from her tree.

About halfway through my deliveries, I stopped at an apartment building close to school. After parking the car, I grabbed the correct bag, walked up two flights of stairs, and found the apartment. The porch light was on. A plastic wreath hung on the door. A string of colored lights twinkled on and off around the window. I knocked. Immediately I heard footsteps running to the door. *Children.* Someone peeked through the curtain. Then the lock turned quickly and the door flung opened. My heart stopped. There standing in front of me was Robbie.

"I was hoping it would be you," he said with a huge smile.

Before I could say hello, Robbie grabbed my arm and pulled me inside. The apartment was warm. The scent of something delicious hung in the air. The window in the kitchen was steamed up. In the corner of the room, a small artificial tree stood on a table. It was smothered with icicles.

"¡Señor Done está aquí!" Robbie shouted. Mr. Done is here.

Robbie's mom walked into the front room, wiping her hands on a dish towel. We shook hands. I had met her once before at our parent–teacher conference. Robbie had translated.

"Merry Christmas," I said, removing my hat. Then I handed her the bags. "These are for your family. From the Angel Network."

"Thank you," she said.

She set the bags down on the table then turned to Robbie and spoke in Spanish. Robbie translated.

"My mom would like to know if you can stay for dinner."

I looked at her. "Oh, thank you. *Gracias.* But I'm afraid I can't." I turned to Robbie. "Please tell your mom that I'd love to but I must get going. I have other deliveries to make."

He explained. She spoke to Robbie again.

"My mom wants to know if you like tamales."

I smiled. "I *love* tamales."

She covered her mouth when she laughed.

Robbie translated one more time. "My mom says that you have to take some tamales home with you."

I put my hand on my stomach and shook my head. "No. No. Thank you." But by then she had already walked into the kitchen. I threw Robbie a smile. He returned it.

As I waited for his mom, I walked over to the tree. Robbie joined me.

"Nice tree," I said. "Did you help decorate it?"

"Uh-huh."

I glanced down on the floor. Presents tied with curly ribbon waited on a tree skirt made from a bedsheet. I pointed to one of the packages. "I recognize *that*." It was a gift that Robbie had made for his mom at school. The wrapping was white butcher paper covered with red and green tempera paint potato prints. Robbie looked up at me and smiled.

Just then a thought popped into my head. I smacked my forehead and turned to Robbie. "Oh my goodness," I said loudly. "I just realized that I left one of the bags in the car. I'll be right back."

Quickly I left the apartment, ran down the steps to my car, and searched through the remaining bags. After finding the one I was looking for, I grabbed it and raced back upstairs. Robbie was standing in the doorway.

"Sorry 'bout that," I said, out of breath. I pulled a present from the bag and handed it to Robbie. His face brightened. "This is for you."

At that moment his mom walked into the room holding the tamales. He turned and showed her.

"Would you like to open it now?" I asked.

He looked surprised. "Now?"

"Sure. Why not?" I glanced over at his mom. Her smile was wide. "It's almost Christmas."

Immediately Robbie knelt down on the floor and started ripping open the paper. It was off in five seconds.

"Whoaaaaa!" he shouted, squeezing his gift.

His mom and I traded smiles as Robbie hugged the new basketball. He didn't take his eyes off it.

"You know," I said, "I hear that this is the *best* present for a nine-year-old boy. Right?"

His eyes were still glued to the ball. "Oh, *yeah*!"

January

"Do you know," Peter asked, "why swallows build in the eaves of houses? It is to listen to the stories."

—*Peter Pan*

READING

One day I was reading *Charlie and the Chocolate Factory* with my class. Everyone had his own copy of the book. I read aloud while the children all followed along. After a couple of minutes, I stopped and looked around the room for a kid I could have some fun with.

"David, would you read now, please?" I asked.

He began reading. "*'Shut up!' said Mr. Teavee.*"

I stopped him. "What did Mr. Teavee say?"

"Shut up," David answered, matter-of-factly.

I pretended to be shocked. "David, are you telling *me* to shut up?"

"No," he giggled.

I continued my performance. "I *hope* not. Now read it again."

David looked at the text and hesitated.

"Go on now," I nudged. "Start reading."

"Shut up," he laughed.

"DAVID!"

Everyone shouted, "Can I read? Can I read?"

I love to teach reading. It is one of my favorite times of the day. I love when a child comes up to me in the morning and asks hopefully, "Are you going to read to us today?" I love seeing a child look up from his book while I am reading and stare at me with wide eyes and open mouth as though I really am Willie Wonka escorting kids through my chocolate factory. I love flicking off the lights to announce that reading time is over and seeing that brief look of confusion on a child's face because she was lost in her book.

When I was in teacher school, I learned a lot about how to teach the different subjects. But most of what I know about teaching reading, I've learned from my students.

My students taught me that when inviting children to the reading corner, it is much more exciting when the teacher hides a book under his shirt than when he pulls it off the shelf.

They taught me that after gathering kids on the carpet—no matter how many times you say *crisscross applesauce*—someone in the front row will always sit on her knees.

They taught me that when the teacher shows his class a picture from a book, he must always move the book very slowly in front of them or they will whine, "I can't see." And when the teacher is finished showing the picture, he will always have to show it again to one person who says, "I didn't see it."

My students taught me that whenever the teacher reads the word *knock* aloud, he should hit the desk at the same time. When he reads *yawn,* he should make a good loud stretch. And when he reads *cleared his throat,* he should accompany it with lots of noise in the back of his mouth.

They taught me that *choir* and *bury* and *coyote* are hard words to read, that five-syllable words are more fun to clap out than those with two, and that sitting close together on the carpet is as important as hearing the stories.

They taught me that a child can read an entire page out loud and not pause at one single period, and that kids will remember exactly who sat on the beanbag chair during silent reading time yesterday, last week, and two months ago. They will remember who held the stuffed animal last, too.

My students taught me that when everyone has a copy of the same book and the class turns the page together—if there is a picture, always allow time for the children to look at it before you start reading again. Otherwise, the kids will lose their place.

They taught me that when I am reading a book to the children and ask them to predict what will happen next, it is entirely possible that one child will disregard my question completely and announce that she can see the skin above my sock and that my leg is hairy.

They taught me that if an ant crawls onto the cover of a child's book during reading time, she will not flick it off—but will carry the book carefully to the front of the room to show me. When hearing that their lucky classmate has an ant crawling on her book, the rest of the class will jump out of their chairs and run over to see our new visitor. Reading will resume only after the dazed little guest has been carried outside to safety by all twenty children.

As we continued reading *Charlie*, I looked out at my students. Melanie was twiddling her earring. John was swinging his legs back and forth under the desk. Laura was tightening her ponytail. Sarah was straightening her curls. Conner was sucking on his bookmark. This made sense, of course. These things make reading more enjoyable to kids. It's instinctive—like eating the frosting in Oreos first. In fact, I have learned that children have their *own* set of reading strategies:

Reading Strategy Number One: Fiddle

As soon as you hand an eight-year-old boy a book, his free hand will immediately reach into his desk and grab the nearest small object—a marble, a ruler, a coin, a paper clip. Because children know that holding things helps you read better. If you don't believe me, watch what happens when they drop the marble or ruler or coin or paper clip. Their reading will come to a screeching halt until they find it.

Reading Strategy Number Two: Balance
With the book in one hand and the paper clip securely in the other, he will lean on the back two legs of his chair and stay there as long as he possibly can until the teacher comes over and pushes the chair back to the floor or the student falls over. When falling, he may let go of the book—but *never* will he let go of the paper clip.

Reading Strategy Number Three: Curl
When an eight-year-old girl starts reading, she will immediately begin twisting her hair around her fingers or twirling her bangs around her pencil. If her hair is already curly, she will pull on it like a Crissy Doll with hair that grows and grows.

Reading Strategy Number Four: Slide
The longer a child reads at his desk, the closer he will sink to the floor. If he is sitting on the reading couch, he will take the sofa cushion down to the floor with him.

Reading Strategy Number Five: Hide
When it is time for children to break into pairs and read together, you will see them run to the corners of the room, hide behind the piano, crawl under the desks, disappear under tables, and squeeze into their cubbies. Reading is more fun for kids when the teacher can't see them.

Reading Strategy Number Six: Gnaw
Have you ever observed a classroom full of third graders sitting at their desks with books in their hands while you are reading

aloud? It's a regular all-you-can-eat buffet out there. They're chewing on collars, pigtails, marker caps, pink erasers—you name it. One day during reading time, John was eating his pencil as if it were a dog bone. I stopped reading.

"John, you're going to get lead poisoning if you do that."

He just snickered and kept on chewing.

Look at my pencil box if you don't believe me. Right now I only have one pencil in there that still has any yellow paint on it. All the pencils are covered with baby teeth marks. Some have been chewed in half. By the looks of those things you'd think I teach a bunch of beavers.

I stood up and walked over to John. "Okay, hand it over." John took the pencil out of his mouth and gave it to me. It was all slimy. "YUCK!"

Laughter sped around the room as I wiped my hands on my shirt and took a seat. Then I picked up my book and resumed reading. Pretty soon John was nibbling on his eraser. Trevor was gnawing his fingernails. Conner was sucking his watch. Chloe was braiding her bangs. Dylan was sucking the string on his hoodie. And Gina was teething on her headband. Just as I was turning the page John yelled out, "When's lunch? I'm hungry." I reached over to my desk and threw him another pencil.

THE DIET

The first week back from winter break, I have my students write their New Year's resolutions. Kids' resolutions don't change much from year to year: "I want to improve in my times tables." "I would like to get better at cursive." "I'm going to make my bed every day." "I won't fight with my brother." This year Angela wrote, "I want a new puppy."

"Uh . . . Angela, this isn't really a resolution." I explained, "A resolution is something you want to improve in or a change you'd like to make."

She rewrote it: "I want to change the way my mom feels about having a new puppy."

My own resolutions are the same every year, too: I want to exercise more. I want to learn how to play the piano with more than one hand. I want to lose a few pounds. Actually, hoping to lose weight is my room moms' fault. They don't know what to buy Man Teachers for Christmas so they send in platters of homemade fudge.

This week as I was looking around Barnes & Noble, I checked out the diet section. I was shocked at how many different books there were. On the covers were photos of low-cal appetizers, light salads, lean entrées, and guiltless desserts. After a couple of minutes I had to get out of there. All that food was making me hungry.

I went online and found a site called The Calorie Calculator. It gives calorie expenditures for hundreds of different activities. I typed in my weight and started scanning the list:

Activity	Calories Burned Per Hour
Moving heavy objects	225
Lifting items continuously	230
Sitting in meetings	38
Walking on the job	75
Caring for animals	125
Heavy cleaning	175
Playing outdoor games	200
Using heavy power tools	375

Hmm, I thought. *I wonder how many calories I burn up in a day at work.* I grabbed paper and pencil and started making a list:

Today I led my kids to the cafeteria, followed my class to the library, and marched five third graders straight into the principal's office (walking on the job). I lifted three fifth-grade boys off a pileup on the field when they were supposed to be playing touch football (moving heavy objects). I sharpened two packs of pencils in the electric pencil sharpener (using heavy power tools).

I wrestled the class bunny out of the cage so I could clean it (caring for animals). I scrubbed the hairs on the paintbrushes that had morphed into rocks because I forgot to wash them yesterday (heavy cleaning). I turned the jump rope at recess (outdoor games). Actually, I can count that one twice. We played Double Dutch.

But that was just the beginning. According to the Web site, I burn up calories whenever I pass out a worksheet, push the paper cutter, pull down the white screen, pin on a name tag, pick up a backpack, press a thumbtack, pump up a rubber ball, or even unpeel an orange.

At the end of the day, I added everything up. "Oh my gosh!" I screamed, hitting the final equals sign on my calculator. I burn more than three thousand calories in just one day at work! I'll work this fudge off in no time. Heck—I don't need to go on a diet. I've already got one! I teach.

PRINCIPAL

Whenever Bob my principal is going to be away at a conference or a seminar, he asks me to be the teacher in charge. It's fun. A substitute takes my class, and I get to do the things that principals do. In the morning, I greet children as they step off the bus and get dozens of leg hugs from the kindergartners. At recess, I make sure kids are not sitting on the tetherballs hanging on the poles. During the day, I walk around the classes and snatch candy from their estimating jars. At lunch, I open stubborn mustard packets with my teeth. After school, I stand at the bus stop and get dozens more leg hugs good-bye.

Once when I was the teacher in charge, a kindergartner walked into the office after the bell rang.

"Are you tardy?" I asked.

"No," he answered. "I'm Tommy."

Another year when I was supervising kids in the cafeteria, one rascal read the menu on the wall, put his hand on his forehead, and proclaimed, "What? No wine list?" Last year I was standing out at the bus stop with a colleague when she spotted one of her first graders walking away from school.

"Mindy," the teacher called out, "aren't you a bus rider?"

"No," she shouted back, "I'm a street walker."

This week the day after Bob left for a training session, our school's furnace broke down. I work in an old building. This wasn't the first time it had broken. The heater seems to break down every winter. I had spent most of the morning with maintenance trying to get the heater fixed. At lunchtime, Kim poked her head in the boiler room. I was talking with the mechanic.

"Uh . . . excuse me, Mr. Done," Kim said, "I think you need to talk with a few of my cherubs."

"Why?" I asked.

She breathed in. "We had a bit of a problem in the boys' bathroom."

"What happened?"

"Well . . . four of my boys decided to put their willies onto the heating grate."

The whites of my eyes doubled in size. The mechanic started laughing.

"*What?*" I asked.

"You heard me."

"*Why?*" I said, rubbing my forehead.

Kim smirked. "They said they were trying to heat 'em up."

I looked at the mechanic. "See why we need to get this thing fixed." I turned back to Kim. "Can't this wait till Bob gets back?"

She shook her head.

I took in a big breath and let it out. "Okay, send them to me."

A couple of minutes later, four second graders marched into the principal's office with their heads down. I sat on the corner of the desk. They sat two to a chair. Among their eight shoes, only three were tied. After learning their names, I gave them the Keep Your Zippers Up Speech in my best Judge Wapner voice.

"So, do you boys understand?"

They nodded vigorously.

"And is this going to happen again?"

They shook their heads.

Then I handed each one a piece of paper and a pencil. "Now, you boys are going to write letters to your parents." (I sure wasn't going to call home and explain.) The boys looked surprised and stared at the papers. "Come on now. Get going."

"What do we write?" Matthew whined.

I pursed my lips. "Well . . . explain what happened and that you won't do it again."

The boys started writing.

After a few moments, Tyler raised his hand.

"What is it?" I said.

"How do you spell *wee-wee*?" he asked, matter-of-factly.

I gaped at him.

"I know," declared Alex. "W-E. W-E."

"Uh . . . that's close," I said, "but not quite." I looked over at Tyler. "It's *W-E-E. W-E-E*."

Tyler raised both palms. "Wait. Slow down."

I repeated it slowly. "*W-E-E* space *W-E-E*." (I know there is a hyphen in between those two *wee*s, but I did not want to confuse the little guy.)

"I'm done," Matthew announced, sliding out of his chair.

"Already?" I asked.

"Yeah."

"Let me see it."

Matthew handed me his paper. It read: "I poot my pee pee in the hetr."

Well, at least he got "pee pee" right.

"That's a good start," I said. "But I think you can write a little bit more." I gave Matthew his letter, and he took a seat.

Nicholas made a loud sigh while erasing his paper.

"Nicholas, you need help?"

He looked up. "How do you spell *jigger*?"

My eyeballs froze in their sockets. *"JIGGER?"*

"Yeah."

I scratched behind my ear. *How many words are there for this thing?*

"I know," Alex piped in.

"Thanks, Alex. I got it covered." I turned to Nicholas and started spelling the word. *"J-I-G . . ."* And then it hit me. Here I was giving an unforgettable spelling lesson to three boys who had just had a wienie roast in the bathroom. *No wonder my boss goes to conferences.* I covered my mouth to hide my smile.

Suddenly the bell rang. The boys looked up at me. I finished helping Nicholas as I got up and opened the door.

"Okay, you kids may go back to class now."

They jumped off their chairs and headed out of the room.

"Hey," I said, stopping them with my voice. "No more jiggers in the heater. You hear?"

"Okay!"

MAGIC

One of my favorite stories is Peter Seymour's *The Magic Toyshop*. In this book, all the toys come to life late at night after the shop has closed. At the first glint of dawn, they return to their shelves and freeze. When the shop reopens, the toys sit perfectly still and watch the customers. When I read *The Magic Toyshop* to my students, I often think of a small children's bookstore right here in my hometown. Because it is magic, too.

The shop sits nestled on the corner of a quiet downtown street two blocks off the main road. It has been there since the giant magnolia trees that line the sidewalk were planted over fifty years ago. Outside the store, green-and-white-striped awnings shade two large bay windows. Sunlight and shadows of magnolia leaves dance on the oft-cleaned glass. Behind the windows, books stand up in plastic snow or Easter grass or mounds of sand—depending on the season.

The front door has two sections, a top half and a bottom. When the weather is nice, the top is usually open. A bell on the door tinkles when customers step inside. In summertime, an arbor of untamed morning glories frames the entrance. When you push the door, it feels as though you are opening a garden gate.

Inside the store, narrow aisles weave around tables and cases and cardboard displays stacked with books. The shop smells of new paper. Posters of Clifford and The Magic School Bus and Eloise hang from the ceiling. And like the toys in *The Magic Toyshop,* stuffed animals and dolls sit on the shelves and watch the customers. Last summer, a morning glory vine sneaked into a crack above the door and started climbing inside the shop. Wisely, the owners let it grow. They called it Jack's beanstalk.

I like to stop by the bookstore on Saturday mornings around ten o'clock, if I can. Across the street from the shop there is a dance studio. Every Saturday a few minutes after ten, a dozen or so little girls wearing pink leotards and slippers chassé into the store after their ballet class. The young ballerinas grab their books, scatter around the shop, and sit and read. I call them the Saturday-morning girls.

One Saturday when I was in the shop, I heard a scream. A squirrel had found its way into the store. All the dancers chased the squirrel around the room as if it were a leprechaun. Another morning just a few days before Christmas, the girls all flew in wearing pink netted tutus and silver wings, their hair pulled up in tight buns. It looked like a bunch of angels had descended on the shop for silent reading time.

Whenever I am in the bookstore, I make sure to visit Mary. Mary is a retired teacher. She taught first grade for forty years. Her skin is crinkled like crepe paper, the lines by her mouth deep from smiling, her earlobes droopy from years of wearing holiday jewelry.

Mary often asks about my students.

"How's Trevor?"

"Still Trevor."

"And Christopher?"

"Never absent."

"And Brian?"

"Still digging to Alcatraz."

Over the years, Mary has helped hundreds of teachers, parents, and grandparents at the bookstore. But her favorite customers are children. When a child walks up to her and says he needs help finding a book, Mary flashes a smile, claps her hands, and holds them together as though she has just received the loveliest bit of news. Then she leans over and asks the child what kinds of things he is interested in and likes to read. After she has a general idea, she says, "Follow me!" and darts off like Dolly Levi on her way to a parade. The child must hurry to keep up.

Mary works her way through the maze of shelves until she reaches her destination. There she runs her finger along the spines of the books like a stick along a picket fence. The child crouches down beside her—excited to be a part of this hunt. Of course Mary does not need to look hard for the book. She knows exactly where it is. But she also knows that discovering something after a bit of a search makes it all the more delicious.

Soon Mary announces, "Here it is!" and pulls the book off the shelf. But she does not hand the book over right away. She makes him wait. She holds it close to her chest while she tells the child a bit about it. Sometimes she'll even open the book up, put on her glasses, then read the first page or two. Not too much—just enough to whet his reading whistle. Then slowly, as though she is presenting him with a golden treasure on a pillow of red velvet, she hands over the book with both hands and a wink. Magic.

FAIRY TALES

Gail, my kindergarten buddy, reads fairy tales to her students every year. She's always doing something clever — like throwing a party after Sleeping Beauty wakes up or holding a knighting ceremony for the Seven Dwarfs because they rid the kingdom of the evil queen. Once Gail had her kids build the Three Little Pigs' houses, decorated her hair dryer like the wolf, and tried blowing them down.

This month, Gail's class put on a wedding reception for Cinderella. Her students invited mine. Gail made a cake and served sparkling apple juice in plastic champagne glasses. The cage of white mice and the pumpkin carriage were there as well. (Gail cut out little doors and pinned on four cardboard wheels.) My students brought a class gift. After much debate, we finally decided to give Cinderella a shoe box padded with cotton balls. We figured she'd need it for those glass slippers.

We study fairy tales in my class, too. The kids and I read lots of stories, analyze different versions, look at parodies, and perform little plays. One year we had a mock trial: *The State v. Hansel and Gretel*. Puss in Boots, Chicken Little, and even the Emperor (he wore clothes) acted as witnesses in the case. Another year, after acting out Rapunzel, I asked, "So, who can tell me the moral of the story?" Amy said, "Not to have long hair."

During our fairy-tale unit, my class compares and contrasts several tales. When discussing their similarities, the children mention the existence of magic, witches, castles, elves, spells, curses, royalty, good versus evil, and so forth. But they always leave out one very important commonality—food. Have you ever noticed how hungry those fairy-tale characters are? They're starving! The Wolf gobbles up Little Red Riding Hood's grandmother. Goldilocks breaks in and eats three bowls of porridge. The Bremen Town musicians perform for their supper. A mean old giant swallows Tom Thumb down like a pill. And all the Troll wants to do is devour one of those billy goats.

I think I've figured out why I like teaching fairy tales so much. I relate to the characters. So many of them act just like teachers. Take Snow White, for instance. She cleans all day and sits in furniture that is too small for her. People bring her apples. And what about that witch in "Hansel and Gretel"? She bribes kids with candy and wants to lock the boy up in a cage. The Pied Piper leads kids in line. The elves at the Shoemaker's place are up all night working. The Little Mermaid loses her voice. The princess with a pea under her mattress has trouble sleeping. And every year when my students beg me to tell them my middle name, I feel like Rumpelstiltskin. In fact, the only fairy-tale character I can think of who doesn't act like a teacher is that poor, unlucky giant in "Jack and the Beanstalk." He has lots of gold and can eat children.

STRESS

My local community center is offering a stress management class. I decided to sign up for it—figured I could use it. This morning when I greeted my students at the door, Robbie was licking the railing. After we walked inside, Dylan started playing Pass the Teacher's Mug. While on yard duty, five second-grade girls decided Jump on the Teacher's Shadow was more fun than jumping rope. In class, I burned Emily's treasure map while trying to singe the edges to make it look authentic, found a handful of Q-tips lodged in my giant ear model, and unwound a rubber band that was cutting off all the circulation in Brian's purple finger. At the end of the day, Stacy had a nervous breakdown when I carried our dying betta fish out of the room and returned with an empty net. And after school when I sat down at my desk to grade papers, I ate half the Hershey's Kisses from my goody jar instead. A typical day.

Actually, I've heard that out of the ten most stressful jobs, teaching is number one. I wouldn't doubt that. It beat out police officers, stockbrokers, and air traffic controllers. I'm sure we beat out Evel Knievel, too.

When I walked into the stress management class, the room was full. I spotted two other teachers in the audience immediately. They were correcting papers and had tote bags covered with kids' handprints.

Our instructor's name was Connie. One of the first things Connie asked us to do was list all the stressors in our lives. That was easy. I wrote five words—all boys' names under the age of ten.

"It's important," Connie explained, "to remove your stressors whenever possible." I laughed to myself. *If I removed my stressors, most of my students would be sitting out on the blacktop.*

Next, Connie taught us deep-breathing exercises. Everyone lay on the floor and closed their eyes as Connie walked around the room guiding us through the steps.

"Picture a balloon under your belly button," she announced. "As you draw in air, imagine that balloon expanding. Then very slowly let the air out."

All I could visualize was a great big giant balloon floating in the Macy's Thanksgiving parade. The balloon looked just like me. My students were holding the strings.

Throughout the day, Connie shared lots of ideas for relieving stress. She talked about the calming effects of music, power naps, and aromatherapy. Peppermint and ginger, she informed us, are relaxing scents. She explained that certain colors like pink are soothing, how caring for animals reduces blood pressure, and that smiling can actually ease tension. When we smile, she said, nerve impulses from our facial muscles transmit to our limbic system, and we experience peace. Connie also recommended sitting under soft lighting and advised eating lunch outside whenever possible. When she said this, I leaned over to the woman next to me. "If I eat my lunch outdoors, I'd be surrounded by five hundred children who need their thermoses opened."

I decided to give a couple of Connie's suggestions a try at school. What did I have to lose? Maybe her ideas would calm some of my students down, too. So after the class, I drove to Target and bought a relaxation CD of wind and rain, a scented air freshener, and even a lamp and some soft bulbs.

The next day, I set my lamp up on the back table and plugged in the air freshener. When the kids walked in, the wind-and-rain CD was playing.

"What's that smell?" Christopher asked, his nose crinkled. He had a Washington apple sticker on his forehead.

"It's air freshener," I answered. "You like it?"

"It smells like marker breath."

I decided to not ask why. "It's peppermint."

In the morning, the children practiced their math on pink paper. While they were working, I petted our class bunny to reduce my blood pressure. Unfortunately, I had to turn off the relaxation CD. The sound of rain made me want to use the bathroom.

During the first recess, I decided to take a quick power nap. After excusing the kids, I lowered the blinds and turned off the lights. I sat in my chair, leaned back, and closed my eyes. I could hear the children playing outside. I pictured the balloon under my belly button and inhaled slowly. I exhaled completely like Connie taught me. Suddenly there was a loud knock on the door.

Bam. Bam. Bam.

"Mr. Done!" someone hollered.

I pretended not to hear it. *Exhaaaaale.*

Bam. Bam. Bam.

"Mr. Done, are you in there?"

Inhaaaaale.

Bam. Bam. Bam. Bam. Bam.

"MR. DONE!"

"Go away!" I shouted back. My eyes were still closed.

BAM. BAM. BAM. BAM. BAM. BAM. BAM.

I got up, grumbled on my way to the door, and pushed it open. It was Christopher.

"Why was the door locked?" he asked.

"Because I am taking a rest. What do you want?"

"A ball."

I waved him in and watched him squeeze all the balls to find the one with the most air.

"They're all flat," he said.

"Christopher, hurry up."

He looked up. "Why is it dark in here?"

"I am trying to relax."

"Why?"

I grinned broadly. But I did not sense any nerve impulses from my facial muscles transmitting to my limbic system. "Out!"

Christopher grabbed a ball and left. I walked back to the chair and sat back down. I closed my eyes and inhaled slowly. I held my breath then began the exhalation.

BAM!

The wall shook and I bolted upright. "What the—"

WHAM!

The wall shook again.

I'm going to strangle that kid.

I jumped up, yanked open the door, and marched to the side of the building. Christopher was standing on the lawn with David.

"How many times have I told you boys not to kick balls against the side of the classroom?" I raised my hand and pointed to the field. "GO!"

They bolted.

Pretty soon the bell rang, and all the children ran back into the room. I wrote their new spelling words on the board, and the class began practicing in their notebooks. After a couple of minutes I heard a loud *SNAP!*

I turned around and looked out at the kids. "What was that?"

No one answered.

I waited a second then continued writing on the board.

SNAP!

I whipped back around. "What's that noise?"

Gina looked over at Christopher.

Aha! I walked over to him. He was holding a sheet of bubble wrap. "Where did you get that?" He pointed to a box on the floor. I held out my hand. "Hand it over." He surrendered it.

Just then I spotted my new lamp on the back table. I looked at Christopher, then back at the lamp, then at Christopher again. I pointed to the back table. "Go sit by the lamp."

"Why?" he asked, surprised.

"Because soft lighting is calming."

"Huh?"

"Never mind." I pointed. "Move."

Christopher grabbed his stuff and moved to the lamp.

I turned to the class. "Okay, everyone, back to work."

The kids returned to their spelling. I walked to the front of the room. *Soft music and smiling and aromatherapy, my foot.* I plopped down in my chair and stared at the bubble wrap in my hands. Slowly a smile spread across my face. I glanced out at the children. I looked down at the bubble wrap. Then I squeezed one bubble.

SNAP!

Twenty surprised faces looked up at me.

"Mr. Done!" they shouted.

I smiled. *This is fun.*

SNAP!

"MR. DONE!"

SNAP. SNAP. SNAP.

"Mr. Done, stop that!"

SNAP. SNAP. SNAP. SNAP. SNAP.

Way better than peppermint.

February

Most of the people who will walk after me will be children,
so make the beat keep time with short steps.

—Hans Christian Andersen

100TH DAY

To celebrate the hundredth day of school, young children all over the country sing songs, shout cheers, read books, count numbers, chant poems, make murals, and string Froot Loops necklaces. When I was a kid, no one celebrated 100th Day. Now it's huge. Our kindergartners measure stacks of 100 pennies, do 100 jumping jacks, lick lollipops 100 times, and try to stand still for 100 seconds. (Most don't make it.) The first graders blow out candles on 100 cupcakes, pop 100 balloons, and discuss what they'd do if they had $100. (It's amazing how far their money goes. One kid bought a Ferrari.)

The second graders write what they'll be like in 100 years and draw pictures of how they will look (some just draw tombstones). Kim brought some of her kids' papers into the staff room to share:

"When I'm 100 years old, I will wear pink lipstick, blue eye shadow, and a pearl necklace."

"When I'm 100 years old, I will watch TV with my dog."

"When I'm 100 years old, I will have glasses and dye my white hair black."

"When I'm 100 years old, I will have false teeth and play golf."

"When I'm 100 years old, I will plant peppers in my garden and spend money on taxis."

All our first and second graders bring in bags of 100 things. You name it, the kids haul it in: LEGOs, pretzels, sugar packets, leaves, bottle caps, Skittles, Ritz Crackers, rocks, stickers, hair bows, Cheerios, cotton balls, jelly beans. Last year one child brought in 100 bars of soap. Most from the Marriott. Dad travels a lot.

Even our staff gets into 100th Day. Gail wears a hat covered with 100 pins. (One says, "I Survived 100th Day!") Kim sewed 100 buttons on her jean jacket. (The kids count her all day.) Lisa blacks out her teeth and dresses like a 100-year-old woman. Bob parades into each classroom wearing a Zero the Hero hat and says he has ninety-nine brothers and sisters. And Ellen hands out certificates at the assembly to the students who walk into the office and take the 100th ice pack, open the 100th Band-Aid, and have the 100th stomachache.

I wonder who the teacher was who started 100th Day. Did she have any inkling that her cute little idea would turn into a national event? Could she have ever imagined that her little brainstorm would cause Froot Loops' stock to soar on Wall Street every February?

I must admit, I'm not really into the 100th day of school— though once I tried having my students not talk for 100 minutes. (It doesn't work.) Fortunately for me, by third grade most kids have pretty much outgrown it. Every couple of years, however, I get a class that absolutely does not want to let go of it. This year is one of those groups.

"What are we doing for 100th Day?" Brian asked.

"Nothing," I replied.

"We're *not*?" he said, shocked.

"I wasn't planning on it."

Joshua looked worried. "Can we bring things in if we want to?"

"Aren't you getting a little old for that?" I said, lowering my chin.

"NO!" several shouted.

"*Please* can we bring stuff in!" Melanie begged.

"Okay," I said with a shrug, "if you really want to. But only small things."

The next morning, Christopher brought in 100 poker chips. Trevor pulled out 100 plastic green army men. Kevin carried in 100 marbles. Chloe rolled in a huge black suitcase that was almost as big as she was.

"What's in there?" I asked.

"A hundred stuffed animals," she answered, proudly.

"I told you to keep it small."

"I did. I brought my Beanie Babies."

I vowed to myself at that moment that if I ever celebrated 100th Day again (which was highly unlikely), all collections would have to fit inside a Ziploc bag. Sandwich size.

A couple of minutes later as I was taking the roll, the door swished open and in waddled Trevor. He was twice his size and looked like the Michelin Man.

"Trevor, what happened to *you?*" I spluttered.

His smile went from one ear to the other. "I'm wearing 100 things!"

Melanie giggled. Several stood up for a better view.

I fixed him with a look. "Trevor, that's impossible."

"Really!" he defended.

Then right there in the middle of the room he started stripping. The class began counting out loud.

"One! Two! Three! Four!"

I responded with a Frozen Teacher.

"Five! Six! Seven! Eight!"

Trevor was having the time of his life.

"Nine! Ten! Eleven! Twelve!"

Waves of laughter surged with each new number.

"Thirteen! Fourteen! Fifteen! Sixteen!"

After removing one down vest, two gloves, five scarves, a pair of earmuffs, two shoes, four socks, six wristbands, and three ski caps, Trevor started unbuckling his belt.

"Okayyyyyy," I said, walking over to him. "That's enough now."

"No!" several retorted.

"I'm only on twenty-four," Trevor whined. "I'm not done."

I picked up one of the ski caps and pulled it over his head. "Oh yes, you are."

WRITING

As a rule, third graders like to write. Ask them what they'd do with three wishes and their third will always be for more wishes. Tell them to keep a pirate journal and one boy will make all the girls walk the plank. Let them make coupons for their moms on Mother's Day and they'll expire in a day. Have them write about their dream vacation and they'll cast their teacher as the chauffeur.

There is no question that third graders write with flair. They make twenty-five exclamation marks where there should be one. They dot their *i*'s with hearts. They fill their papers with words like *bonk, conk, crash, pow, smack, splat, thwap, slam, whack, varoom, splash, zoom,* and *arf arf.* Their friendly letters end with ten *PS*s. If they're writing in print, they'll switch to cursive to make a word stand out. They put ™ next to their signatures. And just in case you weren't sure they were finished with their story, *The End* will fill up half the page.

Whenever we start writing, I always set my rules. "Okay, boys and girls," I announce, "no blood. No farts. No burps. No toilets. And no machine guns."

"Can we have pistols?" Trevor asked.

"No!"

When the Goosebumps books were popular, my students wanted to write gory stories. When the Captain Underpants books were all the rage, half the kids' papers had battling toilets. When Harry Potter first appeared, their main characters had lightning bolts on their foreheads. When *Pirates of the Caribbean* came out in theaters, everyone wanted to write about Johnny Depp.

I usually have my students write two copies of everything—first a rough draft (the sloppy copy) that we edit together, then a final draft. When I'm editing their papers, I spend a lot of time putting in periods, fixing spelling mistakes, turning lowercase letters into capital ones, adding quotation marks, and explaining that commas are on the ground and apostrophes fly.

Sometimes third-grade papers are not all that easy to read. Eight- and nine-year-olds will write forty lines of dialogue with no quotation marks, place apostrophes in every word ending with an *s*, hyphenate one-syllable words, write sentences that are two pages long, and—if they're running out of room—scrunch ten words into a one-inch space and act shocked when I say I can't read it.

My students don't type many final drafts. Typing their final copies in computer lab can be quite a challenge. Third graders type about three words a minute. They don't put spaces after periods. They don't put spaces after commas, either. All they want to do is play with the fonts. And if the computer has grammar check, God forbid a green squiggly line appears under one of their words. They can*not* continue typing until that green squiggly line goes away.

This year I made the mistake of showing my kids some of those emoticons—you know, those little faces you can make using numbers and symbols on the keyboard. Well, you'd have thought I showed them how to type naughty words. Pretty soon emoticons were popping up all over their papers wearing sunglasses 8-), sticking their tongues out :-P, and wearing braces :-#. There was one I didn't know though. Melanie had typed :-)X.

I touched the screen. "What's that, honey?"

"You!" She pointed to the X. "See the tie."

*　　*　　*

When third graders hand in their papers, they are usually a stapled mess, and I have to perform surgery on them to get the staples out. Have you ever seen third graders staple two pieces of binder paper together? They can't. Rebecca's papers all come apart because she pushes the stapler so gently that the staple never goes through the last page. Robbie pounds the stapler so hard that the handle, the staples, and the shiny part you put the staples into all transform into a whole new thing—like a metamorphic rock.

Jennifer staples her papers in the upper *right* corner. Laura likes to staple two eyes, a nose, and a mouth before handing her papers in. Joshua hasn't figured out that his pages are supposed to line up, so after stapling them together the corners end up three inches apart. And Danny's papers have more staples in them than my bulletin boards. This means that I have to hunt for my staple remover—which I usually find in Christopher's desk because he likes to hold it up to Chloe's face and pretend it's rattlesnake fangs.

In spring, I buy a bunch of hardback books with blank pages inside. My students create their own adventure stories then write their final drafts in them. The kids love making their own books. They feel like real authors. When they're finished, we have an Authors' Tea where all the final copies are on display. All the parents come. The kids serve their parents tea in china cups and sign autographs. Everyone dresses up. Last year, Brad wore a navy blue jacket with brass buttons that his mom got him at a secondhand store. He called it his tux.

This year soon after we started writing our adventure stories, I began holding individual conferences with each child. Brian was first.

"Nice work, Brian."

"Thanks."

Something caught my eye. It was a *c* with a circle around it.

"What's *this*?" I asked, smiling.

He smiled back. "I copyrighted it."

Kevin's writing conference was next. His dedication page said, "To Wally."

"Who's Wally?" I asked.

"My hamster."

Laughing, I turned the page. He started off with dialogue.

"Nice beginning," I said. "I see you've used quotation marks here. Good for you." I pointed to one of the sentences. The period was outside the quotation mark. "Kevin, periods always go inside the quotation marks."

"Why?"

I thought about it for a second. "Well . . . think of it this way—the periods are too little to play outside."

He liked that.

John walked up after Kevin. His paper was empty.

I tapped his blank paper with my pen. "Uh . . . what seems to be the problem here?"

"I have a severe case of writer's block."

"I see. And how long do you think this will last?"

He shrugged. "Maybe a couple of months."

"I'll give you five minutes."

David followed John. His story was three lines long. At the end he had written *to be continued*.

I gave him a questioning eyebrow. "You need to write more than this."

"It's a cliffhanger," he replied, grinning.

I pointed to his desk. "Back to your seat."

Emily was next. Her first page looked like a text message. On it she had written *great* as *GR8*. *Because* was *BC*. *Later* was *L8R* and *People* was *PPL*.

I screwed up my face trying to understand. "Uh . . . honey, you have to write these out. This is a book—not a cell phone." She giggled. I spotted one abbreviation that I didn't know. "What's *FTASB*?"

"Faster than a speeding bullet."

Melanie stepped up after Emily. I looked over her story. One sentence began, *"And Anastasia wore a a a a a a a a a a a a a silver gown."*

"Melanie, why did you write all these *a*'s?"

"I was thinking."

Dylan had the last writing conference of the day. Dylan loves to write stories. He has a good imagination. I laughed when I read his title: *Mr. Done in Outer Space*. Dylan illustrated some of the pages, too. He drew me sitting in a spaceship with my briefcase. I was holding my coffee mug.

"Nice drawing," I said.

He giggled.

Dylan reminds me of myself when I was a kid. When I was his age, I also liked to write stories. Not too long ago, I came across my very first book. I wrote it in third grade. Actually, Winston Churchill showed me how. It was spring. My class had just gone on a field trip to the zoo. After school, I sat down at the kitchen table with my paper and pencil and wrote a story about the trip. I drew pictures, too. When I was all done, I folded it and stapled the edges. But I wasn't happy with it. Something wasn't right. It didn't look like a real book. So I went to the family room and stared at the shelves. I pulled down a copy of *My Early Years* by Winston Churchill and examined it. Then it dawned on me—real books have hard sides. Winston Churchill hid his staples. I ran into the garage, found a cardboard box, and cut it up. I glued my story into the cardboard and wrapped it with a brown lunch bag. Now it was real.

The week before this year's Authors' Tea, my kids started working on the dust jackets for their hardcover books. I gathered the children on the carpet and shared a stack of books that had received awards and become bestsellers. I explained what reviews are and pointed out examples. We talked about how special it is for an author to get a review from a big paper like the *New York Times* or the *Chicago Tribune* or the *Wall Street Journal*. Then I asked the children to write their own reviews on the back of their dust jackets. The kids ran back to their desks, grabbed their papers, and started writing. But they didn't want to write critiques from the big newspapers. They had their own ideas in mind.

Angela wrote from Santa Claus: "As good as milk and cookies." Stacy was complimented by Mary Poppins: "Better than a spoonful of sugar!" J. K. Rowling adored Sarah's book: "This is WAY better than any of mine!" Randy Jackson raved about Kevin's: "Yo! Check it out baby. This is awesome, dawg." And Gina drew a giant circle on her cover and wrote, "Oprah Book Club."

As the kids were finishing up, I looked over John's shoulder. He had just written "Ruff! Ruff! Ruff!" on the back of his dust jacket.

"Why did you write that?" I asked.

John looked up and smiled. "It's from Scooby-Doo. He loved it."

LOVE

This year I have a student who absolutely adores sticky notes—Laura. She is crazy about them. In her desk, Laura keeps stacks of Post-its in different sizes and colors. At the beginning of the year, she was shocked when I told her that she couldn't pass notes to her friends in class. But she got over it soon enough. She just started sending them to *me*! In fact, it became her preferred method of communicating.

I'd find sticky notes on everything. She'd put them on her tests: *Why are you doing this to me!* I'd find them on my desk: *You've worn that tie three days in a row.* She'd stick them on the whiteboard: *Mr. Done, you look very nice today. Can we have no homework tonight?*

I am an excellent note detector. Whenever I intercept one, I read it. As far as I'm concerned, notes passed in class can be treated like postcards. If it's not in an envelope—it's fair game. Over the years I have discovered that all notes passed in class fall into three categories. There are the after-a-playground-scuffle notes (*Are you mad at me?*), the when-we-have-a-substitute notes (*Don't tell her about the math!*), and of course the love notes.

Whether they admit it or not, most third graders have a crush on someone in their classroom. And most of the time teachers know *exactly* who likes who. Right now I know that John likes Sarah, David is smitten with Gina, and Laura writes David's name on her folders. I know that Jennifer is crazy about Dylan (he's oblivious), Joshua can't decide between Lisa and Rebecca, and half the boys are goo-goo over Angela.

Oftentimes my students just come right out and tell me. Take Emily and Melanie, for example. One day we were walking to the school library when Emily said, "Mr. Done, you know who I like, right?"

I shook my head. "No."

"Danny," she proclaimed.

"Well, he's a nice boy." I turned to Melanie. "What about you, Melanie? Who do you like?"

She stopped dead in her tracks and put her hands on her waist. *"You don't KNOW?"*

I shrugged and cringed. ". . . I don't think so."

"I like Robbie!"

"Oh yes . . . Robbie." I nodded. "Right. Sorry. I forgot."

Sometimes my students reveal who they like in their journals. The children write in them twice a week and I write back. Some even ask my advice. When they do, I feel like Ann Landers.

February 2
STACY: *Mr. Done, I like Trevor but he is not nice to me!!!!*
ME: *What do you mean?*

February 5
STACY: *He keeps chasing me.*
ME: *Honey, when a boy does this it means he likes you.*

February 9
STACY: *IS THAT REALLY TRUE??????*
ME: *Yes. Trust me.*

February 12
STACY: *I asked my mom and she said you're right.*
ME: *How are things going with Trevor?*

February 15
STACY: *I like Conner now.*

Some kids are more secretive about who they like. But there are signs: When you are going to go on a field trip and he asks to sit in the same car that she is riding in. When she shares her bag of double-stuffed Oreos with him at lunch and doesn't ask for anything of his. When he looks up every time the teacher calls her name. When she puts four conversation hearts in his valentine instead of two like she gives everyone else.

Some of the crushes in my room have been going on for years. Christopher, for example, has been in love with Laura since kindergarten. Laura knows. The whole class knows. The entire third grade knows. But Christopher will never talk with Laura. If I catch him fooling around, all I have to do is glance over in Laura's direction then look back at him with a smirk like I'm going to make him go sit by her. He straightens up immediately.

Of course sometimes the kids have crushes on their teacher. My own first teacher crush was in grade one. Her name was Mrs. Ranada. She wore her hair in a beehive and used lots of hair spray. From September to June, her hair never moved. When the morning bell rang, I waited by the door so I could be first in line when Mrs. Ranada opened it. When she called us to the reading rug, I'd run so I could sit right by her. If she wore new earrings, I noticed. If she had a run in her nylons, I told her.

One afternoon Mrs. Ranada was standing by the door excusing her students at the end of the day. My mom was waiting for me outside. As I walked out of class, Mrs. Ranada said, "Phillip, thank you again for the beautiful flowers."

I didn't respond.

"What flowers?" my mom asked.

Uh-oh.

My mom looked at Mrs. Ranada. "Phillip brought you flowers?"

"Yes, every day this week," she replied. "Your garden must be looking pretty bare by now." She laughed. "I couldn't get them all in one vase." She turned to me. "How many vases do I have now, Phillip?"

"Three," I muttered, looking down.

My mom raised one eyebrow at me. "May I see them?"

"Of course," said Mrs. Ranada, cheerily.

Not good.

We walked inside. There on the teacher's desk sat three vases full of daisies, daffodils, tulips, calla lilies, snapdragons, geraniums, marigolds, and yellow mustard weed.

"Well," my mom said, "they're beautiful." She gave me a pointed look. The other eyebrow was up now. I did not make eye contact. "But they're not from my garden."

Mrs. Ranada looked puzzled.

My mom breathed in deeply. *Here it comes.* "Phillip, *where* did you get these flowers?"

I cringed.

"Answer me," she said with the same voice she used when I put lime Jell-O powder on our dog for St. Patrick's Day. "Phillip, where did you get those flowers?"

Gulp.

"At the neighbors," I mumbled quietly.

"*Where?*"

I shifted my feet. "At the neighbors."

"*What* neighbors?"

There was a beat of silence.

"On the way to school."

Her voice grew louder. "You cut flowers on the way to *school?*"

I nodded faintly.

Suddenly Mrs. Ranada made a quick snorting sound through her nose then covered her mouth. I had never heard her snort before. My mom shut her eyes tight and opened them again the way grown-ups do sometimes to see if they are hallucinating.

"With what?" my mom asked.

I looked up at Mrs. Ranada. She was biting her lip now, but I could tell that she was trying not to laugh. She wasn't mad at me. I reached down, unzipped my backpack, and pulled out a pair of rusty kid scissors with rounded edges. All of a sudden, Mrs. Ranada clutched her stomach and started laughing. Then she held the edge of the desk, leaned over, and laughed some more. I watched her closely. Her hair never moved.

INSTRUCTION MANUAL

This week our local opera company came to school and performed a couple of scenes from *La Bohème*. The whole school packed into the multi for the performance. I sat on a metal folding chair by the wall with Dylan beside me. The performance would last an hour. This was a long time for Dylan to sit still. I wasn't sure how he would respond to an hour of opera. Fortunately, the audience seemed to really enjoy it. For the most part, Dylan was a good listener, too. I only had to remind him two or three times to pay attention. When the show ended, Dylan sprang up on his knees and clapped loudly. *Wow,* I thought, *he really enjoyed it.* As he was applauding, Dylan turned to me with a big smile and shouted, "It's over! Mr. Done, it's *finally over*!"

Not always sure what's going on in your students' heads? Need help figuring them out sometimes? Here's a guide to help:

Your student is sitting with her back straight and her eyes on you.
> **You think:** What a good girl.
> **What's actually going on:** She wants a Jolly Rancher from your goody jar.

As you stand in front of the room and read a book in different voices, your students laugh.
> **You think:** I'm funny.

What's actually going on: Your shirt is unbuttoned and they can see your tummy.

Your student's eyes are staring straight ahead while you're writing on the overhead projector.
    You think: She is focused.
    What's actually going on: You're writing two feet off the screen.

Your student got all the spelling words right on his test.
    You think: He studied.
    What's actually going on: You left all the words on the board during the test.

Your student waves his hand wildly.
    You think: He is so involved.
    What's actually going on: He has to pee.

As you look for kids to dismiss for recess, your student is smiling angelically with his hands crossed.
    You think: My management system is working.
    What's actually going on: He's trying not to let the soccer ball roll out from between his feet.

Your student begs you to tell a story.
    You think: She loves me.
    What's actually going on: She doesn't want to take the math test.

Your student is jumping up and down.
    You think: He is motivated.

What's actually going on: He's thinking about the chocolate pudding that his mom put in his lunch.

Your student asks to go to the bathroom.
   You think: He has a weak bladder.
   What's actually going on: He wants to play in the rain.

Your student is using a magnifying glass to carefully examine the rocks that you have set on a paper plate.
   You think: He is really into the science lesson.
   What's actually going on: He's trying to see if he can burn a hole in the paper plate.

After passing out seeds to each child and explaining that a plant must break through the seed coat as it reaches for the sun, you witness your student removing the coat from his seed.
   You think: He is fooling around.
   What's actually going on: He's trying to help the little plant so that it won't have to push so hard.

SUGAR

One morning Gina walked into the classroom carrying a plate covered with aluminum foil.

"Is it your birthday?" I asked.

"No," she answered, "it's my half birthday."

I smiled. "Your *half* birthday?" I pointed to the plate. "Don't tell me. You have half of a cake under there, huh?"

"Uh-huh."

"Does this mean that in three months you'll bring in a *three-fourths* birthday cake, too?"

"Mr. Done!"

At the end of the day, I cut Gina's half-birthday cake and called the kids up to my desk a row at a time. David grabbed one plate—then another.

"David, I said to take the first one you touch."

"I touched two."

Some elementary schools are starting to ban sugar from their campuses. Might this mean no more having to buy seven boxes of Girl Scout Cookies because I have seven Girl Scouts in my classroom? Could this be the end of all geometry as we know it today? Every teacher knows that Tootsie Rolls are cylinders, Whoppers are spheres, and Brach's caramels are cubes.

I'm all for healthy eating and watching what we eat, but school without sugar is hard to imagine.

"Happy Halloween, kids. Here are your cupcakes. They're frosted with avocado."

"Happy holidays, Christopher. What do you mean you don't like tofu candy canes?"

"Happy Valentine's Day, boys and girls! I dropped celery sticks into your mailboxes."

Besides, I like when moms send in two dozen Krispy Kremes for their child's birthday and three kids are absent so I *have* to eat the extras. We wouldn't want ants.

And what about my goody jar? Grade school teachers understand that the goody jar is one of *the* best management tools. It helps us keep control. If the kids are wiggly, just walk near the goody jar and they will quiet down. If the children are really loud, walk near it and pick up the lid. If they're absolutely bonkers, take the lid off, lift the jar to your nose, and take a long, loud whiff. Complete silence.

If we outlawed sugar in schools, I'd worry about the new teachers most. They would never experience the thrill of scraping their students off the ceiling on November 1 because their mommies let them bring half their Halloween loot to school for snack. New teachers would never learn all the places on a child's head where a piece of candy corn can be lodged. New teachers would never see how sharp the tip of a candy cane can get when sucked into a weapon. They would never get to observe a student dump an entire box of conversation hearts into her mouth at the Valentine's party. And they'd never witness boys like David scarf down two pieces of half-birthday cake then go right on eating the plates.

THE ANGEL

My students and I open and close each day with a song. The children sing while I plunk out tunes on an old beige piano that's missing a pedal, has two broken keys, and tilts because one of the wheels fell off. I hit more wrong notes than right ones. The kids think I'm a professional. Each month I teach the kids a new batch of tunes. In February, the kids learn "Yankee Doodle," "You're a Grand Old Flag," "America the Beautiful," "This Is My Country," and the national anthem. But I don't call it "The Star Spangled Banner" anymore. For me it will always be Michael's Song.

I first met Michael at morning recess on the first day of school many years ago. I was on yard duty. Michael was not in my class yet. He was still a second grader. I was standing on the blacktop making sure that kids didn't run up the slide. Michael was saving a potato bug.

"You're Mr. Done," Michael said, looking up. His freckled nose was peeling. His cowlick was standing straight up.

"You're right," I replied. I began rubbing my chin. "And you're . . . let me see . . ." I closed my eyes and tapped my forehead. "Wait . . . it's coming to me. You're . . . you're . . . Michael."

"How'd you guess?" he asked.

"Teachers know everything," I said, smiling.

He forgot that he was wearing a name tag.

*   *   *

The following year, Michael was in my class. It didn't take me long to realize that he was a special little boy. When a student returned after being absent, Michael would explain what she had missed. If someone forgot a lunch, Michael shared his. When we read picture books with our kindergarten buddies, Michael held his buddy's hand. The day Michael showed me a new badge on his blue Cub Scout uniform, I wasn't surprised. It was for "kindness."

Once I asked Michael what he wanted to be when he grew up. He said a pastor.

I smiled. "You'd make a good one. Hey, wasn't there an angel in the Bible named Michael?"

"Yep."

"And wasn't he the one who told Mary that she was going to have a baby?"

"That was Gabriel."

"Oops. Wrong angel."

After that I started calling Michael "Angel." He liked that. He wrote *Angel* on his name tag. Oftentimes he'd sign his papers *Angel,* too. Little did I know how fitting his new name would become.

Most of the time teachers have to ask their students to stop talking. With Michael I'd have to ask him to stop singing. He loved to sing. His voice was strong, clear, and pure. Every Friday for Show and Tell, Michael would sing us a song. No accompaniment. The other children expected it. Sometimes he would even take requests.

Whenever Michael was our song leader for the week, he would always pick "The Star Spangled Banner." One Friday, after singing the national anthem at eight in the morning for four straight days in a row, I said, "Michael, how about a different song today, huh?" He thought about it for a second then shook his head. He'd have none of it.

One afternoon, Michael's mother walked into the classroom. Her eyes were puffy. Her mascara had run.

"Do you have a minute?" she asked.

"Sure."

I pulled a chair out for her. She took a seat and looked down at her hands. I could see that she was reaching for the right words. Finally she looked up.

"I have something difficult to tell you—about Michael." I waited. Then she took a slow, deep breath. "Michael has leukemia."

I inhaled sharply. For a second I could not find my voice. "Is . . . is it serious?"

She nodded, pressing her lips together. "But we're hopeful. He'll start his first chemotherapy in a few weeks. I'm afraid he'll have to miss school. When he's out, I'll come by and pick up his work."

"Oh, don't worry about that." I paused to take a breath. "Does Michael know that you're here?"

"Yes."

"How's he handling it?"

"Quite well," she responded, forcing a smile. "I don't think he really understands it all yet."

I felt my Adam's apple rise and fall. "Is there anything I can do?"

She took a deep breath. Fresh tears filled her eyes. "We'd appreciate your prayers."

"Of course," I said. "Thank you for telling me."

*   *   *

That week for Show and Tell, Michael told the class all about his leukemia. He brought in little stuffed red and white blood cells that the doctor had given him. The children listened closely. It was hard to believe that what he was describing was his own disease. He looked perfectly fine. After he finished sharing he sang us a song. I had to look away.

Over the next couple of weeks things started to change. Michael began missing more and more school. The chemo made him terribly sick. When he did come to class, he wore a hat. His already small frame looked even smaller. His mother said he had trouble keeping the food down.

Then one day Michael's mom came by and said that Michael wouldn't be coming to school anymore. He was too weak now, and the doctors wanted to make sure that he didn't catch any germs from the other children. I asked Michael's mom if I could visit him. She said of course.

The following week I went to see Michael in the hospital. When I walked into his room, his mom had to stop him from jumping off the bed and ripping the IV out of his arm.

"Hey there, Angel," I said. I handed him a cupcake, though I knew he probably couldn't eat it. "It's Jill's birthday. She brought treats."

My gaze shifted to the plastic bag hanging on a pole beside his bed. Clear liquid ran through a tube and into his little arm.

"What's that?" I asked.

"The chemo," his mother answered.

"*That's* the chemo?" I was surprised. "I didn't realize it looked like that." I was embarrassed that I didn't know.

Then I sat on the foot of the bed. Michael had circles under his eyes now. Pale cheeks had replaced rosy ones. He looked like he was melting away. I tried my best to keep a happy face.

"I miss your voice during music," I said, cheerily. "It's not as loud."

He began to giggle. "What did you sing today?"

"'My Favorite Things.'"

As soon as I answered, Michael started singing. "Raindrops on roses and whiskers on kittens." I joined him, and his mom hummed and tapped her fingers on the arm of her chair. When we finished, Michael's mom clapped. She was trying to keep her happy face on, too.

"Sing another one," she requested.

"Only on one condition," I said, nudging Michael playfully in the ribs. "*Not* 'The Star Spangled Banner.'"

He laughed.

And so we sang. We sang every song I had ever taught him. We belted out "Do Re Mi" and "Food Glorious Food" and "I Won't Grow Up." We sang "Getting to Know You" and "This Land Is Your Land." Even with the needle in his arm, Michael tried the hand movements. Nurses stopped in the doorway to listen. A couple of them joined us. Occasionally, Michael would look over at his mom and smile. And for a few moments, the cancer and chemotherapy and needles were gone. The music had made us forget.

"Do you know any songs from *The Wizard of Oz*?" I asked Michael.

"No."

"You've seen *The Wizard of Oz,* haven't you?"

He shook his head.

I turned to his mom with a surprised look.

"I don't think he's seen it," she said.

"Oh my goodness!" I exclaimed, placing both hands on my head. "You *have* to see *The Wizard of Oz*. It's my favorite movie in the whole wide world."

"We'll have to get it," his mom commented.

Michael grabbed my arm. "Have you seen *Grease*?"

"Of course I've seen *Grease*."

"Do you know the songs?"

I crinkled my forehead. "I'm afraid I don't. It's been a long time."

Then Michael slapped his free hand on his head, too. (He wasn't going to be outdone.) "You don't know the songs from *Grease*? Mr. Done, you *have* to learn the songs. That's *my* favorite movie in the whole wide world."

My lips stretched into a smile. "Fair enough."

The next week after work, I stopped by Michael's house. When I walked in, I handed him a package. His mom reminded him of what to say.

"Thanks!" he said.

"You're very welcome."

Quickly he tore open the paper and held his gift up for his mom to see. It was a DVD of *The Wizard of Oz*.

I crouched down in front of him. "I want you to learn the songs, Angel. And next time I see you we'll sing them together. Okay?"

He beamed. "Okay!"

As the weeks went by, I didn't get to visit as frequently. Sometimes when I'd call to see if I could stop by, he'd be resting. Occasionally his mother would say that it had been a difficult day. I knew what this meant. He was too sick to have visitors.

One night around ten o'clock my telephone rang.

"Hello," I answered.

"Mr. Done?" a voice whispered.

"Michael, is that *you*?"

"Yes."

"Where are you?"

"In the hospital."

"Are you okay?"

"Yeah. I have to stay here overnight."

"Does your mom know you're calling me?"

"No. She left the room."

I chuckled. "How did you get my number?"

"It shows up on our phone when you call. I copied it."

Laughing, I sat down in my living room. The lights were off. It was raining.

"Hey Mr. Done, guess what."

"What?"

"I know all the songs."

"What songs?"

"From *The Wizard of Oz*."

"Already?"

"Uh-huh."

"Good for you. What's your favorite?"

He thought about it for a second. "'If I Only Had a Brain.'"

"Ah, good song." I sang the opening line.

"What's *your* favorite?" he asked.

"Oh, it has to be 'Somewhere Over the Rainbow.'"

"Oh yeah," he remarked. "That's good, too."

At that moment, I looked out the window and thought of him lying there in that hospital room. A wedge of moonlight streamed through the glass and made shadows on the wall over the fireplace. Sadness pressed down on my chest, and I could feel the tears pooling behind my eyelids. Then softly I started singing, "'Somewhere over the rainbow way up high . . .'" I knew that Michael would like it. He sang along with me. My voice wanted to break, but I wouldn't let it.

When we finished singing, I heard a woman's voice. *His mom is back.* There was some muffled conversation, then Michael came back to the phone. "I gotta go, Mr. Done," he said. "Bye."

"Okay, Angel. Talk with you soon."

That was the last time I ever heard his voice.

The memorial service was held at Michael's church. The pews were filled with teachers, classmates, and families from school. I recognized some nurses from the hospital. There wasn't an empty seat.

As the service began, the pastor talked about what a special boy Michael was. He talked about Michael's love for music and God. He told everyone that Michael even planned some of the service—chose the Bible verses, the music, and who would speak. His mother told me I was his first choice.

At first when the family asked me, I didn't want to. I was afraid I wouldn't be able to get through it. But eventually I said yes. For my students. When the moment came for me to walk to the microphone, I looked down the pew at Michael's mom and smiled. She smiled back. Then I walked up to the podium and unfolded my notes.

I talked about the first time I met Michael saving a potato bug. I explained that Michael always chose "The Star Spangled Banner." I told the audience how he called me from the hospital when he wasn't supposed to. At the end of my speech, I folded my paper, looked out at the congregation, and swallowed hard. "I always thought angels wore white robes," I said. "But now . . ." I waited. ". . . now I know that some wear Cub Scout uniforms."

After I took my seat, Michael's mom caught my eye and mouthed *thank you*. Then I heard the shuffling of feet up in the choir loft behind me. The pianist began playing. I froze. *No.* My heart began to race. I whipped around and looked up to the loft. "Somewhere Over the Rainbow" began to fill the sanctuary.

I felt like crying and laughing at the same time. *I cannot believe this,* I thought. *That little guy chose this song for me. I know he did. He picked this song to comfort* me*!* I turned back around and looked up toward the ceiling. I knew Michael was up there singing. I sang with him.

Eventually my students and I got back to our routine. It wasn't always easy to keep it together, but I had to. I had thought about taking Michael's desk out of the classroom, but it didn't feel right. So I decided to keep it where it was. I left his name tag on his desk, too.

In class I spoke freely about Michael. I knew that talking about him was important. Sometimes the kids would talk about him as well. And if the song monitor picked "The Star Spangled Banner," we'd always sing it good and loud for Michael. Eventually, we stopped calling it the national anthem altogether and just called it "Michael's Song."

One afternoon toward the end of the school year, Michael's mom stopped by my classroom. It was the first time I had seen her since the funeral. We chatted for a bit. She was happy to see Michael's desk still in its place. She told me she was going to have another baby. I was happy about that.

"Oh," she said, "I almost forgot." She handed me a bag. "Michael wanted you to have this."

"Thank you."

"Before he died, he bequeathed most of his things." She paused. "Can you believe it?"

I let out a little laugh. "Actually, I can."

"I'm sorry it's so late. I should have given it to you long ago."

I sat on the corner of a child's desk, opened the bag, and looked inside. When I saw what was in it, I threw my head back and gave a good loud laugh. His mom smiled with me. Out of the bag I pulled a well-worn video of *Grease*. On the cover there was a note in Michael's handwriting:

> *Dear Mr. Done,*
>   *Learn these songs! Next time I see you we will sing them together.*
>
> *Love,*
Angel

I stared at the note for a moment and shook my head. Then I looked up at Michael's mom with a big grin. "Well, I guess I know what *I'll* be singing when I get to heaven."

March

MARY POPPINS: Our first game is called "well begun is half done."

MICHAEL: I don't like the sound of that.

MARY POPPINS: Otherwise entitled, "let's tidy up the nursery."

MICHAEL: I told you she was tricky.

—*Mary Poppins*

MATH

I teach math first thing in the morning. Why? Because they say that children are freshest at the start of the day. Well, the kids might be fresh, but when school starts my coffee just hasn't kicked in yet.

When I was a kid, math time consisted of copying a page of problems out of the book and making sure that they were a finger space apart on the paper before I solved them. If I was lucky, the teacher said we only had to do the odd problems.

Math sure has changed. Teddy bear counters have replaced textbooks. Math journals have replaced worksheets. Kids aren't "good in math" anymore; they're "numerate." In the old days teachers said, "Keep your eyes on your own paper." Today we encourage kids to share with their team. I used to ask: "What's the answer?" Now: "Explain your thinking." You know those lists that come out every year saying what's hot and what's not? Here's this year's list for math:

Out	In
Drill	Explore
Memorize	Understand
Procedures	Concepts
Skills	Problems
Answers	Alternate solutions
"That's incorrect."	"You're close."

As a matter of fact, I wouldn't be surprised if the terms *addition, subtraction, multiplication,* and *division* change, too. If they go, I have a good idea what their new names would be:

Addition would be *Bouncy Fists.*

"Gina, what's 8 + 7?" I asked.

She held up her fist then started opening it up one finger at a time. Each time she stuck out a new finger she bounced her hand. "9, 10, 11, 12, 13, 14, FIFTEEN!"

"Good."

Sometimes the kids don't want the teacher to see them counting on their fingers so they hide their hands under their desks just like they do when they sneak in a squirmy worm, a mud pie, or a fistful of Doritos.

Subtraction might as well be *Samurai Warrior.* I don't know why, but when kids borrow and carry they love killing numbers off.

One day when we were reviewing big subtraction problems like 2000 – 1899, Danny was making loud exploding noises at his desk.

"Danny, *what* are you doing?"

"I'm crossing out the numbers like you said."

"They're numbers, Danny. Not targets."

Multiplication would be *Wake Me Up When You Get There.*

"Melanie, what's 7 × 8?"

"51?" she answered slowly.

"No. But you're close."

"52?"

"You're getting warmer."

"53?"

I gasped. "You're *super* hot."

"55?"

"YOU'RE BURNING UP!"

"56?"

"YEAHHHH!"

Of course, multiplication could also be called *Tricky Facts*.

"Mr. Done, what's 7 × 7 again?" Chloe asked.

"The 49ers."

"Mr. Done, what's 8 × 8?" Gina called out.

I started singing. "8 × 8 is 64. Put down the phone and open the door."

9 × 7 is always difficult for children to remember. I thought I came up with a good trick for remembering it, but it's not working so well.

"Boys and girls," I explained, "I was born in 1963. So think of me whenever you see 9 × 7. Okay?"

The following day when Stacy took her multiplication timed test, she wrote 9 × 7 = 36.

"Stacy, why did you write 36?"

"You said 9 × 7 is the year you were born."

"I wasn't born in 1936! That would make me over seventy years old! Do I look over seventy years old?" I put up a single hand. "Wait. Don't answer that."

Stacy gave a heavy sigh. "I can't wait till we start division."

"Why do you say that?"

"Because then I won't have to do multiplication anymore."

I scrunched my nose up. "Well, I hate to break it to you, honey, but you have to know your times tables to do division."

She collapsed on her desk.

There is one math skill that third-grade teachers put off till the very end of the year. *Long division*. In fact, most of us hope the school year runs out before we come to that chapter in the math book. I know that after I introduce long division—no matter how many examples I give—I will have twenty kids lined up at my desk saying, "I don't get it." If long division gets a new name, it would definitely be *Tearing My Hair Out.* (I can think of other names as well, but this is the only one I can put in print.)

In my district, when a teacher needs to be out for the day, we call in to report it on an automated system. We press the number that corresponds to the reason for our absence: Press one for illness, press two for a personal day, and so on. I keep waiting for the recording to say, "Press three for long division."

Take my most recent conversation with Emily. After several sessions together at my desk, she was still having trouble. The problem was 456 divided by 3.

"Okay, Emily," I said. "How many times does three go into four?"

"Once," she answered.

"Good. Put the 1 on top."

"Why?"

"That's where it goes. Remember?"

"Oh yeah." She wrote it down.

"Now multiply the 3 and the 1."

She looked up with a confused expression. "I thought this was division."

"Well, it is. Now multiply the 3 and the 1. What's that?"

"3."

"Excellent. Do you know where you put the answer?"

"On top?"

"No, this one goes below the 4." She wrote a 3. "Next, subtract the 3 from 4."

"Subtract? What kind of division problem is this?"

"I know it seems confusing. Let's keep going. What's 4 minus 3?"

"1."

"Good. Now bring down the 5."

"Where?"

"Next to the 1." Emily stared blankly at the paper. "Okay, how many times does 3 go into 15?"

She paused. "5?"

"Very good. And where do you put the 5?"

"On the bottom?"

"No. It goes on the top."

She shook her head. "Can't I just use a calculator?"

For a lot of kids, solving word problems is right up there with eating vegetables. Have you seen those new cookbooks that teach moms to hide all the veggies kids hate inside the foods they love? It's all the rage. Children are eating zucchini in their macaroni and cheese, squash in their pizza, and broccoli in their chicken nuggets—and they don't even know it. Maybe the word problem maker-uppers can do the same thing. Trick the kids. Write problems about things they absolutely love like Disneyland—and the kids won't even know they're doing word problems! I can just imagine it:

If it takes 45 minutes to stand in line at the Pirates of the Caribbean and 1½ hours to stand in line at Peter Pan's Flight, what is the total number of minutes that you would stand in line?

You buy Mickey Mouse ears ($10), a Goofy balloon ($5), Donald Duck sunglasses ($7), a *Toy Story* T-shirt ($15), and a

Jungle Book backpack ($22). If you have $100, how much change will you get back?

As you journey through It's a Small World, you will hear the song 257 times. If you go on the ride 3 times, how many times will you hear the song?

If you paid $75 to enter the park and half of your day was spent waiting in line, how much did you pay to stand in line?

If the angle of the steepest drop of Big Thunder Mountain Railroad is 45 degrees and the angle of the steepest drop of Space Mountain is 60 degrees, which roller coaster should you *not* go on after lunch?

I don't know about other teachers, but my math period wears me out. My students think math time is playtime. Pass out plastic coins and they'll smuggle them out at recess and try to swindle the kindergartners. Pull out compasses and they'll make shish kebabs with their pink erasers. Distribute thermometers and one will put it under his armpit to make the red line get longer. Hand them calculators and they'll see how many words they can spell. Give them dice and half the boys will kiss the cubes and shout, "Show me the money, baby. Show me the money!"

When I give my students a balance scale and ask them to weigh a pencil, one child will always grab the stapler and the dictionary and the stuffed animals and stack them as high as he possibly can on the scale then come to me and report that the scale doesn't work. When we're learning volume and the kids are supposed to be making three-dimensional rectangular solids with the little cubes, one will always build the Empire State Building then play earthquake.

Last week when the kids were teamed up with partners to

measure their heights, Brian walked up to me with his yard-stick. He looked sad.

"What's wrong?" I asked.

"This yardstick doesn't work. It says Kevin is taller than me, and I know he isn't."

And don't even get me started on rulers. Rulers and third-grade boys should *never* be in the same room together. When I hand out the rulers, I know they will twang them on the ends of their chairs, beat them on their desks like drumsticks, and use them as runways for their erasers that have just turned into rockets.

That doesn't even account for the rulers with holes in them. I'd like to get my hands on the man who invented rulers with holes. What the heck was he *thinking*? Every third-grade boy knows that when you put the tip of a pencil into a ruler hole it turns into a helicopter.

"Mr. Done," Jennifer reported, "Christopher is shooting at me with his ruler."

"Did he kill you?"

"No."

"Good."

I looked at Christopher and put out my hand. He walked to my desk and surrendered the ruler. I didn't have to say anything to him. Third-grade boys also know that when a grown-up stands in front of you and holds out his hand with the palm up, he wants you to hand over whatever you are holding *right now*.

This week as I walked down the aisle, Robbie lowered his ruler in front of me. I stopped.

"Robbie, *what* are you doing?"

He grinned slyly. "You have to pay a toll."

This is a first.

I crossed my arms. "You want to go to recess?"

He sat up straight. "Oh, look at that. The gate is broken!" He raised the ruler. "You may go."

My students also think math time is snack time. It's no wonder. Teachers ask kids to count M&M's, divide piles of Reese's Pieces, sort Lucky Charms, estimate the number of jelly beans in the jar, weigh Hershey's Kisses, measure the circumference of apples, and graph their favorite potato chips. Just this week when Dylan walked into class, the first thing he asked was when we were having math. I smiled. "You're looking forward to math time?"

"No," he answered. "I'm hungry."

THE JAR

"oday's your lucky day," the cashier said as I approached the counter at Starbucks on Monday morning. "Your coffee's been paid for."

It took me a second to realize what she had said. ". . . Huh?"

"The woman ahead of you paid for your coffee. Actually, she paid for five coffees. You're number four."

I stared at her. "Are you kidding?"

"Nope."

Immediately I spun around to see who it might be. *Maybe she's looking at me right now.* Then I turned back. The cashier was smiling. "You said to the top, right?" I nodded, still dazed.

When she left to get my coffee, I looked at every woman in the shop. *What a nice thing to do.* Soon the cashier returned, pressed the plastic lid on my cup, and said, "It's Colombian today."

"Thanks."

She smiled. "Have a nice day."

That morning I gathered my students on the carpet and, with my coffee cup in hand, told them the whole story. They listened closely.

"Do you think that nice woman wanted me to know who she was?" I asked.

"No," several answered.

"I agree. She wanted to be *anonymous*." I repeated the word slowly as I wrote it on the small whiteboard beside my chair. "Can you all say *a-non-y-mous*?"

"A-non-y-mous," they chanted back to me.

"Good. Does anyone know what it means?"

Emily raised her hand. "She wanted it to be a secret."

"Correct. When someone chooses to be anonymous, he doesn't want anyone to know that he did it. For example, if someone sends you a valentine card and signs it with a question mark, he wants to remain anonymous."

"Ohhhh," said Rebecca.

I took a sip of coffee. "So, why do you think she wanted to be anonymous?"

"She didn't want anyone to know," Gina replied.

"Yes, but *why*?"

No one answered.

"Well," I continued, "when you do something kind for your mom—like set the table or take out the garbage—she appreciates it, right?"

"Right," the children echoed.

"It feels good to do something nice for your mom, right?"

"Right," they repeated.

I rested my elbows on my knees and clasped my hands together. "I'll tell you something else. Whenever you do something kind for someone and they *don't know* that you did it, you experience a different feeling altogether—a very special, warm, happy, feeling." I placed my hand on my heart and patted my chest. "Right here."

At that moment I looked over at the closet and stood up. "Wait right here." The students' eyes followed me as I walked over to the back of the room. I opened the double doors, searched the shelves, then pulled out a large empty glass jar with a red lid.

I returned to the carpet, took a seat, and set the jar on the desk beside my chair. The children stared at it. On it two words were written in big red letters: *Kindness Jar.*

"I wasn't going to show you this for a couple of weeks," I said, "but it feels like the right time to begin." I took another sip of coffee. "Now, what that woman did for me at Starbucks was what we call an *act of kindness*. Do you think she wanted anything in return?"

"No," they chorused.

I picked up the jar and set it on my lap. "Starting today, we are going to perform our very *own* acts of kindness—just like the woman in the coffee shop. Over the next week, I'd like you all to do three kind things for anyone you'd like." The children started chattering. "Now wait. Wait. Let me explain the rest." They quieted down. "After you've done something kind, you will write down what you did on a slip of paper and drop it into our Kindness Jar." I held it up and looked inside. "Do you think we can fill this up?"

Everyone answered at once. "Yeah!"

Angela sat up on her knees. "Can we do more than three things?"

"Absolutely," I replied. "You may do as many kind things as you'd like."

"Mr. Done," Melanie called out, "are you going to do it?"

I smiled. "Good idea."

"Do we write our names on the paper?" asked Joshua.

"If you'd like, but you don't have to. You may wish to be ... " I pointed to our new word on the whiteboard and waited for them all to say it.

"Anonymous!" they shouted.

"Very good. If you wish to be anonymous, just put a question mark on your paper after you've described your act of kindness."

For the next ten minutes, we brainstormed all sorts of ways to show kindness. I cut up strips of paper and set them on the table. After recess, there were already a couple of slips in the jar. I typed a note for the parents explaining Kindness Week.

Over the next few days, our Kindness Jar grew fuller and fuller. Each morning, I read the newest slips in the jar out loud. If the kids signed them, I asked them to explain their kind acts. If there was no signature, I just read it and let the child remain unnamed. Most of the kids were eager to share. David collected grocery carts in the parking lot. Laura washed her dad's car. Kevin watered the lawn. Jennifer brought her mom breakfast in bed: toast with chunky Skippy and raisins on top.

"My mom just about fainted," Christopher announced as I was reading the slips of paper.

"Why?" I laughed.

"When she told me to go to bed, I just said, 'Okay' and walked upstairs." He got up and acted it out. "I didn't talk back at all. I brushed my teeth and went straight to bed."

I lowered my chin and puckered my lips in a goofy-looking face. "Don't you *usually* go straight to bed?"

"Well . . . ," he said, grinning.

The kids giggled.

Christopher continued. "She even put her hand on my head to see if I was sick."

"Mr. Done," Melanie piped up, "what did *you* do?"

"Well, I've done three things so far." I counted them off with my fingers. "First, I gave an extra-large tip at a restaurant. Second, I left change in a soda machine."

"How much?" Trevor interrupted.

I threw him a look. "Enough for one soda. And third, I dropped some pennies on the ground."

Danny jumped up. "At *school*?"

"No. Calm down. At a park."

"Darn!"

By Friday, our Kindness Jar was full. I had heard from almost every student. As the kids were leaving at the end of the day, I stopped Brian on his way out.

"Hey Brian, do you need any help thinking of something for the Kindness Jar?"

He shook his head and dashed out of the room. A few minutes later there was a knock at the door. It was Brian's father.

"Excuse me, Mr. Done. Do you have a second?"

"Yes, yes. Of course," I said. "Come in. Come in."

"I'm sorry to bother you," he apologized, stepping inside. "Brian doesn't know I'm here."

"Is everything okay?"

"Oh yes. I wanted to talk with you about your Kindness Week."

"Ah yes," I said, "I just spoke with Brian about it."

"Did he tell you about his act of kindness?"

I looked surprised. "He *did* something?"

"Yes."

"I thought he hadn't . . . What did he do?"

"Well you see, ever since you sent home that letter, the one about Kindness Week, Brian started begging me to take him to McDonald's. I kept saying no. We rarely eat there. But he kept persisting. So last night I took him after soccer practice. When we arrived, he insisted on using the drive-through. We drove in and ordered. When the woman at the window handed us our food, Brian shouted, 'Wait!' Then he unzipped his soccer bag and pulled out a sack full of change. He handed it to the woman and said, 'This is for the car behind us.'"

I sat down on one of the kids' desks. "Wow," I said softly, "That's lovely." I paused for a moment then looked up at Brian's father. "But why didn't he tell me?"

"He didn't want you to know. He doesn't want anyone to know. He'd be upset with me if he knew I was talking with you about this. Brian said he wants to remain anonymous."

"Ahh," I responded with a nod and a smile. "I understand. But I told him he didn't have to sign his name."

"He said that if he wrote anything down at all, you'd recognize his handwriting."

I gave a little laugh. "He's right. I would."

"When we drove away, I asked him where he got the money. I assumed it was from his piggy bank. Some of it was, but most he raised this week."

"How?"

"He gave chess lessons to his friends. He charged a quarter a lesson."

"At *school*?"

"I don't know. I assume so. When I pressed him, he said that he did not want to talk about it. He said, 'Mr. Done told us that if you do something nice for someone and don't tell anyone, you get a very special feeling in your heart.'" I smiled. "So I dropped it. When I tucked him in bed, I asked him if he experienced that special feeling that you described."

"And what did he say?"

Brian's dad smiled. "Well, he still refused to say. So I had to ask his teddy bear."

"And?"

"He said yes."

SIMILES

One day when we were all reading *James and the Giant Peach* (each child held his own copy), I stopped after the sentence *"His room was as bare as a prison cell."*

"Boys and girls," I said, "this is a simile. Similes compare two things using the word *like* or *as*. See the word *as* in the sentence?"

They looked back in the text. "Oh yeahs" popped up around the room.

"What two things is Roald Dahl comparing here?" I asked.

"The room and the prison cell," Laura called out.

"Good." I continued reading. A few minutes later I read, *"Spread out below him like a magic carpet."* I stopped. "Here's another simile. See the word *like*?"

They spotted it. "Yeah!"

A while later I read, *"She was like a great white soggy over-boiled cabbage."*

"Simile!" Brian shouted, raising his hand at the same time.

"Very good," I said, nodding.

"Mr. Done," Brian negotiated, "for every simile that we find can we get a minute of free play?" I give Friday Free Time Minutes, which we add up at the end of the week. These are almost as coveted as No Homework Passes.

"Good try," I said, laughing.

Christopher piped in. "How 'bout for every ten similes we find, we get one minute?"

"Yeah!" they all agreed.

I thought about it for a moment. *How many similes can there be? Surely they won't spot all of them. It might be fun.* I smiled. "Why not?"

"Yeah!"

"When do we start?" Trevor asked quickly.

I shrugged. "How 'bout now?" I looked over at Angela. "Angela, you be our recorder." She ran to the paper basket. We resumed reading.

Teacher Alert: Never underestimate kids' ability to find similes—especially if there are Friday Free Time Minutes at stake. They can sniff them out better than a third-grade teacher can smell a three-week-old Lunchables in the back of a desk.

I couldn't get through a single page without someone announcing, "Simile!" Every time we came to one, the kids would jump out of their seats like jack-in-the-boxes. The farther we read, the more Roald Dahl seemed to sneak them in, too. (I swear he was on some kind of mad simile kick when he wrote this book.)

In *James and the Giant Peach,* nothing Mr. Dahl describes is just fast, flat, high, tall, white, sharp, or furry. Oh no. Everything has to be fast like a torpedo, flat as paper dolls, high as a church steeple, tall as a house, white as clouds, sharp as razors, and furry like the skin of a baby mouse! Stars don't just twinkle. They twinkle like diamonds. There can't just be a swarm. It has to swarm like ants. And no one in the book just jumps. They have to jump around like they have been stung by wasps!

If this weren't bad enough, Mr. Dahl even *repeats* his similes. In chapter 11, he writes *as large as a dog* three times! Yes, three times. ON THE SAME PAGE! Why in the world would he do that? I can only think of one reason. He is trying to help all children in the world get Friday Free Time Minutes. He is on *their* side!

Teacher Alert: When reading *James and the Giant Peach* with your students, do *not* read chapter 11. Go to chapter 12. I repeat. Skip chapter 11. Go directly to chapter 12!

It didn't take long for my students to become simile-crazed. They checked out all the Roald Dahl books from the library. They pointed out similes in their own silent reading books. They started using similes in their own writing. When Laura got caught staying up past her bedtime with a flashlight under her covers, she was reading ahead in *James* searching for similes.

One morning when I read, *"as it went sailing by,"* Kevin shouted, "Simile!"

"Not quite, Kevin. Just because you see the word *as* doesn't make it a simile. *As he was growing up* means *when* he was growing up. Sorry. No points."

Everyone whined.

When I read, *"'Did you like that, James?'"* Emily spouted, "Simile!"

"That's not a simile either, honey. Remember—a simile *compares* two things. Nothing's being compared here. It just means that he enjoys chocolate."

The class grumbled.

When I read, *"The boy's a genius,"* Sarah declared, "Simile!"

"Good try, Sarah. But I'm afraid that's not really a simile."

"But it compares *boy* and *genius,*" she insisted.

"You're right," I agreed. "But a simile has to have the word *like* or *as* in it. If it said, *The boy is* like *a genius,* then it would be a simile. What you discovered is called a metaphor."

Christopher perked up. "Can we get points for metaphors, too?"

"No."

One morning I read, *"The Earthworm looked like a great, pink, juicy sausage."*

"Simile!" Laura boomed.

"Excellent," I said. "Angela, write that down."

Christopher leapt to his feet. "Wait! That's *three* similes!"

"What?" I said, surprised.

He looked back in his book. "It's comparing the Earthworm to three different things," Christopher said, excitedly.

"No way," I said, shaking my head.

John jolted up out of his chair and started talking really fast. "Christopher's right! It says the Earthworm's like a *great* sausage. That's one simile. Like a *pink* sausage. That's another one. And like a *juicy* sausage. That's three!"

I flat-eyed him. "One. Point."

"Three!" everyone shouted.

"No."

More kids stood up. "THREE!"

Suddenly the music *CSI* always plays when the coroner is performing an autopsy began swelling in my head. I pictured the morning's headlines: "Mutiny in the Classroom," "Teacher Flattened Like a Pancake!" "Teacher's Last Words: I Hate You, Roald Dahl!" I gave it to 'em.

FOILED

There are certain things that a teacher must never do: Never give your student the hose at a car wash. Never pour plaster of paris down the sink. Never leave your coffee cup exposed on April 1. Never give an eight-year-old a retractable measuring tape. (It will not retract again.) Never stand on a bathroom scale when teaching your students about pounds and ounces. Never shout, "Hold your balls!" Never throw a wilted flower away in front of the child who gave it to you no matter *how* droopy it is. And never forget to wear green on St. Patrick's Day.

On St. Patrick's Day, children fall into one of four categories— those who cover themselves from head to toe in green, those who wear one or two articles of green clothing, those who forget and wear no green at all, and the tricksters. These are the kids who appear to not be wearing any green. But as soon as you point this out to them, they shout, "Yes, I am!" then bend over and reveal the two-millimeter stitch of green thread on the back of their sneaker.

Last St. Patty's Day when I saw that Corinne wasn't wearing any green, I felt sorry for her. So I called her up and stuck a green shamrock sticker on her shoulder.

"This is so you won't get pinched," I said.

She frowned.

"What's wrong?" I asked.

"I wanna get pinched."

*   *   *

I have only forgotten to wear green once. It was a Monday morning in my second year teaching. I was running late and arrived at school just as the bell rang.

"Mr. Done, you're not wearing green!" Eddie pointed out as I unlocked the classroom door.

My heart stopped. "What day is it today?"

"St. Patrick's Day!" he announced.

Dang!

"Where's your green?" Eddie asked.

Deep breath. Remain calm.

I forced a smile. "Well . . . I . . . uh . . . I'll show you in a minute."

Inside the classroom, I grabbed a piece of green construction paper and quickly started cutting out a four-leaf clover.

"Mr. Done, where's your green?" Eddie asked again.

"Right here," I sang, holding up my green paper.

"That doesn't count!" retorted Stephanie.

"Sure it does."

"No, it doesn't!" Dominic chimed in.

I finished cutting.

"It has to be attached to you," Brianna stated.

"It will be in a second," I said. I started shuffling through the piles on my desk. "Who took the tape?" Suddenly I heard the scooting of chairs and the stampeding of feet. I looked up. "Get back to your seats!" I screamed. Too late. Ambushed.

This year I had recess duty on March 17. The playground was a sea of green T-shirts, pants, jackets, sweaters, headbands, hats, socks, sunglasses, shoelaces, and spray-painted hair. Hannah and Jocelyn ran up to me. I'd had both girls in my class two years before.

"Where's your green?" I asked Hannah.

"Right here," she said, pointing to her turquoise leggings.

That's green?

It was clear to me that Hannah needed a refresher in St. Patrick's Day basics. Acceptable shades of green on the day of the Irish include: emerald, kelly, forest, apple, lime, olive, neon, chartreuse, teal, mint, jade, pistachio, moss, spinach, and camouflage. Aquamarine and blue-green: pushing it. Turquoise: should get pinched.

As I walked around the blacktop, I spotted a group of first graders searching under the picnic table. I poked my head under it.

"What are you kids doing?"

"Shhhhh!" one of them said, putting his finger to his mouth. "We're looking for leprechauns."

I smiled. "Oh." Then I squatted down beside them. "You *really* want to catch a leprechaun?"

"Yeah," they replied.

"Well," I whispered. "I think I know where one is hiding."

"*Where?*" they whispered back.

"In the office. Under the secretary's desk."

They bolted off. (Ellen thanked me later.)

When recess was over, I walked back to my room. John and Dylan were arguing in line.

"What's the trouble?" I asked.

"Dylan pinched me!" John cried. "And I have green on!" He lifted up his shirt to reveal a green tattoo of the Hulk. "See."

"I didn't pinch him!" protested Dylan.

"Yes, you did!" John shouted.

"I did not!" Dylan exclaimed. "I *fake*-pinched you."

"You *what*?" I asked, baffled.

"I fake-pinched him," Dylan repeated.

I grabbed the back of my neck. "What's *that*?"

Dylan reached out his hand, put his finger right near my arm, and gave the air a big pinch. I stood still for a moment with my head down. *Four years of college and a master's for this?* I looked up. The boys were waiting for a verdict. I rubbed my arm and crinkled my brow. "Ouch."

One of my favorite places to be on St. Patrick's Day is Kim's second-grade classroom. In March, the staff affectionately calls her the Leprechaun Lady. Kim's room is plastered with rainbows and pots of gold and leprechaun stories. (One of her kids wrote, "If I caught a leprechaun, I would sell it on eBay.") But the highlight is her students' leprechaun traps.

On St. Patrick's Day, Kim's room is full of boxes and bottles covered with stickers and glitter and aluminum foil. (Leprechauns like shiny things.) Each trap contains bait and of course something to catch the little pranksters: trapdoors, lids propped up on pencils, webs made out of dental floss, "quicksand" collected from the playground. One year a boy named Hayden decided he'd get the leprechaun to stick. So he covered the inside of a red rubber toilet plunger cup with duct tape rolls then filled it with molasses.

After excusing my students to lunch, I walked over to Kim's room. The traps were spread out on the floor. No signs of leprechauns yet.

"Did you leave the phone message?" Kim asked.

I answered à la Mr. O'Hara from *Gone with the Wind*. "Aye, Katie Scarlett." Kim thought it would be fun to leave a message from a leprechaun on her voice mail and asked me to play the part.

She laughed while shaking her head at me. "Ready to get started?"

I clapped my hands together. "Are you kidding? I've been looking forward to this all week!"

She laughed again. "Now don't get too crazy. Okay?"

"I promise."

After Kim locked the door and shut the blinds, together we tipped over desks, set the beanbag chairs on the bookshelves, threw papers on the floor, and put the overhead projector in the ball box. We clothespinned stuffed animals on the wires, dumped the sharpened pencils into the unsharpened-pencil box, opened the piano lid, spilled out the crayons, set the hamster cage in the sink, and poured green paint in Kim's coffee mug.

I started springing the traps while Kim stamped green footprints by the window, sprinkled glitter paths on the carpet, and set a little note in teeny writing on her desk.

"How many students do you have?" I asked.

"Twenty."

"I counted twenty-four traps."

"Devin made extras."

"How come?"

"For backups."

The last trap I sprang was a shoe box lined with pink marshmallow moons, yellow hearts, and green clovers. The lid was propped up with an Irish flag (a sure lure). Taped to the side of the box was a sign written in large green letters.

"Now *this* kid knows how to catch a leprechaun," I said, chuckling.

"Why's that?" Kim asked.

"He wrote, 'Free Food!'"

"That's Wyatt's," she explained without looking up. "And that was his *second* sign. The first one said, 'Free Beer.'"

I laughed.

Pretty soon the bell rang. Kim turned off the lights and we sneaked out the back.

"May I stay?" I asked. My students' recess ends later.

"Sure."

Kim and I sauntered around the corner as though nothing had happened. A couple of parents were standing at Kim's classroom door trying to act nonchalant while holding their cameras. (She had tipped them off.) Then casually Kim opened the door.

As soon as the first children in line saw the room, they started screaming. In two seconds all the kids were shouting and pointing and laughing and jumping and running. I stood in the doorway while moms took photos and Kim was pulled around the room, pretending to be shocked. No one had caught the leprechaun, but that didn't matter. He came.

In the midst of all the hubbub, one little girl scurried up to Kim holding her trap. On it was a leprechaun scooper made out of green and orange pipe cleaners.

"When's Easter?" she panted, out of breath.

"In a couple of weeks," Kim answered. "Why?"

"Because I'm going to fill this up with carrots and catch the Easter Bunny!"

She dashed off.

After about ten minutes, Kim gathered the children around her desk and read the tiny little note that the leprechaun had left behind. (She used a magnifying glass.) The note said, *"Dear Boys and Girls, Nice traps! But not good enough. See you next year! Toodleoo! Cheerio, Lucky the Leprechaun."* All the kids started chattering.

"Wait!" Kim gasped. "Wait . . . I think there's more." Then she leaned in with her magnifying glass just like Sherlock Holmes. The kids leaned in, too. "I think it says . . . 'Check *your phone messages.'*" Kim looked up with a bewildered expression. "My *phone* messages? What could *that* mean?"

She jumped up and walked quickly over to the phone. The class followed and clumped around her while she dialed in to listen to her messages. Kim quieted them down as she waited. Suddenly her eyes grew huge. On the other end of the line a man's voice started laughing. "You didn't catch me! You didn't catch me!" he gloated. Kim held the phone out for the children to hear.

The boys and girls started bouncing up and down. "It's Lucky the Leprechaun! It's Lucky the Leprechaun!"

As the kids squealed, Kim looked over their heads and gave me a smile. I waved good-bye and slipped out.

The next morning at recess, I stopped by to say hello. Kim was sitting slumped at her desk, her hand leaning on her elbow.

"Well," I said, "did our Leprechaun Lady survive another St. Patty's Day?"

"Barely," she croaked.

"What happened?"

She looked up. "Next year I'm not leaving any messages from any leprechauns."

"You're firing me?"

"Yes."

"How come? I thought they liked it."

"They *loved* it." She feigned a smile. "But do you know how many times I ended up playing that dang message?"

I shrugged.

"*Twenty!*"

"Twenty?"

"Yes." She gave a great heaving sigh. "I had to play it for *each* kid. Then this morning when they walked in, the first thing they did was ask if they could listen to Lucky again."

I bit back a laugh. "Did you play it?"

"No! I told them that leprechaun messages are magic just like leprechauns and the message disappeared."

I walked over to Kim, set both hands on her desk, and made a devilish grin. "Well now, it seems to me that Lucky just may have to make another wee call."

"DON'T! YOU! DARE!"

SPEAKING

Teachers try everything short of back handsprings to get their students to quiet down and pay attention. We flick off the lights, clap patterns, hold up fingers and wait, change the level of our voices, count up to three, count down from five, set timers, brush wind chimes, shake shakers, bribe kids with free play, and seat the boys next to the girls. Gail, my buddy teacher, tells her kindergartners to pretend they have sparkly bubbles in their mouths and if they open them the bubbles will float away. When you walk into her classroom and it's quiet, all the kids have their cheeks puffed out like they're holding their breath underwater.

Many teachers use catchy words to get their students to listen up. When Lisa sings, "Peanut butter," her whole class chants, "Jelly!" When Dawn announces, "Spaghetti," her kids shout, "Meatballs!" When Kim croons, "Abraham!" her students call out, "Lincoln!" Mr. Davis acts like an astronaut and says, "Mr. Davis to class. Come in, class." When my students are getting too loud, sometimes I shout "SALAMI!" (Stop And Look At Me Immediately!) They aren't supposed to say anything back, but once in a while some smarty-pants whispers, "Sandwich."

This year my class sounds like a Chatty Cathy convention. Some days I'd swear they all drank Red Bull for breakfast. I spend half my time saying, "Turn around," "Be quiet," "Get to work," "Do you want to go to recess?" and "Your mom made an egg salad sandwich for lunch? Careful. I love egg salad. Now stop talking." My students are so social that when one is chatting away, I skip right past "Who put a nickel in you?" and ask, "Who dropped in fifty bucks?"

Not every quieting strategy works though. If I jokingly threaten to tape one child's mouth shut with masking tape, the whole class will beg me to tape their mouths. A few days ago when the volume in my class was way too loud, I said, "Okay, everyone, press your Mute buttons." Danny said his remote was out of batteries.

Raising hands before speaking is something teachers are always reinforcing with their students. There are three groups of hand-raisers: (1) students who lift their arms and patiently wait to be called on (the smallest group); (2) those who blurt out at the *same* time their arm is going up in the air; and (3) those who bypass the whole hand-raising thing completely. This year, Brian is in Group Number 3.

"Brian," I said one day, "put your hand up."

He raised it.

"Now put it down."

He lowered it.

"Good," I said. "It works."

"What works?"

"Your arm. I thought it was broken."

You'd think that with all their talking, kids would be perfect little speakers. They're not, of course. Kids mispronounce words all the time.

When I was in the student-teaching program, one of my professors asked everyone in the class to keep a journal. She encouraged us to write down the funny things our students did and said. "Trust me," she explained, "on bad days, you'll be glad you did. It's cheaper than therapy." After I started teaching, I continued to keep up my journal. (Hence this book.) Here is a list of some of my favorite entries:

Olivia called the national anthem "The Star *Strangled* Banner." Russell thought the pirate flag was the *Jolly Rancher*. Fred said he had a *cricket* in his neck. (He meant a *crick*.)

Sean believed that Rudolph was chased by the *Abdominal* Snowman. Alexandra called Peter Cottontail—Peter *Cocktail*. Cameron thought the fuzzy stuff that moms pull out of the dryer was *lent*. Karen said *Harmonica* for *Hanukkah*.

In PE, Melanie referred to The Macarena as *The Margarita*. In computer lab, Deborah called home row on the keyboard the *house keys*. During reading, Abbie said that all words have consonants and *bowels*.

Ronny reported that his dentist recommended that he get a *restrainer*. Dominic called me *psycho* (he meant *psychic*). Madison said *tangerine* instead of *tambourine*. Michelle asked where the table of *continents* was in her book. And Tyler thought thumbtacks were *Tic Tacs*.

Brianna complained that she got up at the *crock* of dawn. Zachary listed the armed services as army, navy, and *submarines*. When I asked Hailey to tell her mother what she had learned about Benjamin Franklin, she reported that Ben had *testicles*. (She meant *spectacles*.) And every year there is at least one kid who refers to that crooked building in Italy as the Leaning Tower of *Pizza*.

We don't have a school nurse anymore on our campus. So Ellen, the secretary, handles all the kids who walk into the office with hot heads, scraped knees, bloody noses, or sore tummies. Over the years, Ellen has heard some funny things come out of their mouths.

William came in and said he had a *platter* infection. Louisa claimed she had *walking ammonia*. Victoria worried that she might have *Shrek* throat. Mackenzie referred to the rainy-day monitors as *thermometers*. Evan explained that he had to have his tonsils and *androids* removed. And when Jordan walked into the office holding his privates, he said that a ball hit him really hard in the *knuckles*.

Ellen says that the kindergartners make her laugh the most. Carlos asked if he had *garlic fever*. Claire told her that she couldn't go swimming because she had *tubas* in her ears. Sydney explained that her grandma had an operation because she had a *Cadillac* in her eye. While Melody was getting her hair checked for lice, she asked if she had *headlights*.

I asked Ellen if she has any favorite patients. She said that one would have to be Hunter. Hunter is in first grade. He's a regular in the office. The first time he came in hurt was at the end of recess. He was holding his ribs. He said he had sideburns.

A couple of months ago Hunter walked into the office with really chapped lips.

"Good morning, Hunter," Ellen said. "What can I do for you today?"

"Mrs. Parks sent me," Hunter replied. Mrs. Parks is Hunter's teacher.

"And what seems to be the problem today?" Ellen asked.

He pointed to his lips. "She wants you to put gasoline on them."

BUBBLES

All teachers have their *time of the month*—even the men. These times are achy and unpleasant. When they occur, teachers take a lot of aspirin and increase our coffee intake. In October it's the week before Halloween. In November it's parent–teacher conferences. In December it's the days leading up to winter break. In January it's the mid-school-year blues. In February it's surviving paper hearts and glitter. And in March it's when we frantically try to get our students prepared for the big state tests. Contrary to popular belief, the term *March Madness* did not come from the basketball court. It originated in elementary school.

One day as I was prepping my students for the exams, I said, "Boys and girls, on the test you have to know the difference between a dictionary, an atlas, and a thesaurus. Who knows what a thesaurus is?"

Robbie shot up his arm.

"Yes, Robbie."

"A dinosaur."

I could see that we had a lot of work to do.

Just before test time, teachers all over the country cram in all the things we haven't taught yet and review everything we know our students have forgotten. But we're not just drilling material. We're also teaching kids how to take a test—and for a good reason. Have you ever seen a third grader take a standardized test? Well, it's pretty much like observing a boy put on his own buttondown shirt and tie. It's a mess. The problem with these tests is those darn bubbles the kids have to fill in. I measured them. Some of those bubbles are only five millimeters in diameter. It is almost impossible for a third-grade boy to fill in a five-millimeter bubble without going outside the line. Our class bunny could do better.

Every year I give lots of practice tests. I have to. Third graders lose their place. They skip questions. They bubble in the wrong answers. They copy the problems down incorrectly on their scratch paper. If they get stuck, they will sit there for the entire length of the timed test staring at one problem. And if you tell them to be careful and check all their answers, one boy will cover his entire test booklet with checkmarks.

By the end of March, I have given so many practice tests that my life starts to feel like one big exam. When Dawn asked me what I was doing for the weekend, I had to think about it. I could:

a. Correct papers;
b. Plan my lessons; or
c. Watch *Survivor.*

I looked at her and answered, "C."

This year our first practice test was in reading. The kids had twenty minutes to read the passages and answer the questions. Each question had four possible answers. Once the kids began, I walked around the room. My first stop was Melanie's desk. She was on question number two, but had filled in seven bubbles.

"Uh . . . Melanie, you can only fill in *one* bubble per problem."

She looked surprised. "But I can't decide."

"Make your best guess, honey."

Next stop—Jennifer. She was on her fifth problem, but hadn't bubbled anything in at all. Instead, she had circled all her answers. I knelt down beside her.

"Honey, you have to *fill in* the bubbles. Not circle them. Otherwise the machine that reads your answers will mark them as wrong."

"Oh."

I left Jennifer and visited Joshua. His test manual looked like a sketch pad. There were more pencil markings outside his bubbles than in them.

"Josh, try to stay in the circles if you can. Okay?"

"Okay."

I glanced up at the clock. We were about halfway through the allotted time. I looked over Laura's shoulder. She was making absolutely sure that every bit of white inside her bubbles was completely filled in. "Laura, this is not an art project. Your bubbles are beautiful. Move on."

Trevor raised his hand, and I walked on over.

"What do you need?" I asked.

He pointed to one of the problems. "None of these answers are right."

I looked down at his packet then shrugged. "Make your best guess."

"But I can't figure it out," he whined.

"Trevor, I can't help you. You know that."

"Well," he said, "which one would you *recommend*?"

I pulled a face. Across the room I spotted Christopher drawing on his test with his crayons. I ran to his desk.

"Christopher, what are you doing?"

"Coloring."

"You can't do that."

"But it says to."

He pointed to the passage. The title was *How to Draw a Cat.* I read it: *First, draw a big circle. Next, put ears on the circle. Then draw a nose, eyes, and whiskers. Finally, color your cat.*

I rubbed my forehead. "Christopher, you're just supposed to *answer* the questions. Not actually *do* it."

"Ohhhhh."

He started erasing the crayon.

When it comes time to give the actual tests, I try to be as pre-pared as I can. I send home flyers reminding the kids to eat a good breakfast and make sure their number two pencils are sharpened. I tape my "Do Not Disturb" sign on the outside of the door and highlight all the "Say Boxes" in my instruc-tion manual.

"Say Boxes" are the directions that tell the teacher exactly what to read: *Open your books. Put your finger on the sample. Read the problem. Are there any questions?* Teachers are sup-posed to say precisely what's in each "Say Box"—and nothing more. But of course we don't always do this. Sometimes we *have* to say more. The test manual leaves some important "Say Boxes" out. There is no "Say Box" detailing how to respond when a child comes running up to you in the middle of the test because he forgot to use the bathroom at recess. And there is no "Say Box" outlining what to say when Jay starts chewing on his an-swer key.

Finally, the day arrived when it was time to begin our first real test. That morning I surprised my students with a pet frog. I had bought it at PETCO the night before. The class had really worked hard preparing for the exams. They deserved it. The kids named her Bubbles in honor of all the circles they had filled in.

Our first exam was spelling. The children had twelve minutes to complete it. It wasn't a lot of time. They would have to work quickly to finish. I passed out the manuals and the pencils and read all my "Say Boxes." I waited for the second hand to reach the 12 then said, "You may begin." The class got right to work. I sat down at my desk and kept my eye on the clock.

About two minutes into the test, I heard a noise in the back of the room. I looked up. The kids turned around. It sounded like trickling water.

"Get back to work," I told them.

The kids resumed working. But soon there was another noise. Everyone wheeled around again. I stood up and walked to the back of the room to see where the noise was coming from.

Splash!

It was Bubbles.

This can't be happening.

Splash!

I scratched my head and faced the kids. Everyone was looking at me and the frog. I glanced at the clock. Five minutes left.

"Get back to your tests!"

They snapped back to work. Then I had a terrible thought. *If Bubbles keeps this up, my students aren't going to finish their tests in time. This frog is going to* ruin *all my test scores.* What would I say if my boss called me into his office? "Uh . . . well . . . er . . . you see . . . it's my frog's fault." I crouched down and glared at Bubbles.

Splash!

I tapped on the glass, hoping this would stop her.

Splash! Splash!

"Stop that!" I whispered.

Laughter.

I turned around. All eyes were on me again. I looked at the clock. Two minutes remaining! *Summon serious teacher voice.* "If you kids don't turn around, I'm taking this frog home and you'll never see her again. Do you hear me?"

They whipped back to their tests. No one dared turn around again. At recess I marched Bubbles straight to the office. It was the first and only time I ever expelled a frog.

April

"It must be tremendously interesting to be a schoolmaster . . . I don't see how you could ever get old in a world that's always young."

—*Goodbye, Mr. Chips*

SCIENCE

M r. Done, when are we going to do science?" Kevin asked. "It's been a long time."

Kevin was right. I grabbed a pen off my desk.

"Watch this," I said. I dropped it onto the floor. "Do you know why the pen fell to the ground?"

"Gravity," he answered.

"Very good." I smiled. "There. We just had science. Now get back to work."

He just stared at me.

I know. I know. It's sad. I love teaching reading and writing and math and history. I love art and music. I don't even mind playing kickball in my dress shoes. The one subject I'm just not crazy about, however, is science. I feel guilty about it.

It's not because I don't know anything about science. I do. Teaching kids has taught me a *lot* of science. I know that mold grows in yogurt cups but not on Kraft cheese slices. I know that seeds are like lunch boxes: Inside is the food for the new plant, and outside is the protective cover. I know that the closer a child puts his hands near the overhead projector light, the larger the dog will appear on the screen. I know from which desk the sound waves are coming with my back turned.

I know the sun does not need to be shining to make smoke with a magnifying glass. I know that when you place a straw in a glass of water, the straw looks like it is broken. Teacher scissors look broken in the glass of water, too. I know that when I discover a long-forgotten potato in the back of my kitchen cupboard, it will look like a potato tree. And I know exactly what a balloon sounds like when you blow it up and let it go.

I've learned that all you need to make a telephone is a piece of string and two Dixie cups and that magnets stick to chair legs, but not to rabbit fur. I've learned that large blades of grass are best for making squawkers, car keys make excellent fossil imprints in plaster of paris, and pumpkins float. Tape dispensers do not.

I've learned that if you put a bar of soap into the microwave, it will expand to five times its original size. If you put a peanut M&M into the microwave, it will spark. And if you place two marshmallow Peeps into the microwave facing each other and stick a toothpick in each one—after thirty seconds they will inflate and stab each other.

Every elementary school teacher has a poster of the scientific process:

1. Ask a Question;
2. Gather Evidence;
3. Make Your Best Guess;
4. Test Your Hypothesis; and
5. State Conclusion.

I've become an expert at using the scientific process. Just this week, I followed it to a T with Robbie and Joshua. The boys were sitting under my desk recording in their science notebooks. My box of Cheerios was open.

1. **Ask a Question:** "Did you two boys get into my Cheerios?"
2. **Gather Evidence:** Robbie is frozen. Josh is frozen, too. Robbie is not responding to my question. Josh is also speechless. Their lips are shut. Their cheeks are full.

3. **Make Your Best Guess:** "You ate my Cheerios, didn't you?"
4. **Test Your Hypothesis:** "Okay, you two, show me your hands."
5. **State Conclusion:** "Based on the presence of Cheerio residue on all four hands, plus the fact that neither one of you has dared to swallow or blink since I walked over here, I conclude that my hypothesis is indeed correct. Now get out from under that desk."

Even though science is not my favorite subject to teach, I do try my best. Kids love it. Bring in a stethoscope and they all want to wear it. Dust off the giant plastic model of the teeth and suddenly everyone wants to brush. Ask them to rub balloons against their heads and I lose complete control of the class.

One day I gathered my students around my giant thermometer. I pointed to the *F*.

"Can anyone tell me what this letter stands for?"

"Fahrenheit!" Jennifer called out.

"Very good. And can anyone tell me what the *C* stands for?" Stacy raised her hand. I pointed to her.

"Cellulite."

Together my students and I have made solar systems out of old tennis balls, punched airholes in jars of caterpillars, and created sedimentary rocks out of peanut butter, jelly, and Wonder Bread. We've traced our shadows with chalk on the blacktop, written invisible messages in lemon juice, and turned off the lights to watch the pupils in our eyes get really big. We've sprinkled salt on ice cubes, created cumulus clouds out of cotton balls, watched carnations sitting in food coloring turn red, and made molecules out of toothpicks and mini marshmallows.

I do my best to stay abreast of the best practices for teaching science. Since the experts have declared that Pluto is not a planet,

I don't teach students *My Very Elegant Mother Just Sat Upon Nine Pickles* anymore. Now I say *My Very Energetic Mom Just Served Us Nachos.*

Kids are natural scientists. Christopher can demonstrate erosion when washing his hands. Trevor illustrates friction when sliding into home plate. Brian is an example of force every time he pushes the door to go out to PE. Recently, Melanie taught us all about static electricity when she ran in late with a pair of "Wednesday" panties clinging to her sweater.

Of course all children are zoologists.

"Mr. Done, look at the ladybug. I found it at recess."

"Mr. Done, I gotta cricket. I caught it on the way to school."

"Mr. Done, I found a snail. It was outside the classroom."

"Mr. Done, look at my cockroach. You need more? We have tons at home."

Sometimes my students' science knowledge is a bit off. Over the years, I have clarified that the famous man who studied gravity was not *Sir Fig Newton,* that the earth does not revolve on its *axel,* and that a *sense of humor* is not technically one of the five senses.

I've explained that pistils inside flowers do not *shoot* pollen, that the inventor of the graham cracker was not Alexander Graham Bell, that the only mammal that flies is not Superman, that goldfish eat algae—not *allergies,* and that the Big Dipper is not a *constipation.* Once when I asked the class, "Who knows what migration is?" David grabbed his head and pretended that he had a massive headache. It took me a second until I got it. "That's a *migraine,* David. But you're close."

Of course, I've had my own science bloopers. Teachers never forget the lessons that bombed. This is when we're glad the classroom door is closed and that children are very forgiving. I should have known papier-mâchéing twenty mayonnaise jars into volcanoes then filling them with vinegar and baking soda all at the same time was not such a good idea. I should have realized that sticking twenty vibrating tuning forks into cups of water would soak everything on their desks. Who'd have guessed that one itsy-bitsy candle could set off the fire alarm? And how was I supposed to know that when the directions on the ant farm say to put the ants in the freezer for fifteen minutes to get them moving—it means *fifteen minutes*. Next time I won't forget about them.

When I was a kid, I was actually very good in science. I knew why the entire strand of Christmas tree bulbs went out when one bulb died and how far away the lightning was by counting till I heard the thunder. I could make a xylophone out of my mom's water glasses, Kool-Aid powder dissolve by stirring really fast, and bubbles in my milk by blowing in a straw. On hot days, I could make rainbows in the water when I turned on the garden hose. And I knew that the first letters of the color spectrum (red, orange, yellow, green, blue, indigo, and violet) spelled the man's name ROY G. BIV.

Every spring at my school we have a science fair. On the day of the fair, the children set all their displays out on the tables in the multipurpose room, and all the classes go see what everyone has made.

Before the fair, the children must get their projects approved by their teachers. More than once, I've had to veto an idea. Nathan never got to test if a jump rope lassoed to a ceiling fan could slow it down. Ben wasn't allowed to see what happens when he shines the bar code reader in the class bunny's eyes. I nixed Ronny's idea for measuring the distance water will travel when putting a finger under the faucet. I refused to let Kerry's goldfish swim in apple juice. And I steered Brian away from determining if Coke or Pepsi produces the more gigantic reaction when Mentos are dropped into it.

On the day of the fair, I know before even stepping into the multi exactly what the science projects will be. One will show if houseplants grow better listening to Beethoven or Britney Spears. Another will prove if Tide or Biz does a better job at getting out the stains. And somewhere in the room a group of plants that were exposed to various levels of sunlight will remind me of the Seven Dwarfs. One will be Happy. One will look Sleepy. And one poor fellow will look like he needs Doc. (I'm always tempted to take the droopy ones outside for some fresh air when no one is looking.)

Scattered around the multi will stand displays explaining which paper airplane flies the farthest, why our hands get wrinkly in water, which brand of bubblegum blows the biggest bubbles, and what paper towel is the most absorbent. And there will always be at *least* one project that doesn't work. I'll feel so bad for the guy who made it that I'll stand and wait for him to rebuild his motor invention with his entire LEGO set because he swears that it really did work last night.

No matter what the project is, all the displays have one commonality—the science fair board. In fact, this board has not changed since science fairs began. The board is always folded into three panels. On it is a title along with the words *hypothesis, materials, procedure, observations,* and *conclusion.* Oftentimes one of these words is misspelled. When people walk by the display, it falls over.

At this year's science fair, several classes were in the multi looking at all the exhibits when a large gust of wind came shooting through the open door and blew over a whole row of projects. Like dominoes, board after board began collapsing and falling on the floor. Everyone went scrambling to save them. It was chaos. The science fair was almost ruined. Quickly I assessed the problem. Noticing the strong wind current rushing through the doorway, and understanding the effects of air pressure on cardboard, I walked over to the door and shut it. Immediately the displays stopped falling over. The fair was saved.

I told you I was good in science.

FIELD TRIPS

While driving with my friend Marian one day, we came upon a large group of children walking down the sidewalk in a single-file line. Name tags tied with yarn hung around their necks. Several adults were spaced between the kids. Clearly they were on a field trip.

"Oh look," Marian cooed. "How cute."

"*Cute?*" I protested. I pointed at the man in back of the line carrying three backpacks and giving one kid a piggyback ride. "See that man over there—the one who looks like a coatrack? I'm sure he's the teacher. And I can tell you right now that he does not think this is at all *cute*. You know why? That man will share his lunch today because some kid forgot his. When they stop for a potty break, he will stand in the boys' bathroom making sure that no one empties the entire paper towel dispenser. And when they're walking back to school, he'll get punched in the arm if someone sees a VW Bug." Marian started laughing. "If it's a VW bus, he'll get punched *twice*!" As we drove past the teacher, I rolled down my window and shouted, "God bless *you*!"

Over the years I've led dozens of field trips—to fire stations, factories, farms, libraries, airports, aquariums, and the school parking lot. (I had washed my car and my class wanted to see it.) No matter where a teacher takes his students—there are nineteen universal field trip truths:

1. When you send home permission slips, you will never get 100 percent of them back by the due date.

2. After the teacher makes car assignments, one child will request to sit in a different one.

3. When discussing the trip with your class, one boy will ask if he can bring his Game Boy.

4. When you pull out of the parking lot at school, at least one kid will say, "When will we get there?"

5. If the teacher is driving his own car behind a car full of his students, they will *shmush* their faces against the back window and wave to him for the entire drive. If the teacher opens the window and flaps his arms, they will laugh.

6. If the teacher passes his students on the road, they will scream at their driver to go faster.

7. Ten minutes after you arrive, one child will ask, "When's lunch?"

8. When it's time to eat, she will feed her entire sandwich to the birds.

9. When assigning children to groups at the nature preserve, more kids will want to be in the *falcons* than in the *hummingbirds*.

10. The teacher will spend the entire trip counting his students' heads to make sure everyone is there. (This is like playing Duck, Duck, Goose. For six hours.)

11. If there is a fountain, the children will ask if they can play in it.

12. If there is a gift shop, they will ask if they can buy something.

13. The farther you walk with your students in a line, the more spread out it will become.

14. When taking a group photo, half a dozen moms will hold up their cameras at the same time so you don't know in which direction to look.

15. By the end of the trip half the kids will have lost their name tags.

16. When it's time to hop into the cars and drive home, several will try to renegotiate the seating arrangement.

17. When you go to the theater, one child will have to go to the bathroom just as the lights are dimming.

18. When you say, "I just asked who had to go," he will answer, "I didn't have to go then."

19. As soon as he returns, five others will have to go, too.

Years ago I used to perform in shows at the local community center. I'd bring my correcting basket to rehearsals and the cast would help me grade papers. They thought it was fun. I felt like Tom Sawyer when he gets everyone to paint his fence. One year we put on *Pirates of Penzance* and I got tickets for my entire class to see a performance during Arts in Education Week.

The day before our field trip, I went over the rules for good theater behavior:

1. No talking during the show.

2. Keep your feet off the chair in front of you.

3. No hooting or whistling.

4. No wearing baseball caps inside.

5. No turning around.

6. No sitting on the springy seat when it is upright then collapsing down on it as if you are on the giant water drop ride at Six Flags.

When I was done with my speech, Valerie raised her hand.

"Yes, Valerie?"

"Can we laugh?"

I smiled. "Yes."

Since I needed to be at the theater early on the day of the performance, I arranged for a substitute to cover my class and asked my room moms to drive the children to the show. I'd meet my students afterward.

Finally, the big day arrived. The kids came to school all dressed up. The moms got the kids to the theater and in their seats without any problems. The children giggled when they saw my name in the program. The lights dimmed, the overture began, and the curtain opened. I stood in the wings and peeked out at my students. I could tell they were excited. I was, too. As I waited to go on, I wondered if my kids would even recognize me. I wore a big hat, and the makeup lady had slapped a full beard and mustache onto my face with toupee tape.

Soon it was time to make my entrance. I climbed up on the ship with the other men. The orchestra began playing the pirate song, and we entered singing and swinging our swords as the crew pushed the boat onto the stage. Immediately my whole class stood up en masse and started waving and pointing and reaching for me. One kid started crawling up on stage! The parent drivers frantically pushed the kids back down into their seats. I wanted to jump ship and make them all sit down, but of course I couldn't. I had to act like the happy pirate. Apparently I had left out one very important rule for good theater behavior: Do not stand up when you see your teacher on stage!

I have a great idea for a new reality show. It's called *Teacher Survivor*. On this show, a group of contestants would take a class on a different field trip each week. The show would be based on the true experiences of veteran teachers. I alone could fill an entire season. Here are a few of the real-life stories that I'd submit:

The Art Museum

It was a peaceful spring morning. When we walked into the museum, our docent, Linda, stopped in front of a large statue in the lobby to review the rules and talk about what we were going to see. Immediately all the kids started giggling and laughing. No one was listening to Linda. It was impossible. *Please God*, I screamed inside my head. *Tell me I'm hallucinating. Please God, can we move away from the six-foot naked lady statue?*

The Zoo

My class and I were standing at the railing looking over the bear den when I noticed one of the bears playing with a tennis shoe. I smiled and pointed. "Hey, kids, look at that!" The kids were laughing. *Uh-oh,* I thought. *That shoe does not belong to one of my . . .* Quickly I scanned my kids' feet. Sure enough—Gavin was missing one shoe. "Gavin," I screamed. *"What happened?"* He looked down at his sock and shrugged. "It just fell off."

The Pumpkin Patch

One beautiful autumn morning, we loaded five cars with students and drove to the local pumpkin patch. When we arrived, one of the chaperones put sunscreen on her kids' faces. The next day those five children looked like they were wearing war paint. They had orange streaks on their noses and cheeks and foreheads and chins. The helpful mommy had used her Tan in a Bottle by mistake.

The Historical Society (For Sweeps Week)

The room was filled with artifacts from the local Native Americans. Our docent was a nice little old man named Al. I could tell that he hadn't worked with young children much. Some of his explanations were a bit over their heads. But I didn't mind. The artifacts were wonderful: baskets, tools, arrowheads, a papoose. There was even a canoe.

As we were walking through the museum, Joshua pointed to some objects in one of the display cases.

"What are those?" Josh asked.

I looked in the case. There were about a dozen small carvings stacked in a pyramid. Each looked like a thick cigar. I had never seen them before.

"Well," Al explained, stepping toward the case, "the women in the tribe carved these. They would set them in front of the huts of a newly married couple on their wedding night."

My jaw dropped. My body stiffened. My heart stopped. If it had been hooked up to a monitor, all you would have seen was a flat line.

They're not. They can't be. Those are NOT stone wienies.

Al continued. "The Native Americans believed that the more of these placed in front of the hut—the more children the couple would have."

THEY ARE!

My sweat glands started to kick into overdrive. I could feel heat coming off my face. Al walked closer to the case. The children started to follow. My heart began pounding like a warrior drum. *NO! DON'T EXPLAIN MORE! STOP!* Just then I spotted some baskets.

"Oh my goodness!" I sputtered. "Look!" Everyone turned. "What are *these*?"

Trevor gave me a funny look. "They're baskets."

I clapped my hands and stepped closer. "Oh, they're *beautiful*! Could you please tell us about *these*?"

Al walked over to the baskets. He forgot about the wienies. Thank God.

THE CONFERENCE

Last week the third-grade teachers at my school attended a big literacy conference at a nearby hotel. I love going to conferences. I get to walk straight into the men's bathroom while fifty women line up in front of theirs. I get more than thirty minutes for lunch. Once I even got to eat at a real live restaurant. And if I want to, I can even slip out and make a personal phone call! But my favorite part about conferences is all the free stuff. In between workshops, I run around to all the vendors and load up on pens and calendars and key chains and bookmarks and candy. It's like trick-or-treating for grown-ups. At each booth I act like I am interested in the materials. But really I am just waiting for them to start the raffle.

The last session of the day took place in the grand ballroom. There were about a hundred teachers. The room was full (rumor had it that the instructor hid door prizes under the chairs). I sat at a round table with my colleague Sandy and eight others. I was the only man at the table. There was nothing under my chair. Sandy slapped me when I tried to see if anything was under hers.

"Okay, everyone," our instructor Barbara said, "for our first task, I'd like you all to do a quick-write about your most embarrassing teacher moment." The crowd chuckled. "You'll have about five minutes."

Everyone started writing. Except me. Not because I didn't have anything to write. I have plenty of embarrassing moments. The problem was that I had *too* many to choose from. It was like trying to select something on a menu when you're starving and everything looks good. Immediately I started going through the slide show of embarrassing moments in my head.

Slide One: Teacher notices wasp on inside of classroom window. Teacher grabs dictionary and slams it against glass. Window cracks. Wasp is fine.

Slide Two: Teacher stops car at red light while singing at top of his lungs with windows down. Teacher looks left. Teacher sees his student and student's mom sitting in next car.

Slide Three: Teacher loans Austin a die to play board game at home. Teacher writes reminder on board. Austin's mom walks into classroom and sees "Austin—die!" written on whiteboard.

Slide Four: Teacher plays *National Geographic* video in class about cheetahs without previewing it first. Midway through movie, cheetahs start "going at it." Teacher grabs remote to skip segment. Instead of hitting Stop button *then* Fast Forward, teacher presses Fast Forward. Students watch *everything* in fast motion.

Slide Five: Teacher returns tie in Macy's that Sophie gave him for Christmas. While standing at counter, teacher spots Sophie with whole family. *What are the odds?* Teacher screams at clerk to hide tie, grabs shirt off return pile, and pretends to buy it.

Slide Six: Teacher greets students as they enter classroom at start of school. Christina's mom says, "Have a good day, sweetheart." The teacher, who mistakenly thinks that Christina's mom is talking to *him*, smiles awkwardly, and says, "Uh . . . thanks. You, too."

Slide Seven: Teacher runs to bathroom in between two parent–teacher conferences. On way back to classroom he cuts across field. Halfway across grass, automatic sprinklers come on. Teacher does next three conferences soaking wet.

Slide Eight: Teacher plays tag with class on play structure. Teacher hears loud ripping sound. Teacher looks down, sees boxers through ten-inch hole where seam used to be in pants. Teacher orders two children to hand over their sweatshirts, ties them around his waist, and teaches like this for rest of day.

Slide Nine: Teacher steps out of shower at gym and hears familiar voice call his name. Teacher turns and spots student. Teacher cups hands over front, grabs towel, and runs to locker.

"Just a couple of minutes more," Barbara sang in the microphone.

I looked around the table. Sandy was already finished writing. So were several of the other teachers at my table. I still had nothing on my paper. Then all of a sudden Slide Ten popped into my head. *Bingo.* I started scribbling.

Barbara walked around the tables one more time then asked us to wrap it up. I continued writing. "Okay," she announced. "Now I'd like you to turn to the person next to you and share what you've written." We all laughed nervously. Quickly, I finished up my last sentence then turned to Sandy.

"You want to start?" I asked.

"No," Sandy said. "You go first."

"Okay." I sat up, cleared my throat, and started reading. *"My most embarrassing teacher moment. One day I was in a huge hurry to get to work. I grabbed my lunch sack, threw in a drink from the fridge, and raced to school. When lunchtime rolled around, I sat down in the staff room and started chatting away. As I was talking, I pulled my lunch out of the bag. Audrey tapped me on the arm and said, 'Hard day?' 'Why do you say that?' I asked. She stared at my can. I followed her gaze.*

'Ahhhhhhh!' I screamed. I grabbed the can and threw it back into the bag. It was a Budweiser."

Sandy started cracking up. I could feel my face getting hot.

"You're blushing," Sandy said, in between laughs.

"I know." (I turn red faster than a thermometer stuck in boiling water. Can't control it.)

Just then Barbara walked by our table and put her hand on the back of my chair. "Looks like you two are having a good time over here."

"You've *got* to hear Phil's story," Sandy said, wiping her eyes.

I shook my head broadly. "Ohhhhh no."

"Come on, Phil," Sandy prodded. "It's funny."

By now the others at my table had stopped reading and were listening to us. I shifted in my seat.

Barbara leaned over my chair. "I have an idea. Why don't you share it with the whole class?"

"Yeah!" Sandy said, patting me on the back.

"No way!" I refused.

"Come on!" another piped in.

I could feel my face turning redder. I turned to Sandy. "The only reason you want me to read it is so that you're off the hook."

She laughed.

All of a sudden one of the other women at my table started chanting. "Phillip! Phillip! Phillip!"

"Stop that!" I whispered through gritted teeth.

The others joined in. "Phillip! Phillip! Phillip!"

The last time I was in a pickle like this, I was on a cruise with a group of friends. They pushed me up on the stage during the karaoke competition and I was forced to sing "Ain't Nothing But a Hound Dog" to half the ship.

"Oh all right!" I grumbled. (This had to be easier than singing Elvis.) Sandy started clapping. I shot her a look. "I'll kill you later."

"Okay, everyone," Barbara said, excitedly. "Please listen up. Listen up, please." The room became quiet. "Phil is going to share his most embarrassing teacher moment." She handed me the microphone.

I stood up slowly, looked out into the audience, and gave a half smile. "Is my face red?"

A hundred people answered, "Yes."

Then I took a deep breath and swallowed. "Well," I said staring down at my paper. "Uh . . . this really isn't my most embarrassing moment anymore." I looked up and paused. "I'm having a whole new one *right now*."

LUNCHTIME

When I was in third grade, I asked my mom if you have to be a lady to work in the cafeteria. She said no. "Good," I responded. "Because when I grow up I want to be a cafeteria man." I used to love eating in the cafeteria. The lunch ladies made cinnamon rolls and large, soft, uneven peanut butter cookies from scratch. Every St. Patrick's Day we had chocolate cake with green icing. The day before Thanksgiving, they always served turkey and mashed potatoes. I told my mom that hers was as good as the school's.

I don't eat in the school cafeteria anymore. The food is sent in. At lunchtime I usually drive to a little Mexican restaurant down the road and grab a burrito. If I time it right, I can get there, order, and return to school just before the bell rings.

One afternoon I had just picked up my burrito and was on my way back to work when I heard a loud noise behind me. I looked in my rearview mirror. Blue and red lights were flashing. *Dang!* I pulled to the side of the road, parked, and rolled down my window. I was right beside the school.

"Hi, Officer," I said meekly as he stepped up to my car.

He removed his sunglasses. "Do you know why I pulled you over?"

I shook my head.

"You were doing thirty-five in a school zone." He pointed to the campus. I decided to not tell him that I worked there. "May I see your driver's license and registration please?"

I reached into the glove compartment and handed him the papers. As he walked back to his car, I glanced at my watch. The bell would ring in five minutes. *Please hurry.* If I didn't get back in time, my kids would not let me hear the end of it.

Suddenly I spotted children walking down the sidewalk. *Eek.* The kindergartners were out. They were walking home with their mommies. I grabbed a paper off the floor, slid down in my seat, and covered my face. *Please, don't anyone recognize me. Please no one start waving at Mr. Done.*

I glanced at my watch again. Two minutes till the bell. I shook the steering wheel. *Hurry, Mr. Policeman.* Finally, the officer walked back to my car. He was studying my driver's license. When he reached the window, he pointed to the school and asked, "Do you work there?"

How does he know that? "Uh . . . yes."

All of a sudden his face broke into a giant smile. "Are you Mr. *Done?*"

My eyes grew big. "Uh-huh." Immediately I started flipping through the Rolodex in my head. *Is this guy one of my former students? Is he the officer who spoke to my class at the Bike Rodeo about safety on the road?*

"I'm Laura's dad!" he announced, patting his chest. I opened my mouth but nothing came out. "Laura *loves* your class." I knew that Laura's father was a police officer but had never met him. He didn't come to Back to School Night.

Just then I heard the school bell ring. Lunch was over.

"Sorry I was going so fast," I said. "I was trying to get back to school in time."

"Oh yes. Of course." He handed me back my license. "Just watch the speed. Okay?"

"Yes. Yes. I will. Thank you, Officer. Thank you very much. Nice to meet you, sir." He started walking away. "Uh . . . excuse me, sir." He turned back around. I cringed. ". . . would you mind not telling Laura about this?"

He laughed. "I promise."

I quickly grabbed my burrito, locked the car, and flew to my classroom. The kids were waiting for me in line. Rebecca spotted me first.

"You're *late*!" she scolded.

"*Where were you?*" they all shouted.

"We've been waiting for an *hour!*" Trevor whined.

"I'm sorry. I'm sorry," I said, searching for my keys.

"Why are you late?" several asked as I unlocked the door.

"Well . . . I . . . uh . . . I . . . (*Ding!*) . . . I was having a parent–teacher conference."

TEACHER MODE

This year for spring break I splurged and flew to Paris. I adore Paris. I went with my good friend Heidi. She is not a teacher. On our first day in the city, we visited the Eiffel Tower and took the elevator up to the observation deck. After about twenty minutes, Heidi said, "Phil, you're doing it again."

"What?"

"That . . . that teacher thing."

"What are you talking about?"

"Well, since we've been up here you've helped a kid look through the telescope, pointed out a girl's untied shoelace, picked up litter, and when a boy ran by—you patted your pocket looking for your whistle."

I laughed. "I did?"

"Yes. And when we were waiting in line to get up here and some woman stepped in front of us, you shouted, 'No cuts!'"

"Well," I huffed, pretending to be offended. "I can't help it. I'm a teacher. And *that's* what teachers do."

Heidi was right. I was in Teacher Mode. It turns on automatically whenever children are near and goes into overdrive when it senses busy streets, mud, gum, or bloody noses.

As our week in Paris continued, my Teacher Mode got worse. I played crossing guard at the Arc de Triomphe and nearly fell into a fountain trying to retrieve a boat that sailed out of reach. At the Louvre, my camera was almost confiscated while I tried taking photos of the *Mona Lisa*. When I explained to the guard that the pictures were for school, Heidi pretended that she didn't know me.

One afternoon when Heidi and I were strolling by some souvenir shops near the Moulin Rouge, I spotted some "I Love Paris" pencils in a window. *My students would love those,* I thought. I turned to Heidi. "Just a second. I'll be right back."

Well, I really should have known better than to walk in there. No one should ever walk into a souvenir shop when he is in La Mode de Teacher. The shop was a teacher's paradise, packed with a veritable smorgasbord of goodies I could use for school. I grabbed a basket and started filling it up with postcards of Notre Dame, a miniature bust of Napoleon, a map of France, a Monet calendar, a chef's hat, a Picasso tie, Eiffel Tower sticky notes, Moulin Rouge magnets, the French flag, a beret, and a Paris Metro mouse pad.

"There you are," I heard a voice say as I was counting out my "I Love Paris" pencils. It was Heidi. "What's taking you so long?"

I pointed to my treasure. "Look at all this great stuff!"

Her eyes grew wide. "You're buying all *that*?"

"Yeah. Isn't this fantastic?"

Heidi made a face and threw up her hands. "Here we go again."

"What do you mean—here we go again?"

"Remember when you came home from Boston?"

"Yeah."

"You brought back everything short of Paul Revere's horse."

My mouth fell open. "I teach American history."

Heidi knelt down and started rummaging through the basket. First she held up a mug. "How many of these do you have?"

"None." She looked at me like I just told her the dog ate my homework. I snatched the mug out of her hands. "Well . . . none with the Paris Metro."

Next she pulled out a stack of bookmarks shaped like baguettes. "Why do you need so many of these?"

"They're for my students. I can't go to Paris and not bring back something for my kids."

Heidi shook her head and reached into the basket one more time. She pulled out a shot glass and gave me a look.

"For my boss."

I bent over the basket and picked up the calendar and the Eiffel Tower sticky notes. "Heidi, just *look* at all this! Where else could I get this stuff?"

She crossed her arms. "Target."

I threw back the sticky notes and snatched up the basket. *Clearly* she did *not* understand.

"Listen," she lectured, "don't ask me to put any of this into my suitcase. And don't come whining to me when you have to pay a hundred bucks extra because you're over the weight limit."

I hadn't thought of that. I looked down at all my goodies, pursing my lips. "Well . . . maybe you're right. Maybe it is a bit much." I gave a loud sigh. "Okay, I won't buy it all." I reached into the basket and put back the Van Gogh night-light. Then I turned back to Heidi. "*There*. Satisfied?"

I REMEMBER

All teachers have those days when we think the cashier's position at Wal-Mart is looking pretty good. But then just when we're about to lose our minds, a student does or says something that reminds us of why we went into this profession in the first place.

When I spotted Eleanor praying over a dead baby bird by the bike racks—I remembered. When Erin asked if the stars in the sky are pointy like the ones we draw—I remembered. When I asked Carolyn how she came up with the words *chestnut brown* in her story and she said it's on her mom's box of hair dye—I remembered, too.

When Brianna wrote "I love you more than pancakes" in her dad's valentine, when Sarah asked me how blind people write Braille in cursive, and when I told everyone to partner up with a buddy for their math game and Jason asked, "Can we have a three-way?"—I remembered.

When Caleb pinky-promised me that he'd do his homework, when Blake covered his eyes while labeling the states on his blank US map (I had asked him to fill it in without looking), and when Alex wanted to bring me an apple for Teacher Appreciation Week, but didn't have any at home so he gave me a ripe avocado wrapped in foil instead—I remembered.

I remembered when Luis called an exclamation mark *the excitement point,* when Ji Eun scratched her mosquito bite and said, *"It inches,"* when Jerod thought an autobiography was a story about cars, when Tae Hun called toast "jumping bread," and when Ricky asked me to draw him a horse and I told him I didn't know how. So he asked me to draw him a sand-blaster instead.

I remembered when I handed out the multiplication timed tests and Ralph said, "Do you want it fast, or do you want it accurate?"; when I said "Gesundheit" after Vanessa sneezed and she told me her mom speaks French, too; and after Christopher asked why we always have to end a sentence with a period and Trevor answered, "Because it's a commandment."

I remembered when the class broke out into a heated discussion over whether or not girls can be elves, when Michele wanted to know how wine can be dry, when Kohei said the time was "*Two o'watch,*" and the day Sebastian walked up to me with a bruise on his arm so I took a look. "What happened?" I asked. "I was sucking on it," he answered. He had given himself a hickey.

When I asked the class where french fries come from (I was looking for *potatoes*) and Eric said *McDonald's*, when Ronny wanted to know if there is such a thing as a *left angle*, when Evelyn was shocked to find out that I get paid, when I asked the class to give me a synonym for *laugh* and Greg said *LOL*, and when Juan looked at my cuff links and said, "My dad wears handcuffs, too"—I remembered.

When Aaron thought covered wagons were called station wagons, when Marci asked me how to spell *DVD*, when I couldn't get the TV to work and Christopher announced, "Houston, we have a problem," and when Theresa (a kinder-gartner) dropped her name tag and asked me to pin back her "price tag"—I remembered.

When I said I'd like to see "some new hands" in our class discussion so Adam lowered his right arm and raised his left; when a first grader ran up to me on the blacktop and shouted excitedly, "Mr. Done! I have diarrhea!"; and when I passed out marshmallows for multiplication and Skyler announced, "I just *love* when we eat what we're learning!"—I remembered.

When Kyle, unsure if he should write *which* or *witch,* pointed to his paper and said, "Is this the good witch or the bad witch?"; when Layla wrote that the main character in her story was *tall, blond, beautiful, and lactose-intolerant;* when Crystal said that her sister can say all the presidents *in a line* (she meant *in order*); and when Isabelle was reading to me about beavers and refused to read *dam* because it was a bad word—I remembered.

I remembered when I asked Mark why he was a mile away from his desk and he replied, "I got lost," when Brian wrote in his science journal, "The first person to orbit the earth was a dog," when Andrea explained that the difference between molecules and atoms is that "Molecules are small. Atoms are itsy-bitsy," and when I pointed to the edge of the rug and said, "This is the *exterior.* Who knows what the center is called?" Tyler answered, "The mush pot."

I remembered when Laura asked why a ship is a "she," and Dylan proclaimed, "'Cause the men are on it," when Brian was bouncing because he couldn't wait for his birthday (it was in three months), and when I walked into class one morning grumbling that the coffee machine in the staff room was broken and a couple of minutes later Gabriella handed me a drawing of a full cup of coffee and a doughnut. With sprinkles.

I remembered when Rachel said she was tardy because her mom couldn't get her eyelashes on, when Steven taped an *Enter at Your Own Risk* sign on his desk for Back to School Night, when Jill said that I was her first boy teacher, when Chloe's mom couldn't find a shoe box at home for a school project so she went out and bought herself a new pair of pumps, and when I asked Carolyn what she liked best about her new fifth-grade teacher and she answered, "He sticks a pencil behind his ear."

I remembered the day I asked for a volunteer and Paige begged me to be the "bunny." (It took me a second to figure out that she wanted to be the guinea pig.) I remembered the day I moved the hands on the plastic yellow teaching clock and asked Allison what time it was. She replied, "Happy Hour." And I remembered when Ronny walked up to me during the last week of school and said, "Mr. Done, you could probably teach fourth grade. You're smart enough."

May

"Wa, wa, wa, wa, wa, wa, wa. Wa, wa, wa, wa, wa, wa, wa."

—Charlie Brown's teacher in *Peanuts*

CHANGE

I'm starting to feel like a relic. The movies I grew up with are on the Classic Movie Channel. The Speed Racer lunch pail that I carried in second grade is in a collection at the Smithsonian. One of the new hires in the district is a former student of mine. (I had her when she was seven.) Christopher just about had a heart attack when I told him that I saw *Star Wars* when it first came out. And out of all the valentines that my students gave me this year, there was only one Snoopy, one Spider-Man, and one Tinkerbell. All the rest were of Orlando Bloom.

Sometimes I feel like my students and I don't speak the same language. When I said, "Wax on. Wax off," no one got it. When I sang, "Two all-beef patties, special sauce, lettuce, cheese, pickles, onions on a sesame seed bun," they looked at me like I was completely nuts. Recently when I was explaining to my class how kids used to clean chalk erasers by going outside and banging them together so the dust would fly all around, Danny asked, "What's chalk?"

Once in a while I even need a translator—like the day John walked into the classroom after recess with his hair soaked and sticking straight up.

"John!" I cried. "What did you do to your *hair*?"

"It's a swirlie," he answered, proudly.

"A *what*?"

"A swirlie."

I thought swirlies were what they serve at Dairy Queen.

"You don't know what a swirlie is?" Trevor asked, shocked.

"No. What is it?"

The kids started laughing at me. I got the same response when I told them that I had never visited Club Penguin and couldn't name all three of the Jonas Brothers.

Kevin piped up. "It's when you stick your head in the toilet and flush it and it makes your hair look like that." He pointed to John's head.

This week Joshua and Robbie completely lost me.

"Jinx!" they called out at exactly the same time.

"Personal Jinx!" they cried in unison.

"Rainbow Jinx!" they announced together.

"Toilet Jinx!" they shouted. Josh was a split second faster than Robbie. Robbie stomped his foot.

I stood there dazed. "What's Toilet Jinx?"

Josh cracked a smile. "Robbie can't go to the bathroom or say anything until I say his name three times."

So much has changed since I was a kid. When I was my students' age, we turned the dial on phones, found books in the card catalog, waited a whole year to see *The Sound of Music* on TV, unfolded car maps to find directions, and painted typing mistakes with Liquid Paper.

We dropped the needle on the spinning record and hoped we'd hit the beginning of the song on the very first try, waited for the cassette to beep before turning the knob on the filmstrip projector, and changed the due date in the librarian's stamp when she wasn't looking.

Of course *nothing* has changed like technology. Kids TiVo their favorite television shows, text on cell phones, shuffle tunes on their iPods, ride in cars with GPS, Skype their grandparents, snap digital photos, appear on their moms' blogs, play Nintendo Wii at their birthday parties, and have virtual food fights on the Internet. Today's children are as familiar with Google, Yahoo!, Craigslist, Mapquest, Netflix, eBay, and Amazon as they are with Mickey Mouse, Donald Duck, Goofy, Jiminy Cricket, and Dumbo. This year, five of my third graders already have their own Facebook pages. Melanie's ballet recital is on YouTube. And Dylan's dog has a profile page on Dogster—a MySpace for canines. No doubt Fishter, Birdster, and Class Bunnyster will be here soon.

As one who grew up with scratchy records and watching the Emerald City on television in black and white, I feel lost in the twenty-first century. I only know what three of the twenty-seven buttons on my remote mean, would starve if the microwave didn't have the *potato* setting, and drive my car around with the wrong time for half the year just so I don't have to reset the clock when we go off Daylight Saving Time.

It's not my fault really. When I was in teacher school, my technology class consisted of changing the bulb in the overhead, making sure the slides in the carousel weren't upside down, and feeding film into the movie projector so it didn't spill out all over the floor.

A *bug* was something you brought in from recess to show the teacher. A *desktop* was something you scraped dried Elmer's glue off of with your teacher scissors. *Hard drives* were on Monday mornings. *Viruses* kept you home from school. *Backups* were what you called the custodian about when the toilet overflowed. *Monitors* cleared the boys out of the bathrooms on rainy-day recess. The *mouse* was something you forgot to feed. *Zip* was what the teacher told you to do to your jacket on a cloudy day. *Windows* were what you opened with a long pole. And *cursors* were sent to the principal's office.

Do I worry that I'm becoming a relic? Am I concerned about becoming outdated? Not at all. Because I know that every morning when I read my students a story on the carpet, they will sit transfixed and scoot closer. And every afternoon when I set the song on the overhead projector, they will sing their hearts out. These things will never change. Good things usually don't.

MUSEUM

In May, the third graders put on a Wax Museum. It's like Madame Tussauds in miniature. We invite the parents. The other classes visit, too. To prepare for the day, the kids read biographies about famous men and women then write mini reports which they memorize. On the morning of the Wax Museum, the children come to school dressed up like the people they have studied and take their places all over the multi. Each third grader stands frozen until someone touches the green construction paper "button" pinned on his shoulder. When the button is pressed, the frozen figure comes to life and begins speaking. After he is finished, he refreezes until someone else walks over and starts him up again.

Among this year's famous people were Davy Crockett, Rosa Parks, Benjamin Franklin, Amelia Earhart, Mark Twain, Laura Ingalls Wilder, Charles Schulz, Theodore Roosevelt, Joe DiMaggio, Annie Oakley, Henry Ford, Walt Disney, and Black Beard. Black Beard was Trevor's second choice. He really wanted to be the Hulk, but I explained that the Hulk was not quite the famous historical figure I had in mind.

As the children performed, I made my way around the multi. Laura was dressed up as Amelia Earhart. She'd borrowed her dad's leather jacket and wore an old swimming cap and goggles on her head. She looked more like she had swum across the Atlantic than flown over it.

Sarah was Shirley Temple. When I pressed her green button, she sang "On the Good Ship Lollipop" and tapped out a little routine in her black Mary Janes. Her hair was a mop of exactly twenty-three ringlets which Sarah reported when she walked into class. Chloe wanted to count them, but I said I was sure that Sarah was right.

John came as Vincent Van Gogh. He painted a canvas of sunflowers while delivering his speech. Paintbrushes stuck out of his pockets like a porcupine. His hair was spray-painted red. His left ear was covered with a bandage.

As Vincent was wrapping up his talk, I noticed a crowd of second graders gathered around Black Beard. I walked on over. One child was holding down the pirate's green button while the others laughed. Black Beard was talking really fast like a Chipmunk.

"Okay," I said, breaking through. "What's going on?"

"I'm fast-forwarding him," one of the onlookers giggled.

I turned Trevor off and shooed his audience away.

Over the next half hour I listened to Thomas Edison describe the lightbulb, Dr. Seuss read *Green Eggs and Ham,* Harry Houdini reveal how to break out of handcuffs, Jim Henson sing with Kermit, and Louis Armstrong play "Hot Cross Buns" on his trumpet.

One of my last stops was Abraham Lincoln (played by Brian). Lincoln sat in a chair next to Shirley Temple. He wore an old tuxedo jacket that his mom had bought at the Salvation Army Store. Dark sideburns were drawn on his cheeks with eyebrow pencil. His top hat was made out of an oatmeal box. I pressed his green button.

Slowly, Lincoln rose out of his seat. He grabbed his lapels then began reciting the Gettysburg Address. As he spoke, a parent came by and pressed Shirley's On button. Immediately Shirley launched into "On the Good Ship Lollipop." Lincoln snapped his gaze at Shirley and cast a disapproving look. Shirley, oblivious to his stare, kept right on singing. Soon she started doing time steps on the tile floor. Lincoln spoke louder. Then Shirley started shuffling off to Buffalo right in front of the president. Her twenty-three ringlets bounced like Slinkys on her head. Well, that was it. Lincoln turned to the child star and without missing a beat declared, "Little girl, would you kindly stop singing that ridiculous song. Can't you see I'm trying to win a war here." Shirley stopped cold. Lincoln went right back on giving his speech.

I have always loved museums. When I was eight, I went around the house gathering up knickknacks and dishes and odd stuff and hauled it all upstairs to my bedroom. I set it out all over my bed and desk and dresser and labeled everything. After the room was ready, I invited the public in. The sign on my door said "Museum. Admission: ten cents." My mom paid to view the exhibit. My brother would not give me a dime, so he didn't get to see it.

The United States has a lot of odd and unusual museums. Across the country there are museums of mustard, barbed wire, Pez containers, bananas, Band-Aids, dental instruments, and squished pennies. There is even a Museum of Dirt. People send in all different kinds of dirt from around the world. Someday I'll mail in a jar of my own. It will be labeled: "Mud Tracked in on Rainy-Day Recess."

Actually, I'm surprised that no one has built a Teacher Museum yet. If there were one, I know just what it would look like. The lobby would be covered with first-day-of-school photos. "You're a Grand Old Flag" would play on the speakers. Visitors would store their bags in cubbies. The tour guides would wear smocks.

The museum's permanent collections would include the Hall of Excuse Notes, the Student of the Month Bumper Sticker Gallery, and the Confiscated Item Salon. In the Room of Records, visitors would see the smallest working pencil, the highest correcting basket, and the longest-lasting red rubber ball (three weeks). The museum would also house the world's largest collection of bells, whistles, apples, hamster cages, and Partridge Family lunch pails.

One entire wing of the museum would be dedicated to teacher apparel. Here hundreds of sweatshirts appliquéd with teddy bears, wooden block alphabet necklaces, Christmas tree pins, and plastic spider earrings would be on display. The walls would be covered with teacher T-shirts with messages like: "Just be thankful I'm not your mother," "Teacher by day. Deadly ninja by night," "The dog ate my lesson plan," and "I do not do decaf!"

In the gift shop, silhouettes traced on black construction paper, baby food jars decoupaged with tissue paper and Vano starch, and postcards of the Zaner-Blaser cursive alphabet would be available. At the museum café, visitors could choose from sloppy joes, pizza, grilled cheese sandwiches, fish sticks, or toasty dogs (a buttered slice of white bread lined with a slice of processed cheese, wrapped around a hot dog, held together with a toothpick then toasted). Side dishes would include Tater Tots, canned peaches, celery filled with peanut butter, fruit cocktail, and shredded carrots in green Jell-O.

THINKING

I like to teach my students a little about archaeology. It helps them develop their thinking skills. Besides, what child doesn't enjoy solving mysteries and hunting in the dirt? I used to bury arrowheads, beads, baskets, and bones (that I bought at the butcher) in the sandbox and pretend it was an ancient Native American site. But I don't do this anymore. I got tired of telling the kids that the Happy Meal Toys they found in the sand were *not* Indian artifacts.

This year I decided to try something new. I walked around the school and gathered various items out of wastebaskets. Back in my classroom I set these "artifacts" out on the round table in the corner of the room: broken crayons, pencil stubs, ink cartridges, Styrofoam cups, and lunch trays. When the kids walked in, I was wearing my white lab coat. They knew something was up. After I took roll and the attendance monitor returned from the office, I began the lesson.

"Does anyone know what an archaeologist is?" I asked.

"Like in *Jurassic Park*," Dylan said.

"That's right. Archaeologists are like detectives. They solve mysteries. Would you like to solve some mysteries today?"

"Yeah!" they cheered.

I invited them to the corner of the room where they gathered around the table—kids in front on their knees, the back row standing. Then I sat down in a chair and waited for them to quiet down.

"Now," I began, "I want you all to pretend the year is 2100.

You are digging at an archaeological site. There are no buildings here. But you believe at one time there were. You're not sure what kind." I pointed to the objects on the table. "You have just uncovered the objects you see in front of you. Things that you find in a dig are called *artifacts*. Everyone say *art-i-facts*." They repeated it. I turned to Chloe.

"How many syllables?"

"Three."

"Good." I looked around the table. "Your job is to determine what kind of place used to be on this site."

"That's easy," someone shouted.

"Not so fast," I said. "You also have to pretend that you don't know what these artifacts are. You've never seen them before. Okay?"

"Okay," everyone answered.

First I held up two crayon stubs—one red, one blue. The wrappers were torn off. "Hmm . . . what do you think these could be?"

"Crayons!" Stacy said.

"Wait," I reminded. "Remember—you don't know what these things are."

I inspected them closely. "Do you think they are some kind of food?"

"No!" Rebecca giggled.

I bit into one. "You're right! Tastes awful."

"EWWWWWW!" they cried.

I held up the crayons. "What do you notice about them?"

"They're different colors," Sarah observed.

"Good," I said. "And what are they made of?"

"Wax!" someone blurted out.

"And what is wax used for?" I asked.

"Drawing!" Stacy called out.

I stroked a piece of paper with the red crayon. "You're right!" I said, acting surprised. "So if these were meant for drawing, *who* might have used them?"

"Kids!" Laura answered.

"Why do you say that?" I questioned.

"Kids like to draw," Stacy remarked.

I looked across the table. "Who thinks there were kids at this site?"

Everyone raised a hand.

"Okay," I said with a nod. I set the crayon down and picked up the ink cartridge. I held it a few inches away from my face to study it. Most of the label was scratched off. "Now, how can we figure out what *this* is?"

"It has writing on it," Sarah pointed out.

I handed it to her. "What does it say?"

"It says *ink*."

"So, what might this be?" I asked.

"An ink cartridge," John volunteered.

"Maybe so," I responded. "But what place would have an ink cartridge?"

"A school!" Melanie deduced.

"Is that *all*?" I asked.

Ideas sprang up around the table.

"An office!"

"A house!"

"A store!"

"Aha!" I smiled. "Now you're thinking." I set down the cartridge. "If you're right and there were children here, do you think the building that was once here was a store or an office?"

"No," several answered.

"Why?" I asked.

Stacy chimed in. "Because kids don't go to offices."

I prodded. "So we're probably at . . . " My voice went up as I stretched out the *a*.

"A house or a school," Trevor concluded.

"You're narrowing it down." I reached for a Styrofoam cup and examined it closely with a furrowed brow. "This looks interesting. What do you think *this* was used for?"

"For holding something," Robbie observed.

"Seems likely." I sniffed the inside then handed it over to Jennifer. "What does this smell like to you?"

She took a whiff. "Coffee."

"What does that tell you?" I asked.

"They drank coffee!" Kevin reasoned.

I turned to him. "The *children* drank coffee?"

"I have!" announced Christopher.

Laura sneered. "I hate coffee."

"Coffee's disgusting!" shouted Dylan.

"Whoa," I said. "Let's get back to our detective work." I looked intently at the cup. "If there were kids here, do you think *they* drank coffee?"

Everyone answered "No" at the same time.

"Ah!" I said. "So, perhaps someone *else* was here besides the children." I lowered my voice. "But who could *that* be?"

"Grown-ups," said John.

"Teachers!" suggested Trevor.

I turned to him. "Why do you say that?"

"Because you can't teach without your coffee."

He got a laugh.

Finally, I picked up one of the lunch trays. "Now, what could this have been used for?"

"It definitely held something," Brian contributed.

I scanned their faces. "Does everyone agree?"

"Yeah!" they answered.

"Some of it is stained," Laura added.

"Good observation." I pointed to its separate sections. "Do you think these held coffee, too?"

"No!" they chorused.

"Why?" I asked.

Kevin touched the tray. "The . . . the holders . . ."

I helped him out. "The *compartments* . . ."

"The compartments aren't deep enough."

"Good point," I said. "You're using your brain." I studied the tray. "So what do you think this tray would have held?"

"Food!" Angela called out.

"But why would you need food at a school?" I asked.

"For lunch!" Melanie chimed in.

"Maybe it's a lunch tray," Dylan proposed. "Maybe the kids put their food in the different compartments."

"Or the teachers," said Laura.

I set down the tray. "Excellent thinking, everyone. You're doing *exactly* what archaeologists do. You're filling in the missing pieces of the puzzle. Well done! I'm proud of you."

I surveyed the artifacts on the table one last time. "Well, we've eliminated the possibility that there was once an office or a store on this site. We think there were both children and adults here." I turned to Laura. "And maybe teachers." I tapped the tray. "We believe that this could have been used for lunch." Then I leaned back in my chair, crossed my arms, and started scratching my chin like Sherlock Holmes. "So . . . what can we conclude from all of this?"

Trevor slammed his hands on the table. "I know!" he exclaimed with a grin.

Everyone looked at him.

"What?" I asked.

"The teachers ate the kids for lunch!"

PE

Every spring, Mr. Bailey the PE teacher hands out physical fitness awards to the fifth graders—certificates for running and jumping and things like that. We don't give out physical fitness awards in third grade. But if we did, mine wouldn't be like Mr. Bailey's. My PE awards would be like the Oscars. There is nothing like physical education to bring out the thespian in kids. Following are the nominees for this year's Academy Awards—including clips from their outstanding performances:

NOMINEES FOR BEST PERFORMANCE BY AN ACTRESS IN A SUPPORTING ROLE

1. Chloe in *Field Magic*
   (*Mr. Done sets up brooms and balls on grass for broomball.*)
   CHLOE: (*seeing all the equipment, speaks excitedly*) Mr. Done, are we playing Quidditch?

2. Rebecca in *Refreshment*
   (*After walking in from PE, Rebecca pulls out a glue bottle that is half full, puts it up to her neck, and squeezes it until a little puff of air comes out.*)
   MR. DONE: (*stares with mouth open*) What are you doing?
   REBECCA: Cooling myself off. Want to try it?
   MR. DONE: No, thanks.

3. Gina in *The Note*

GINA: (*holding note from mom*) Mr. Done, I can't do PE today.

MR. DONE: Why? What's wrong?

GINA: (*looks down at note*) I don't know. I can't read my mom's writing.

NOMINEES FOR BEST PERFORMANCE BY AN ACTOR IN A SUPPORTING ROLE

1. Brian in *Prepared*

MR. DONE: (*leading class in calisthenics*) And *why* is it important to stretch?

BRIAN: (*in the middle of a toe-touch*) So I can reach the mashed potatoes before my brother does.

2. Trevor in *Hanging On*

TREVOR: (*struggling desperately to do one more pull-up*) I hope . . . my insurance . . . covers this.

3. Kevin in *Out of Shape*

MR. DONE: (*demonstrating sit-ups*) Does anyone know the name of the stomach muscles I'm working right now?

KEVIN: A six-pack. (*lifts up shirt, looks at stomach, and sees no six-pack*) Man, I need to get back to the gym!

4. Christopher in *Poor Sport*

(*Christopher stomps off after losing kickball game.*)

MR. DONE: Christopher, get over here.

CHRISTOPHER: (*walks back*) The teams were unfair!

MR. DONE: The teams were not unfair. You're sore because they won. Winning is fun, but it's not the point. What counts is that you tried and had a good time. Understand?

CHRISTOPHER: (*head down*) Yeah. (*raises head*) They cheated!

NOMINEES FOR BEST PERFORMANCE BY AN ACTRESS IN A LEADING ROLE

1. Stacy in *Excuses*

   STACY: Mr. Done, I can't do PE today.

   MR. DONE: Why?

   STACY: I got asthma.

   MR. DONE: I didn't know you had asthma.

   STACY: I got it on the weekend.

2. Angela in *What's in a Name?*

   MR. DONE: Does anyone know what *PE* stands for?

   MELANIE: Play Everyday?

   MR. DONE: Not quite.

   SARAH: Play Everything?

   MR. DONE: Nope. It stands for Physical Education.

   (*Cut to later that day.*)

   ANGELA: (*breathing hard after soccer game*) Mr. Done, I know what PE *should* stand for.

   MR. DONE: What?

   ANGELA: People *Exhausted*!

3. Laura in *We're Off!*

   MR. DONE: (*to Laura*) Did you get new shoes?

   LAURA: (*smiles*) Yeah.

MR. DONE: They're nice lookin'.

LAURA: (*looks down and admires them*) They're really fast.

NOMINEES FOR BEST PERFORMANCE BY AN ACTOR IN A LEADING ROLE

1. Danny in *Dying*

   DANNY: (*sweating after an intense Four Square match*)
   Mr. Done, can I get a drink?

   MR. DONE: In a minute. PE's almost over.

   DANNY: (*feels under armpits*) I'm leaking.

2. Dylan in *Relays*

   MR. DONE: Okay, everyone, put your toes on the line.
   (*Dylan stands an inch over it.*)

   MR. DONE: (*pointing to Dylan's feet*) Dylan, step back. Your
   toes are over the line.

   DYLAN: These are new shoes. I haven't grown into them yet.

3. David in *Tackle*

   DAVID: I want to be a backup quarterback for the NFL.

   MR. DONE: Why not a starting quarterback?

   DAVID: They get hurt too much.

4. John in *The Bones*

   MR. DONE: (*stops in the middle of singing "Dem Bones"
   with class and points to forearm*) Who remembers what
   this bone is called?

   JOHN: (*raising hand*) The . . . the . . . (*shakes hand*) Wait . . . I
   know . . . the . . . the hilarious.

Mr. Done: (*smiling*) Almost. It's the *humerus*. You were close. (*points to his forearm*) Does anyone remember what these two bones are called? (*waits for response; no answer*) The first one starts with an *R*. (*kids continue staring at teacher; teacher helps them out*) Ra . . . Ra-di . . .

Gina: Radius!

Mr. Done: Good. (*teacher points to his forearm again*) Now, who remembers the name of the second bone?

John: (*shoots arm up*) UTERUS!

TELEVISION

"Christopher, is *quickly* an adjective or an adverb?" I asked. He looked up to the ceiling and thought about it. Then he turned to the rest of the class and said, "Can I ask the studio audience?"

Teachers and television share a common goal—keep the kids tuned in. But teachers have a more difficult time of it. We don't get to use special effects and background scores to keep our audiences listening. I do not look like Zac Efron.

"Why are you so tired?" I asked Trevor one morning as he plopped his head down on the desk.

"I was watching *American Idol*," he mumbled, his head lodged in his elbow.

"*American Idol?*" I exclaimed. "That's over at *eleven o'clock*! Does your mom know you were up that late? You should be in bed!"

I can't really blame the kids though. When I was Trevor's age, I was just as bad. At nine years old I could identify the characters on every kid's lunchbox at school. I knew the television theme songs better than my times tables. I could recite the lineup of every show on the three big networks: *Gilligan's Island* followed *I Dream of Jeannie. Mutual of Omaha's Wild Kingdom* preceded *The Wonderful World of Disney. The Partridge Family* came after *The Brady Bunch.* We ate dinner with *Mary Tyler Moore* and dessert with *Bob Newhart.* After *Carol Burnett*—time for bed.

One day I asked my students, "So, how many hours of TV do you watch a day?"

"One," Jennifer answered.

"Two," said Gina.

"Three!" Trevor announced, proudly.

I shot him a look. "You watch *three* hours a day?"

He smirked. "More on the weekends."

I sat on the corner of my desk. "Boys and girls, how would you like to have no homework for a week?"

The room exploded. One night without homework is a big treat, two is super. A whole week off—unimaginable!

"You're the best!" Danny declared.

I tapped the desk till they quieted down. "Now wait. Wait. I'm not just going to cancel homework for nothing. We're going to have a little contest."

They all sat up.

"What do we have to do?" Angela called out.

"Well," I began, "I challenge you to not watch TV for two solid weeks."

Everyone started talking at once. Trevor grabbed his neck and fell on the floor.

"Okay. Okay," I said over the noise. "Quiet down, everybody. Trevor, get up." I sat up in my chair and waited until it was silent. "Raise your hand if you have a question."

Twenty hands shot up.

"Is this just for school nights?" Sarah shouted out.

"No," I replied. "Weekends, too."

More grabbing of throats.

"You don't have to do it," I explained. "It's optional."

"Can we watch movies?" David asked.

"Not on your TV. You may go to the movies. But you may not do anything using your TV."

Kevin dropped his head on his desk.

"Can we use the computer?" Trevor asked.

"*May* you use the computer?" I repeated correctly. "Yes."

Kevin lifted his head. There was hope.

"You may play games on the computer, but you may not watch shows. And no DVDs."

Kevin plopped his head back on the desk.

"Can we TiVo?" asked Robbie.

"If you want to TiVo the shows and watch them later, you may."

"Yes!" Robbie cheered.

"How many days do we get without homework?" Joshua asked.

"Five," I answered.

The room grew animated.

Christopher spoke up over the noise. "If we can't watch TV for two weeks, then we should get *two* weeks off without homework."

"Yeah!" everyone agreed.

"Nope," I said. "One week off."

"WHY?" John challenged.

"Because I'm the boss. And I make the rules."

"Please!" Dylan pleaded.

"Nope. Remember, you don't have to participate."

"How will you know we did it?" Melanie asked.

"Aha," I said, holding up my index finger. I reached for a stack of red papers on my desk and held one up. "Every night that you don't watch television your parents will have to sign this piece of paper." I ran my finger down it. "There are fourteen lines here. In order to have no homework for a week, you need fourteen signatures."

A sly grin spread across Trevor's face. "I'm going to forge my mom's signature."

"You are, huh?"

He nodded slowly.

I reached into my pocket, pulled out my imaginary cell phone, and dialed. "Hello, Trevor's mom. This is Mr. Done." The kids stared at me. Wide grins brightened their faces. "I have this red paper in front of me with fourteen of your signatures." I paused. "You don't know what I'm talking about? Well, according to this, you've confirmed that Trevor didn't watch TV for two weeks." I held the phone away from my ear and whispered to my kids. "She's screaming." They laughed. I put the receiver back to my ear. "What's that? . . . Trevor doesn't get to watch TV for the rest of his life?" Giggles. "Oh my!" I listened some more. "And he's grounded for a *month*?" More giggles. "Okay, I'll tell him. Good-bye." I closed my imaginary cell, looked at Trevor, and shrugged. "I'm sorry."

After the snickering died down, I sat on the corner of my desk and leaned forward. "Imagine," I said, drawing them in with my voice. "One whooooole week without homework. Just think of how nice it will feel when your older brothers and sisters have homework and you don't."

Brian started bouncing.

"Wait!" I shouted, popping up. "I just realized something. If you have no homework for a whole week, that means you can't do your spelling homework. And if you can't do your spelling homework, then you can't have a spelling test on Friday."

Everyone cheered.

I acted upset. "Let's not do this," I said, shaking my head. "Forget the whole thing."

"NO!" they boomed.

"No. No," I continued. "I've changed my mind. We can't go a week without a spelling test."

"Yes we can!" they screamed collectively.

I flopped down in my chair, covered my face with my hands, and heaved a loud sigh of defeat. "Okay, you win."

More cheering.

"So, how many of you are going to participate?" I asked. Everyone but Robbie raised his hand. I looked at him. "Robbie, you're not going to try?"

He shook his head.

"Why not?"

"I won't survive."

I looked back at the class. "Now, there's a man who knows himself."

Next I reached for the stack of red papers and started passing them out.

"When do we start?" Rebecca asked.

"Tonight."

Melanie slammed her hands on her desk. She looked panicked. "What day is this?"

"Wednesday."

"No!" she moaned.

"What's the matter?" I asked.

"*Hannah Montana* is on tonight."

"Sorry, honey. No *Hannah Montana*."

She put her hands on her cheeks and gave a *Home Alone* yell. Stacy raised her hand.

"Yes, Stacy?"

"Mr. Done, are you going to do it?"

"Me?"

"Yeah!" Brian shouted. "If we have to do it, then you have to do it."

"Yeah," Dylan chimed in. "You have to do it, too."

I shook my head.

"Come on," Brian urged.

Laura joined him. "You have to."

I looked around the room then shrugged. "Well, why not?"

Everyone clapped.

Trevor smirked. "And your mom has to sign it."

For the next two weeks, my class ate dinner with their backs to their TV sets, listened to their favorite shows through the walls, and were tortured by siblings who took full advantage of this competition and made sure the TV was on 24/7. And loud.

Each morning I asked who was still in the competition. Each day fewer and fewer hands went up. When someone dropped out, I always asked, "So, what show did you in?"

"*Survivor,*" Chloe replied.

"*Wizards of Waverly Place,*" said Gina.

"*Tom and Jerry,*" John answered.

"*Suite Life of Zach and Cody*" was Emily's response.

"What about you, David?" I asked. "Which show did you in?"

He sighed. "*Dancing with the Stars.*"

Finally the contest was over. Five kids handed me their red papers with fourteen signatures. I felt like Willie Wonka collecting the five golden tickets.

"Congratulations," I said. "Well done." Christopher was one of the winners. "Christopher, I'm impressed. I didn't think you'd make it."

"My mom put the TV in the closet," he grumbled.

"Mr. Done, did *you* make it?" Laura asked.

I flinched. "Uh . . . well . . . Okay, everyone, get your math books out."

"Did you watch TV?" John interrogated, pointing at me.

"Don't point."

"You watched TV!" Stacy screamed, jumping out of her seat. "You watched TV!"

"Stacy, sit down."

Dylan joined her. "You watched TV!"

"Dylan, sit down right now!"

I was trapped. (And I was running out of Teacher Dodges.) I drew in a deep breath. "Okay. I watched TV."

(Cue: laughter.)

"Mr. Done," Trevor inquired with delight, "what show did *you* in?"

"Oh no!" I said, shaking my head. "I'm not telling you that."

"Come on," Kevin bargained. "We told you."

"Uh-uh!"

"Please!" Christopher pleaded.

"Tell us!" Laura begged.

I paused to weigh my options. *Option A: Tell them and get it over with; Option B: Say "Stop asking me that!" for the next six hours.*

"Okay. Okay. I'll tell you."

They started squealing.

"But you have to settle down."

The room quieted down immediately.

"And one more thing," I added. "You *can't* laugh."

Emily sucked her lips over her teeth. David held his breath. Rebecca cupped a hand over her mouth and started to snicker. I looked at her. "You're already laughing." She added the other hand.

I paused for a moment, gave one last look around, then confessed. "I watched *American Idol.*"

(Cue: peals of laughter.)

The room sounded like the station manager had just cranked up the laugh track. To full blast. Trevor sprang out of his seat. "*AMERICAN IDOL?* You watched *American Idol?* Mr. Done, does your mom know you're watching that show? That show is over at eleven o'clock. You should be in bed!"

June

We are your symphony Mr. Holland. We are the melodies and
the notes of your opus. We are the music of your life.

—*Mr. Holland's Opus*

THE SECOND CURRICULUM

This week Sarah's mom walked into my classroom after school.

"Sarah is really upset," she said.

"Why?" I asked.

"Because she didn't do well on her multiplication timed test."

I paused for a moment. "You know something? I actually think this is good for her."

The mom looked stunned. "What do you mean?"

"Well," I explained gently, "things come easily to Sarah. I'd imagine they always have. This is a little bump. She's learning how to deal with it."

I could see that this wasn't what Sarah's mom expected to hear. She was still letting it sink in when she left the room.

There are many things that teachers teach that you won't find written down on any district standards or Back to School Night handouts. I call it the second curriculum. It consists of all the *other* stuff that teachers spend so much time on in school—all the things that we believe kids need to experience. Anyone who works with children has his or her list.

I believe that all children should blow out birthday candles, follow an ice cream truck, eat a hot dog at a professional baseball game, lick mixing bowl beaters, spit watermelon seeds, suck on a lollipop, eat a triple ice cream cone, roast marshmallows, make their own Popsicles, dye eggs, bake a batch of cookies, pick out a pumpkin in a pumpkin patch, turn the handle of a gumball machine, eat at a picnic table, have popcorn at the movies, wave a Fourth of July sparkler, stay up until midnight on New Year's Eve, and get the frosted flower on a sheet cake covered with icing.

I believe that all children should run through the sprinklers, blow bubbles, slide down the stairs, cannonball into a pool, play in the mud, toss a penny into a fountain, swing really high, ride a Ferris wheel, pull as hard as they can in tug-of-war, pillow-fight, talk to stuffed animals, score a touchdown, splash in a puddle, throw snowballs, race across the grass inside a burlap bag, build a fort, somersault down a hill, ring a bicycle bell, run all four bases, trick the teacher, and search for a favorite animal on a merry-go-round.

I believe that all children should give a present bought with their own money, sell lemonade for a cause, care for a pet, wrap a gift, address an envelope, visit a nursing home, and pray for someone in need.

I believe that all children should run away from a wave on the beach, stare at a rainbow, skip rocks on a lake, walk through an orchard, listen to crickets, fly a kite, wait for a tug on a fishing line, ride a horse, have a secret hiding place, feed ducks, sleep under the stars (and wish on one), build a sand castle, count spots on a ladybug, hike with a stick they just found, make a snow-man, collect seashells in the sand, climb a tree, dig in the dirt, witness a sunset, hunt for four-leaf clovers, press flowers, and walk in the rain without an umbrella.

I believe that all children should pick up trash that isn't theirs, make their own beds, pull weeds, clean an animal cage, whisper in the library, learn to say *please* and *thank you*, wait while an adult is talking, lose a game, and take down the flag and fold it.

I believe that all children should play an instrument, mix colors in a watercolor tray, mold something out of clay, listen to

Mozart, wear a costume, see *The Nutcracker,* hammer a nail, draw a family tree, hear a live orchestra, see the circus, sing on a riser, dress for the theater, take piano lessons, perform in a play, applaud without hooting, watch Donald O'Connor sing "Make 'Em Laugh," and go backstage after a show and meet the performers.

I believe that all children should learn the difference between a daisy and a rose, take apart a flashlight, see the Statue of Liberty and the Lincoln Memorial (or pictures of them), observe a caterpillar turn into a butterfly, visit their parent's place of work, search for the Big Dipper, read *Charlotte's Web,* study a second language, talk to a military veteran, look through binoculars, fall off a bike and get back on again, struggle with a math problem, speak with someone who immigrated to this country, get their own library card, and hear a favorite story over and over again.

I believe that every child should hear his teacher say *I'm sorry* when he is wrong, see her teacher smile while reading her story, spot his teacher in the audience at the school play, stand beside her teacher when he tells Mom how wonderfully her child is doing in school, and see his teacher smile every morning when he opens the classroom door.

WHAT I HAVE LEARNED

The old adage "By your students you'll be taught" is definitely true. I have no doubt that I've learned as much from my students as they've learned from me. Here is the postgraduate education I've received so far:

Teaching is like cutting open a pumpkin. It can be a messy job. Pumpkin seeds, like kids, are not always easy to keep under your thumb.

After children find their desks on the first day of school, they will look to see where their friends are sitting. Then they will see how close they are to the ball box. The kid by the door is happy because he is the one who gets to turn off the lights.

Red rubber erasers can get stuck in plaster arm casts. Scissors are not good at getting erasers out of casts.

It takes a third grader half a glue stick to mount one paper doily onto a valentine. Pounding the doily with your fist makes it stick better.

By April there will be more balls on your classroom roof than in the ball box.

Stink bombs are made from spraying deodorant on snowballs. Snowballs always hit the nearest head.

There is a hierarchy of classroom jobs. *Line Leader, Paper Passer,* and *Messenger* are much more sought after than *Floor Cleaner.*

When dropped, cupcakes covered with frosting always land upside down.

Parent–teacher conferences are like the first Thanksgiving: two groups coming together at a table in November to celebrate after months of hard work.

Dogs like to dig up time capsules. Hamsters like to chew computer cords. Guinea pigs do not like to be decorated for Christmas. Bunnies do not like Pringles.

An inflatable globe can take out a fluorescent light cover. One little tea candle in a jack-o'-lantern can set off the fire alarm.

When playing Bingo with your students, they will always announce what number they need before you pull the next piece of paper out of the basket.

If the sign on a railing says "Wet Paint," one child will touch it to make sure.

If you color your watch crystal with yellow Magic Marker, you can still see what time it is. Red Magic Marker doubles as lipstick. Black Magic Marker does not taste like licorice.

If you turn your shirt into a kangaroo pouch, you can carry more markers back to the supply table than if you hold the markers in your hands.

A beanbag chair is not really filled with beans. The custodian does not like beanbag chairs.

If you take a piece of bologna, fold it over and bite the center, you have a bologna monocle.

There is a difference between a drizzle, a sprinkle, a shower, and a downpour. If it starts raining in the middle of lunch recess— leave the kids outside if it's anything less than a downpour.

When a child has his cheeks puffed out, either he is holding his breath or he just stuffed two packs of Tic Tacs into his mouth.

A table of eight-year-old boys waiting to be excused from the cafeteria can come up with eight different ways to make farting noises.

When a child gives you a pink Easter Bunny, always check before you bite into it. Crayola should not make sidewalk chalk that looks like Easter candy.

Principals are like grandparents. They get to have fun with the kids then leave.

When you are waiting for a tadpole to turn into a frog and spot what looks like a leg—it might just be a poop.

Kids are like punctuation marks. The loud ones are exclamation points. The boys who cannot pass a basketball net without jumping up to touch it are apostrophes (apostrophes are always in the air). The children who are always asking for help are question marks. And the quotation marks never stop talking.

Your students will not believe you when you say the crust has all the nutrients, or that a watermelon will grow in their stomach if they eat too many seeds. They will not believe you when you tell them that April 1 is really March 32, either.

Ketchup packets can be squirted, dotted, smeared, or smashed.

When a child gets the hiccups during class and you tell her to go get a drink of water, she will hope that the water does *not* do the trick.

TV carts pick up speed when pushed down the hall.

Pencils make excellent paint-stirrers. Cafeteria trays make excellent bases in kickball. So do library books.

When mud dries on the knees of your jeans, you can scrape your initials in it with scissors.

Goldfish crackers do not look like goldfish after being dropped in water. Gummi bears melt when plunked into coffee.

There are two ways to fold a piece of paper in half—the long way and the short way—or the hot dog way and the hamburger way (or the shower way and the bathtub way).

If you jab a pencil into a globe and push it all the way in, the globe will rattle when you spin it.

The morning after Halloween, kids will tell you how long they were out trick-or-treating and exactly how many pieces of candy they got.

The occupational hazards of teaching include: bad back, sore neck, tired eyes, and piano recitals.

The most coveted crayon in the room is the one that you only have one of.

Oklahoma looks like a gun. Michigan looks like a mitt. Kentucky looks like a piece of fried chicken. And Tennessee looks like someone stepped on it.

It takes twenty-seven seconds for a child to find z on the keyboard, thirty twists of a glue stick for the inside part to fall out, five spins of a tetherball for it to wrap completely around the pole, and one roll of toilet paper to cover the teacher up like a mummy at the Halloween party.

Always believe a child when he says that he has to throw up.

There are two remedies for almost everything: a Band-Aid and an ice pack. Wrapping wet paper towels around your arm with masking tape is just as good as an ice pack.

Pencils do not sharpen in electric fans.

It is impossible for a third-grade boy to hold a ball in line without dribbling, throwing, bouncing, dropping, or sitting on it.

After explaining to your students that if they make a valentine for one friend they have to make them for the whole class, one child will raise his hand and ask if he can make a valentine for himself.

The kids who give you the toughest time are the ones you love most. The students who receive the perfect attendance awards at the end of the year are the ones you wish would stay home once in a while.

On rainy days the classroom will smell like a room full of wet puppies. The carpet will have more footprints on it than the cement squares in front of Grauman's Chinese Theatre in Hollywood.

If you twirl a pencil in a handheld pencil sharpener very slowly, you can make a pencil sharpener flower. If you tell the child who has just given you three pencil sharpener flowers that they are beautiful, you will receive more.

The water cycle is not evaporation, condensation, and precipitation. It is evaporation, condensation, precipitation, and play Heads Up 7-up.

Parents are more nervous than their children at the school play.

When a mom hands you a tie box for Christmas and says, "I'm sorry"—her child picked it out himself. When a child gives a tie to her teacher, she will wait for him to wear it.

If you bend a paper clip around your teeth, it looks just like a retainer. If you wrap a piece of white construction paper around your arm and slide a rubber band over it, you can make a cast.

When there are treats in the staff room, women teachers will break a brownie in half before taking a piece. Men teachers eat the whole brownie.

You will run into your student at Safeway when your shopping cart contains three packs of beer.

The length of one school year is approximately 180 days—or nine months. Same as a pregnancy.

If a child cannot think of what to write, he will shake, twirl, tap, drum, and poke his pencil. The longer it takes to think of an idea, the more shaking, twirling, tapping, drumming, and poking there will be.

Students are like dogs. They make lots of noise when their master is away, display frantic greeting behavior when he returns, and follow him around the classroom when he's back home.

At some time in a teacher's career he will have said the following: "Don't write on your arm," "Do not karate chop your sandwich," "Please get out of the trash can," and "We do not eat our glue sticks."

No matter how many students you have in your classroom, there are only eight types. *Speedy* finishes everything lickety-split. *Chatty* is always turned around. *Sporty* is not always a good sport. *Dreamy* is often thinking about what he can build with his LEGOs. *Sloppy* can't find anything. *Smarty* corrects the teacher's math mistakes. *Silly* loses it when you're pouring paint and the container sounds like a fart. And *Pokey* is always the last to finish cleaning up. If you tell him he's as slow as molasses, he will ask, "Who's molasses?"

GOOD-BYE

I would know it's the last week of school—even if you didn't tell me. There are signs: The ball box is empty. The Lost and Found is full. There's a number in the corner of the whiteboard counting down the days left of school. All the backpacks—once crisp and perky—have lost their shape. Most of their zippers are broken. Pants that used to be long on the children are too short now. The caps on my glue bottles are so crusty they won't turn. The bulletin board paper around the sink is splattered. Half the markers don't color anymore. The pencils have no erasers. The supply room is low on paper. The copier repairman comes by more regularly. Flip-flops have replaced sneakers—I see more toes. When we clean our desks out, I find three thousand pencils.

This year on the last day of school, I try to make it like any other day. We sing. I read my students a story. Thirty minutes before the last bell rings, I bring my kiddos close to me on the carpet one final time. We reflect on the year and talk about our favorite activities. Stacy promises to visit me every single day next year. Danny asks me to be his teacher in fourth grade. I laugh. "Aren't you tired of me yet?" I ask. "NO!" they shout. Finally, the last bell rings. The year is over. Just like that.

After I hug my last child good-bye and close the door, I begin cleaning the room. It is time to put the classroom to bed. I pick papers up off the floor, pack presents that the kids brought me into a box, and move the furniture so the custodian can clean the carpets over the summer. As I'm moving chairs, I notice a yellow sticky note in Laura's desk. I pull it out and read it. "Welcome to your new classroom. This desk that you are sitting in belongs to Laura. You are only renting it!" I chuckle and stick it in my pocket.

As I reach for the next chair, I spot another sticky note in Dylan's desk. "Dear new student, I'll give you some advice. Don't touch Mr. Done's coffee mug." I smile and slide it into my pocket, too. As I move down the row, I discover sticky notes in all of the desks. *Why those little sneaks.* I read each one.

Melanie gave homework tips. Gina drew a cursive chart. David wrote, "If you have to go to the bathroom say *May I go* not *Can I.*" Angela made a map of the room with arrows pointing to the reading rug, the piano, and the goody jar. Jennifer advised, "Don't say anything about Mr. Done's messy desk." Danny wrote, "Mr. Done is forty-five years old and drives a white Toyota." The last desk I open is Christopher's. I smile when I look inside. Eleven stickies are lined up in a row, a single word written on each one: *Dear future third grader, you are going to love it here!*

Acknowledgments

Endless thanks to my agent, Janis Donnaud, and my editor at Center Street, Christina Boys. I am deeply indebted to you both. I also wish to express my graditude to the following for their support, encouragement, and assistance: Jill Asher, Marion Beach, Doug Connell, Phillip Irwin Cooper, Judi Cotant, Erin Dare, Mary Done, Elisabeth Doxsee, Shelley Ganschow, Caryn Garia, Vicki Garson, Colin Geiger, Robyn Gimbel, Jennie Grimes, Doug Grude, Richey Grude, Kim Guillet, Dorothea Halliday, Grace Hernandez, Caitlin Hoffman, Pia Jensen, Laura Jorstad, Marilyn Kanes, Mary Jo King, Piotr Konieczka, Troy Lapham, Monica Lehner, John Lents, Whitney Luken, Peter Ohm, Elisa Camahort Page, Sarrie Paguirigan, Barbara Parks, Elaine Saussotte, Dawn Scheidt, Eva Schinn, Tommy Kay Smith, Sarah Sper, Patsy Timothy, Carol Velazquez, Beth Wang, Lisa Wilson, and Laura Wright. Last, the hugest thanks to my dear friend and right arm, Heidi Fisher. As E. B. White wrote in *Charlotte's Web,* "It is not often that someone comes along who is a true friend and a good writer." Heidi is both.